D0524354

TO COIN A PHRASE

TO COIN A PHRASE

A Dictionary of Origins

Edwin Radford and Alan Smith

PAPERMAC

First published in 1945 by Rider Publishers under the title
Encyclopedia of Phrases and Origins

Revised edition *To Coin a Phrase* (Hutchinson) 1973

Published in 1981 by
PAPERMAC
a division of Macmillan Publishers Limited
4 Little Essex Street, London WC2R 3LF
and Basingstoke

Reprinted 1982, 1983, 1985
New edition 1989
Reprinted 1990

Associated companies in Auckland, Delhi, Dublin,
Gaborone, Hamburg, Harare, Hong Kong, Johannesburg,
Kuala Lumpur, Lagos, Manzini, Melbourne, Mexico City,
Nairobi, New York, Singapore and Tokyo

ISBN 0-333-49946-8

A CIP catalogue record for this book is available from the
British Library

Printed in Hong Kong

To E. M. H.

Acknowledgement

This book was the original conception of Edwin Radford, who, among other activities as an author and journalist, found time to edit for some years the 'Live Letters' feature column of the *Daily Mirror*. During that time he received thousands of letters asking 'Why do we say it?' and spent many hours in research to find the fascinating answer. Since he combined fine scholarship with a ready wit, the result of his studies was a unique analysis of the language we speak rather than the language of books – what people really say and the reasons why. Enjoying an active retirement too much to devote the time to the revision necessary since the years of its first publication, he entrusted the task of preparation of the new edition of 1973 to a colleague, Alan Smith. Edwin Radford died in November 1973, but Alan Smith has continued the research necessary to amend and update this new Papermac edition.

Introduction

Language is a living, ever-changing thing, moulded, not only by its own inner laws of development, but also by the outside influences of the human society it serves. The English language has had fifteen hundred years of unbroken evolution in Britain, not to mention the parallel growth of variant forms of English in territories overseas. The language as it exists today is like a geological record of the experiences of our ancestors right down to those who lived only yesterday. Such a phrase as 'caught red-handed' takes us back to the days of primitive tribal law, when the obvious guilt of the killer with his victim's blood still upon him made further investigation unnecessary. Giving 'chapter and verse' for our opinions only became possible in the sixteenth century when the text of the Bible was so divided. If we set about a task 'like billio' we are recalling the energy and enthusiasm of a seventeenth-century English preacher. If we talk about our chance of a job 'going West' we use an idea with an ancient history but which, nevertheless, did not emerge in the form of a popular phrase until the First World War.

These are some examples of outside events leaving their mark on the language; other forces, however, are also at work. For example, *folk etymology* translates the unknown into the everyday and familiar. The alien asparagus becomes 'sparrow grass' and the doctor's diagnosis of bronchitis became in the countryman's mouth 'brown kitties'. Sometimes the alien was accepted on its own terms and remains with us as a last relic of some long-abandoned theory. The belief that diseases came from bad air gave us 'malaria', and the suggestion that the influence of the stars was to blame, 'influenza'. Both words testify to the former reputation in England of the doctors of Italy.

Derived from the Greek 'to speak fair', *euphemism* is the practice of calling something distasteful, or deemed vulgar, by some name more socially acceptable. 'To pass away' was a phrase once widely used instead of 'to die'. What the eighteenth century called the 'necessary house' became, as plumbing brought water into the home, the lavatory (literally 'washing place'), which in turn became 'toilet'. In the same way in the United States 'bathrooms' and, in public buildings, 'rest rooms' are not quite all that their names suggest. Euphemism is a tenacious growth and has given many strange words and phrases to the language. Related to it is *genteelism*, the preference for certain words or turns of phrase believed to be those favoured by a dominant or influential social class. The cottage home had its 'room' or 'front room'. A little higher up the social scale the word was 'parlour' or 'sitting room'. All these have been supplanted by the middle-class 'lounge'. Even the upper-class 'drawing room' (originally 'withdrawing room') has been fatally damaged by it. Much in the same spirit is *ostentation*, from the Latin 'to expose to view', the preference shown for foreign words and phrases. Once a smattering of Italian was the sign of the man of culture, then French came into favour and a crop of 'French' expressions often unknown to the authentic French language sprang up. Similarly, *group jargon*, the words and phrases specially used by some well-defined body, the armed forces for example, is often popular with people wishing to advertise, claim or even merely to suggest a connection with the group in question. The glamour of the Royal Air Force clung for many years after the war and was a great influence on popular speech, the enthusiastic 'Wizard!' being a good example. Group jargon in the old is often nostalgic and sometimes rather pathetic.

Another source of enrichment of the language is *technical terms* that escape from their home ground and find a life of wider usefulness. 'To turn over a new leaf' and 'to blot your copy book' are simple examples from the classroom. 'Keeping a straight bat' or 'hitting him for six' are but two of the many examples of British sporting expressions being put to such uses. 'A flash in the pan' had to wait for the invention of the musket and no one could really 'let off steam' before the Industrial Revolution. In a world rapidly filling with new inventions all requiring names, new coinages abound but often change their shape before finding popular acceptance. Wireless telegraphy first lost its second element and then found itself ousted by radio. Television contracted into TV almost instantaneously. Such *contraction* or 'telescoping' is much more common in Russian or German than it is in English, but is still a force to be reckoned with especially as technical terms multiply. Related to contraction is the creation of *acronyms*, words made up of the initial letters of some inconveniently long expression, usually political or organisational. NATO (North Atlantic Treaty Organisation) and UNO (United Nations Organisation) are obvious examples.

Finally, there always has been and doubtless always will be *slang*, colourful coinages first used by cliques of self-admiring 'in-groupers', next spread by the mass media of the day to a wider public and then usually disappearing after a comparatively short life, puzzling both the student of language and the foreigner who seeks to master practical English. The lexicographer will never keep pace with the flood of fashionable colloquialisms. The book aims to explain some of the many curiosities of the English language wherever it may be spoken. It gives the stories that lie behind odd and puzzling words and phrases we may never really have thought about while using them every day. English is one of the great languages of the world and its exploration can be a fascinating—and rewarding—voyage of discovery.

A.W.S.

A

A1   This expression, meaning 'First rate, best of its kind', derives from the usage of *Lloyd's Register of Shipping* in which the quality of a ship's hull is denoted by letters and that of its fittings by numbers. 'A1 at Lloyd's' therefore means 'of the best and most reliable quality throughout'.

A B *Short for Able(bodied) Seaman*   A ship's crew was divided into the skilled Able Seamen, the unskilled Ordinary Seamen and the Boys who were the inexperienced beginners, whatever their actual age. In American usage A B is sometimes found as a variant of B A, the university degree of Bachelor of Arts.

aback, *taken*   One of the many English expressions taken from the world of the sailing ship. We are taken aback when momentarily stopped by a sudden surprise. A ship was taken aback when a strong gust of wind forced square rigged sails back against its masts, thus halting it in its course.

above board   Anything not above board is suspected of being fraudulent. The term derives from the practices of cheats in card games. Board is an old word for table. To drop your hands below the table could be in order to 'lose' an unwanted card and replace it by something better kept in reserve, but if all play was 'above board' this was impossible. See CARDS for related phrases.

abracadabra   This magical 'word of power' was believed to take its strength from the concealed (Hebrew) initials of Father, Son and Holy Spirit. The earliest reference to it is in the writings of Severus Sammonicus in the second century A.D. He used it as a charm against ague (malaria) but the word survives today as a type of any magical incantation.

'Absence makes the heart grow fonder'   This oft-quoted senti-

1

ment comes from the song 'Isle of Beauty' by T. H. Bayly (1797–1839).

academy The name comes from a garden in the suburbs of ancient Athens where Plato taught 'among the groves of Academe'. Nowadays the word academic suggests either belonging to the world of university scholarship or, more popularly, something of more interest to the pure scholar than to the practical man.

Achilles, *heel of* A vulnerable spot. The metaphor comes from ancient Greek mythology. When Thetis, mother of Achilles, dipped him into the River Styx to make him invulnerable she held her son by one heel which, being untouched by the water, remained liable to injury. It was in this heel that Achilles received a mortal wound whilst fighting at Troy.

Achilles tendon The sinew running along the heel to the calf of the leg. It takes its name from the above legend.

acid test, *the* The test that proves something beyond all doubt. Gold, 'the royal metal', resists the effects of ordinary acids and only succumbs to 'the royal water', Aqua Regia, a mixture of concentrated nitric and hydrochloric acid. The term goes back to the days of medieval alchemy.

acme (*the acme of* . . .) The high peak of effectiveness. Originally a medical term but now in wider use. Greek doctors saw each illness as having four characteristic phases: arche (beginning), anotasis (increase), acme (height of attack) and the paracme (decline).

acre Now a standard measure of ground but originally no more than an Old English word meaning 'field'. Shakespeare was still using it in this sense in the line 'Between the acres of the rye' (*As You Like It*, V iii).

Adam's ale (*sometimes Adam's wine*) Water. The first created human being obviously had nothing else with which to quench his thirst.

Adam's apple The visible bulge of the larynx characteristic of male throats is said to be a reminder that Adam accepted a piece of the forbidden fruit from Eve in the Biblical story of the Garden of Eden.

Adelphi A group of streets and a terrace on the south side of the Strand, London, laid out and constructed by the famous Adam brothers in the late eighteenth century. Most of the area has now been rebuilt, though the original name survives. Adelphi is Greek for 'brothers'. In the USA Philadelphia means '(city of) brotherly love'.

adieu Contraction of an old French expression 'I commend you to God (*à Dieu*)'. Many other languages have parallel phrases, e.g. our own 'Goodbye' is 'God be with you'.

admiral One of our many borrowings from the Muslim world. The word comes from the Arabic *amir el bar* meaning 'ruler of the sea'. Medieval Latin turned this into *admiralius*. The first English form was, more accurately, 'amyrel', but, as has often been the case, a more 'learned' form based on the Latin was ultimately preferred.

adroit This word, meaning 'manually skilful', is, like its parallel form 'dexterous', one of a group showing our preference for the right-handed person as the desirable norm. In French *droit* means 'right'. Its opposite, *gauche* (French 'left'), is used to mean awkward. Dexterous is of Latin origin (*dexter* is Latin for 'right hand'). Its opposite, 'sinister', carries even more unpleasant implications than *gauche*.

advowson The right of appointing a parish priest to his position, from the Latin *advocatio*, a summons. Advowson is now purely a legal term.

aegis The origin of this phrase is in mythology. Aegis is the Greek for goatskin, the skin in question being of the goat that suckled Zeus. Preserved by him as an object of power and symbolic of the god's protection, it is sometimes depicted as a cloak and sometimes as a shield. (Athena, daughter of Zeus, also carried the aegis-shield.) For all its exalted ancestry, today's use of the phrase can be quite mundane, 'The new project is under the aegis of the County Council' for example. See also AUSPICES.

affluent society   In 1958 John Kenneth Galbraith, a Canadian political economist, published *The Affluent Society*, an analysis of the contemporary scene which pointedly commented upon the relationships of 'private affluence and public squalor'.

'After us, the deluge'   Louis XV of France received a letter from Madame de Pompadour in reply to one of his own, written after the defeat of France and Austria at the Battle of Rossbach, 5 November 1757. She wrote 'Après nous le déluge', and the saying gained currency from being quoted by Madame de Hausset in her *Mémoires*. The 'deluge', of course, took the shape of the French Revolution, in which Louis XVI was overthrown.

agenda   This word familiar to anyone who has ever sat as a committee member has a double origin. In form it is pure classical Latin and means 'things for doing' or 'things to be done'. *Addenda* meaning 'things to be added' is a similar formation. However, the modern usage of agenda is due to the example of Jeremy Bentham (1748–1832), the social philosopher, whose political approach was based on the vital need for a practical and systematic attack on social problems. His seizing upon the word *agenda* and giving it its present currency is symbolic of his whole outlook.

Aggie Westons   This was the popular naval nickname for the 'social centres' for naval ratings established at Portsmouth, Devonport and Chatham by the late Dame Agnes Weston. The English holiday resort of Weston-super-Mare was also sometimes punningly referred to as 'Aggie on horseback'.

aghast   This word simply means 'frightened' and comes from an Old English original, *gaestan*, 'to frighten'. The 'h' crept in from some false idea of a connection with 'ghost'.

4

agnostic Coined by Professor Thomas Huxley in 1869 to express the position of those who disclaim any knowledge beyond that capable of proof by normal means. The agnostic modestly bows out of discussions of the existence or non-existence of God, leaving the expression of positive opinions to the theists and atheists.

agog Of Old French origin, *En gogues* once meant 'mirthful'. If you are all agog you are happily anticipating some interesting new development.

aigrette A diamond head ornament worn by women in full traditional evening dress. It was originally the white plume of a heron. The egret is a species of heron. Note the preference for the French form.

aisle (*of a church*) A much misused word. It should not be used to describe the central 'gangway' of a church. Aisle derives from Latin *ala* and French *aile*, both meaning 'a wing', and refer to those widenings of the church north and south of the central nave, usually being separated from it by rows of pillars. 'To go down the aisle' is an old expression meaning to be married.

alarm From the Italian *all'arme*. The old 'alarum' is an unjustifiable form.

Albert A heavy type of watch chain running from one waistcoat pocket to another via a special vertical buttonhole. It was popularised by Prince Albert, the husband of Queen Victoria, who was presented with such a chain by the jewellers of Birmingham in 1849.

alderman In the local government of England and Wales a senior member of a borough or county council, elected to the office by his fellow councillors; under the local government reorganisation of the 1970s the office was scheduled to disappear almost completely. In the United States municipal corporations in some towns still have aldermen. The name has an Old English original, *ealdormann*, meaning a regional governor. In obsolete slang an alderman was 'half a crown', equivalent of the decimal currency 12½p, a reference to the high standing of the Saxon official. Among thieves an alderman was a short crowbar, box opener or jemmy, a heavier version being called 'a Lord Mayor'.

allergic To be allergic to something is to react abnormally to it. This medical term came into circulation on the eve of the First World War. Properly applied, it referred to the special sensitivity of some individuals to certain foods or even to dusts or pollens leading to such conditions as 'hay fever'. Now, in its popular sense, it is used to indicate dislike. A typical example would be 'The trouble is that John is allergic to work!'

all my eye and Betty Martin Traditionally said to be a British sailor's garbled version of words heard in an Italian church, '*Ah mihi, beate Martini*', meaning 'Ah grant me, blessed St Martin'. The phrase now means that something is no more than nonsense. 'It's all my eye . . .'

all serene Everything is all right, usually in the sense that 'the coast is clear', and some agreed action may be proceeded with. The countersign '*serena*' was used by Spanish sentries to indicate that all was well.

all Sir Garnet A reference to the brilliant military successes of Sir Garnet Wolseley during the brief war with the Egyptians in the 1880s. To answer 'All Sir Garnet' means that everything is well in hand.

all the go A phrase from the drapery trade meaning that the thing in question was popular and 'going' (that is selling) well. 'It's all the rage' is a variant of this.

aloof One of the many English expressions derived from the sailing ship. To hold aloof meant keeping the vessel away from a dangerous shore towards which it was being blown. Now it just means to avoid involvement in something of which one is perhaps suspicious. The modern sailing term would be a-luff.

altogether, *in the* This well-established US colloquialism for 'naked' can be traced back to the 1890s and was at that time also in use in Britain. It is a coy euphemism beginning as 'altogether, utterly naked'. Compare the English upper-class 'starkers'.

amazon A term used of a tough, well-built woman. In Greek mythology Amazons were a race of female warriors living on the shores of the Black Sea. The name itself means 'without a nipple', because the Amazons were said to mutilate themselves in this way lest their efficiency as archers should be imperilled. The South American river was so named because its Spanish explorer, Orellana, thought he saw female warriors there in 1541.

amok 'To run amok' is a Malaysian term and means to be seized with a sudden, blindly destructive frenzy or, to use a parallel of Viking origin, 'to go berserk'.

anathema In the current phrase anything anathema to us is rejected as hated and obnoxious, but this usage is incorrect. In ancient Greece *anathema* were accepted offerings 'set up' (the literal meaning of the word) in temples. 'Rejected' offerings were declared *an*anathema, and this is the word that should be used in the sense described above.

Ancient Lights Seen on notice boards these words are a traditional and legally recognised claim to continuing unrestricted light through a window that has had an open aspect for at least twenty years previously.

Andrew Millar Variant forms are 'The Andrew' or 'Andrew Millar's regiment' and it means the Royal Navy. Although it has been connected with the name of a firm supplying food to the fleet the weight of naval tradition favours the idea of Andrew Millar as a notorious leader of the press gang in the days when that was a major source of recruits.

angel The expression 'to write like an angel' is sometimes used in praising a writer's style. In fact, it should refer to beautiful handwriting, and derives from the name of Angelo Vergece, the Cretan calligrapher employed by the French kings Henry II and Francis I in the sixteenth century. In the theatre world an angel is a play's financial backer. The term came from the United States and was first used in England in connection with the people who backed Wylie and Tate musical comedy in London in the 1920s. Apocryphal stories connect its first use in America with various named individuals, e.g. a certain Al Wood, but an evolution from the idea of 'guardian angel' seems more likely.

Angry Brigade, *the* Name assumed by a 'propaganda by deed' group convicted of responsibility for a number of bomb and firearm attacks in and around London 1970–2. In December 1972 four of the eight accused were given heavy prison sentences after the longest ever Old Bailey trial. The name would seem to derive from 'angry young man'.

angry young man This phrase, first used as the title of Leslie Paul's autobiography in 1951, soon became a label attached to the 'antiheroes' portrayed by such novelists as Kingsley Amis, John Braine and John Wain. Especially it was used to describe the type made famous by John Osborne's Jimmy Porter in *Look Back in Anger* in 1956. The abbreviated form 'an angry' is sometimes found.

Annie Oakley, *an* This is circus and theatrical slang for a free ticket because such tickets were commonly punched with a hole before distribution to prevent recipients selling them. The reference is to Annie Oakley the famous American rifle-shot (1860–1926). She appeared in circuses with the Buffalo Bill show and specialised in shooting the centre 'pip' out of a playing card.

8

Antipodes   Of Greek origin and meaning 'opposite feet'; the people living on that part of the globe directly opposite to our own. The word proves that Greek scholars were quite familiar with the idea of a spherical earth. The theory was also known in the Middle Ages, but the idea of Antipodean people was rejected as inconsistent with certain Biblical texts. Nowadays the expression simply means Australia and New Zealand.

Apache   Originally (and still) the name of a Red Indian tribe and properly pronounced as 'apatchi' it became applied in France c. 1900 to members of the criminal subculture of Paris. (Compare the Mohocks of eighteenth century, London and later 'street Arabs'.) From this background there evolved the night-club/variety theatre act 'the apache dance' in which two stereotyped figures engaged in bizarre courtship. It can have done the image of France no good!

apartheid   This word for the policy of 'separate development' of the races in the Republic of South Africa derives from two Afrikaans words whose English equivalents would be 'apart hood'. It is correctly pronounced apart-hate!

apocryphal (*an apocryphal story*)   Although the word derives from the Greek *apokrupto*, 'to hide away', its major usage relates to certain books 'between the Old and New Testaments' included in some ancient texts of the Bible, though not in others and therefore concluded to be not of the same authority. An apocryphal story, then, is one perhaps worth retelling but of doubtful authenticity and certainly not 'to be taken as gospel'.

apple cart, *to upset the*   Apparently no older than the 1790s, this phrase would seem no more than a vivid picture of surprise and confusion drawn from an incident of everyday life. 'Apple cart' was then wrestlers' slang for the body and to 'upset the apple cart' was to throw a man down.

apple of his eye, *the*   A phrase from the Bible. It meant at first simply the pupil of the eye, from its roundness, and was then applied by extension to anything precious and protected.

apple-pie bed A classic practical joke in which the bottom sheet of a bed is doubled upwards, so that the user cannot stretch out his legs in the normal way. A folk corruption of the French *nappe pliée*, 'a folded sheet'.

apple-pie order Everything in its proper place. Possibly derived from Old French *cap à pie*, meaning (fully armoured from) 'head to foot'.

argosy This quintessentially romantic term for a ship is a mangling of the name Ragusa, historic port on the Adriatic coast. It came to English via Italian.

Arsenal The original 'Arsenale' was in the dockyard area of Venice and derives from the Arabic *darsina'a*, 'house of industry'. (See also MAGAZINE and QUARANTINE for words of similar background.) Arsenal is now most commonly heard as the name of a London football team (nicknamed 'the Gunners') taking their designation from the Woolwich Arsenal where the original club began.

Ashes, *the* When an English cricket team was beaten by Australia in 1882 The *Sporting Times* announced the death of English cricket and said, 'The body will be cremated and the ashes taken to Australia.' When in the following year England won, some Melbourne ladies presented the team with an urn containing the ashes of the stumps and bails. The urn is still with the M C C at Lord's and is never moved even when Australia wins a Test and 'regains the Ashes'.

assassin The original assassins were a religious sect founded in Persia in 1090 by Hasan i Sabah, who, from his inaccessible mountain stronghold, sought to dominate the Islamic world by a campaign of 'assassination'. Each successive leader of the sect was known as 'The old man of the mountain'. The word assassin itself comes from the hashish used by the leaders to 'brainwash' newcomers to the cult.

Atlantic Charter The name given to an eight point declaration of war aims by President Roosevelt and Prime Minister Winston Churchill in August 1941 after a four-day conference at sea. The term is now sometimes used for any proposed agreement between the U S and the powers of Europe.

augury (*a good augury for the outcome of the contest*) The augur was a Roman official whose job it was to check that the days chosen for public enterprises would be lucky ones. This he did by looking for traditional omens. Caesar said he did not know how one augur could pass another in the street without laughing.

auspices (*under the auspices of*) Like augury another usage from the ancient world. A priest called an 'auspex' also sought omens for the future of an enterprise by ritually observing the flight of birds. If the results were good, the initiator of the plan would take responsibility and 'give the go-ahead'. The venture was now 'under his auspices'.

automation Coined by John Diebold in his 1952 book *Automation: the Advent of the Automatic Factory*. Diebold derived his term from the pre-existing 'automaticisation' which he said he could not trust himself to spell!

A W O L Acronym contraction for 'Absent without leave', a term with a long history (doubtless because the offence was so common) in both American and British armies. The question of one's intentions about returning distinguish this from the more serious offence of desertion.

axe (*another axe to grind*) Said of those who offer help or friendship with a view to their own advantage. Franklin tells the story of being persuaded by flattery to turn the heavy grindstone for a man who wished to sharpen his axe. The job done, he was abruptly dismissed. In later life he often asked himself whether flatterers were not perhaps simply men who had 'another axe to grind'.

11

B

bachelor An unmarried man. The most probable origin seems to be from a late Latin word meaning 'herd boy', the common juvenile occupation of primitive societies.

Bachelor of Arts Holder (whether male or female) of the first or lowest degree of a university and inferior in status to what was once the full degree, that of Master.

back-room boys The name given by Lord Beaverbrook, Britain's Minister for Aircraft Production in the Second World War, to the Research Department of the Air Ministry. He said, in 1941, 'To whom must praise be given? I will tell you. It is the boys in the back room. They do not sit in the limelight, but they are the men who do the work.'

bacon, *to bring home the* To win the prize, to succeed in some contest. Country fairs for centuries included pig-catching events and a pig was the traditional prize in bowling competitions.

bacon, *to save one's* To avoid punishment, to come out unscathed. Of Old English origin, *baec* meaning back or body.

bafflegab A term coined in 1974 by Hugh Brogan for the official/intellectual jargon that frequently bewilders us. It neatly sums up all that Sir Ernest Gowers was campaigning against in his *Plain Words*.

baggage (*applied to a woman*) This usage derives from the female camp-followers of traditional armies who travelled not with the fighting men but with the baggage train.

baldheaded, *to go for someone* The traditional story is that the Marquess of Granby when fighting at Minden in 1759 was so incensed at having his wig shot off that he 'went for the enemy baldheaded'. The scene is depicted on some inn signs. Another suggestion sees the phrase as a perversion of the Dutch *bald dadig* meaning 'audacious'.

balk To balk anyone is to thwart them. A door could be barred against an unwanted visitor by fixing a balk of wood across it inside. The word is Old English.

balloon (*when the balloon goes up*) This phrase, meaning when anticipated trouble or fighting begins, is of First World War origin when the first sign of impending action might be the sending up of observation balloons.

ballyhoo Originally noted *c.* 1910 this soon became a stock Hollywood term for sensational large scale publicity activities. It seems to derive from a catchphrase of the old music hall world 'the Ballyhooly truth', one of those many expressions based on the alleged characteristics of the Irish.

balmy A popular term for being mentally deranged. This incorrect spelling conceals the derivation which is from **barm** or yeast, which froths and ferments. It is, however, interesting to note the former existence of a Balmes House Asylum in Hoxton on the east side of London.

banana republic This derogatory phrase seems to have been first applied to Panama by those critical of the dominant position enjoyed there by the American-based former United Fruit Company.

bandsman, *to cop a* This old London phrase meaning 'to suffer unmitigated disaster' derives from a formerly well-known heavyweight boxer, known as Bandsman Rice, defeated three times in title fights by Bombardier Billy Wells. At their final meeting (December 1915 in Liverpool) Rice was knocked out in the first round but gave a phrase to the language!

bandy, (*to bandy words with someone*) Bandy is a kind of primitive hockey and the ball was 'bandied' to and fro as are the harsh words of an argument.

Bannister, *to do a* On 6 May 1954 Dr Roger Bannister

became the first man to run a mile in less than four minutes. The phrase 'to do a Bannister' was soon being used facetiously for anyone displaying an unusual turn of speed. Bannister's record has long been superseded, but the phrase structure with some appropriate contemporary allusion is still often heard. See SMITH, *Harvey*.

banting A method of losing weight by strict diet control, named after its exponent, William Banting, a London cabinet-maker, in 1864.

barbarians As originally used, the name had no necessary implication of cruelty or even of brutality, but was a Greek name for what they thought of as the 'lesser breeds' who spoke incomprehensible languages, sounding like 'bar bar'.

barley sugar This oddly-described sweet gets it name from the French *sucre brulé* (burnt sugar) but is now sold in France as *sucre d'orge*, 'barley sugar'.

barracking This term for the noisy interruption of cricket, football matches, etc. by discontented spectators emerged in Australia in the 1890s and soon crossed to Britain. Its origin is obscure, but the best authorities suggest some blending of the aboriginal *borak* 'fun' with the London cockney *barrikin* 'nonsense words', and the bad reputation for crowd behaviour of those matches played at the Victoria Barracks ground, Melbourne.

Bath chair First used in Bath, the English spa town, to take invalids from their homes or hotels to the baths for treatment. Bath chairs were much more substantial than modern invalid chairs. Made of covered wicker-work, they had high solid hoods and hinged side-pieces that closed across the lap for extra protection. They were pulled by a man holding the T-shaped rod attached to a small front wheel. The use of these chairs spread from Bath to other spa towns, and to such seaside resorts as Brighton or Bournemouth which were favoured by invalids.

14

batman An army officer's servant gets his name from the Old French *bât*, or 'pack saddle', which was once in his charge.

battle-axe Used of a formidable elderly woman, this term goes back to the early American women's rights movement which published a journal called *The Battle Axe*.

battle royal A term ultimately derived from cock fighting. Sixteen birds fought in couples, then the winners were matched and so on by elimination until only one survived. Today, however, it often means no more than 'spectacular contest'.

batty One of the many euphemisms for 'insane'. Fitzherbert Batty, an eccentric barrister of Spanish Town, Jamaica, attracted some public notice in London in 1839 when he was certified insane. 'Batty', however, also calls to mind that evocative phrase, 'he has bats in the belfry'.

bear A Stock Exchange term for the man who sells shares he has not got, gambling on a fall in price that will enable him to acquire them in time to deliver and still make a profit. Is there a reference to the man who sold the skin of the bear before killing the animal? A big profit is still a 'killing', but what about the 'bulls' who do the opposite?

bear up It is hard to relate this phrase which means 'keep up your spirits', 'do not despair', to the maritime usage which involves keeping the head of the vessel away from the wind. It is more probably connected with the 'bearing rein' which forced carriage horses to hold their necks in a 'smart' arched manner.

beat generation, *the* Coined by American writer Jack Kerouac in the 1950s and carried abroad by such messengers as poet Allan Ginsberg this expression successfully captured the feeling of many young people in California and elsewhere that they were simply overwhelmed by the pressures and complexities of the contemporary world, 'dead beat' as it were. They sought relief by 'opting out', restless wandering and resort to oriental techniques of meditation, in particular the cult of Zen Buddhism. False etymologies involving '*beat*ification' and *beat* music show characteristic associations of ideas. See HIPPIES.

Beefeaters Nickname for the Yeoman Warders of the Tower of London. In medieval times 'eater' was synonymous with 'servant' and a loafeater was a menial servant waiting upon higher ones. These latter were 'beefeaters' who enjoyed a superior standard of living. This makes better sense than a derivation from 'buffetier' – a servant attending the sideboard.

beefing Used in the sense of complaining or making an unnecessary fuss, this American usage stems from the slang of the London underworld. The traditional 'hue and cry' of 'stop thief' was mockingly parodied as 'Hot beef, hot beef', hence the use of 'beefing' to mean making a fuss.

beer and skittles Popularly symbolic of the easy life. To say 'Don't think it will be all beer and skittles', conjures up the image of a pleasant country inn. Shakespeare in his *Twelfth Night* uses the similar phrase 'cakes and ale'.

behind the eight ball Meaning to be in an awkward situation, derives from the game of pool or snooker. The eight-ball should be the last left on the table, hence to be behind it creates difficulties.

bell, *as clear as a* Once used to indicate audibility, because of the carrying power of a bell's tone, the phrase has been meaninglessly perverted to refer to the visual clearness of a bright sky.

bell, book and candle The symbols used when a person was solemnly excommunicated from the Roman Catholic Church. The bell was rung, the book closed, the candle extinguished.

Bench, *the* As a term for magistrates or judges sitting

16

together this derives from the medieval usage whereby judges had a bench while plaintiffs and others stood. In Westminster Hall the traditional site of the original King's Bench from which he dispensed justice was long pointed out. Later the name was given to the court, wherever it was sitting 'the Court of King's Bench'. 'To be raised to the Bench' is to be appointed a judge.

berserk A word used to describe the state of frenzied Viking warriors who went into battle either 'bare to the shirt', i.e. without armour, to show their contempt for death or possibly clad only in a magic *bear* skin. See AMOK for a related idea from another culture.

bicycle From the Latin *bi'*, 'two' and Greek *kyklos*, 'a circle'. The first real bicycle in Britain was made by Fitzpatrick Macmillan in 1840 but cycling only became general with the invention of the 'penny farthing' in 1872. The remarkable thing about the bicycle is that it took so long to invent, for its theoretical basis has existed since antiquity.

Big Brother is watching you Often used as an ironical reminder that authority has you under its eye, the phrase derives from George Orwell's horror-novel of the future, *1984*, first published in 1949. Although *1984* undoubtedly expresses Orwell's revulsion at Stalin's regime in the Soviet Union, it is an equally damning indictment of trends, especially those made possible by recent technology, in the so-called 'Free World' as well.

bikini Here we have a clue to the way in which the human race preserves its sanity. Just as the memory suppresses the horrific, but retains and indeed develops the happy recollection so, too, does the speech of the man in the street. It is a kind of protective censorship or, better, therapeutic trivialisation, of dangerous material. In 1946 Bikini Atoll in the Pacific Marshall Islands was the scene of a series of atomic bomb tests. The word *bikini* leapt to the headlines as evidence of the new destructive power available to mankind, but, in an astonishing psychological twist, the classical meaning of *atom*, as the then smallest conceivable unit, reasserted itself. Mankind was diverted from dreams of universal doom by the appearance of the smallest possible two-piece swimsuit that could still be legally considered as clothing. Overnight the original French name *le minimum* was displaced by *bikini*, for what, indeed, while retaining its essential identity could possibly be smaller? Since these words were written, something smaller has developed, and the name *monokini* is applied in French to the more essential lower half, when even this is retained!

billio, *like* This expression, indicating energy and enthusiasm, comes from one Joseph Billio, Puritan divine, who founded the Independent Congregation at Maldon, Essex, in 1682. Forgotten as a man, his name survives as a monument to the zeal which impressed all who knew him.

billycock hat What in England is called a bowler and in the United States a derby was originally a billycock. The famous London hatters, Lock's of St James's, claim to have made the first 'bowler' *c.* 1850 for Mr Billy Coke a Melton Mowbray sportsman who thought the style would be more suitable for riding than the traditional 'topper'. The style is still known as a 'Coke' in the trade and it still keeps something of its sporting associations.

Bingo In the 1700s this was the name for the King of Dominoes game, which only the most skilful players ever attempted, so complicated was the method of play. The modern game named Bingo was known before 1914 as Keno or Loo. During the First World War it became a popular pastime with soldiers under the name Housey-Housey. It requires no skill at all. In the 1960s a Bingo craze swept Britain and the Bingo Hall, often a converted cinema, is an accepted social institution.

Bircher, *a John* In the United States a supporter of strong anti-Communist views and a subscriber to 'conspiracy theories' as, for example, that President Eisenhower was a Communist agent. The name derives from the John Birch Society founded in 1958 by Robert Welch, a sweet manufacturer, 'to oppose Communism in the name of Christian Civilization'. John Birch was a U S army officer killed in 1948 by a group of Chinese Communists and thus claimed as 'the first victim of the Cold War'. The full story of what happened, released in 1972, suggests he virtually provoked his own death, perhaps in the hope of precipitating US action against the Chinese Communists.

biro This word for the ball-point pen derives from the name of its inventor Ladislao (Lazlo) Biro, a Hungarian. The first patent was in 1938 in Hungary, but Biro then went to the Argentine to continue developing his idea. Towards the end of the Second World War he found a British backer for his product, but the company was taken over by the French firm of Bic, which in turn gave its name to the ball-point in France just as Biro had done in the English-speaking world.

bistro In France a wine bar but in Britain more often used for an intimate restaurant this name is said to date from the usage of Russian troops in Paris after the fall of Napoleon in 1815 when their cries of *Bweestra*!, 'Quickly!', gave rise to the first 'fast food' establishment.

bitter end, *right to the* This phrase, meaning 'to the very last point, to the furthest possible extent' is, like so many, nautical. The bitts were oak pillars firmly fixed to the deck and used for securing the anchor cables. To 'pay out' the cable 'to the bitter end' was, then, as much as one could do. The normal meaning of the word 'bitter' has, however given the modern phrase sombre implications.

blackballed To have one's application for membership of a society rejected. The original vote by ballot was by means of a small ball placed in an urn, a word still used in some countries for a ballot box. In certain clubs and societies, when a new applicant for membership was under discussion, existing members voted on the question with a black or white ball. If even one ball in the urn was black, the would-be member was rejected. He had been 'blackballed'.

blackguards Originally the sooty scullions of a great man's kitchen. In course of time the idea that all servants were dishonest led logically to the idea that the humblest were the worst. The word villain has a similar history.

blackmail The crime itself is probably timeless, but our word derives from the bad old days of border warfare between England and Scotland. 'Mail' was once a normal word for rent or tax. 'Black' mail was the 'protection' money paid to the gangs of outlaws who flourished in frontier conditions.

Black Maria Colloquial name for the police van used to take away arrested men. Of American origin, it was supposed to derive from Maria Lee, a powerfully built Boston Negress who kept a sailors' lodging house and often assisted the police in removing the drunk and disorderly. Another American variant is 'paddywagon', a reflection of the bad reputation of the early Irish immigrant. In Vienna the equivalent vehicle was called 'the salad basket' because of the mixed nature of its contents.

black-out Now most commonly used as a synonym of fainting fit or sudden loss of consciousness, the word originally meant the compulsory darkness imposed on cities in the Second World War in an effort to hinder the identification of targets by enemy aircraft.

blarney The Irish art of persuasive speech. When Cormach Macarthy was besieged in Blarney Castle near Cork in 1662 his verbal evasiveness, or diplomatic skill, stood him in good stead. The wall of the castle now contains a memorial stone. Those who kiss this stone are said to acquire the art of persuasion. This is the traditional story of the word's origin. We must note however that 'blarney' cannot be found in print before the nineteenth century, when we must associate its appearance with the increasing Irish immigration to England.

blazer The man's jacket once colourfully striped though now more usually navy blue takes its name from a ship of the Royal Navy, *HMS Blazer*, whose Captain, J. W. Washington, in 1845 dressed his boat's crew in blue and white striped jackets. The new style was much affected by rowing clubs and the fashion spread to schools and colleges.

blighty From the Hindu *bilayti*, 'far away', and used to mean home or the homeland first by soldiers in India and then on the battlefields of the First World War. The word can also refer to the wound that ensured a rapid return to the homeland.

Blimp, Colonel Cartoon character invented by David Low of the London *Evening Standard*. Blimp, depicted as an ex-Indian Army man, represented the forces of utterly uninformed, unimaginative and blind reaction.

blimp As a name for the non-rigid type of airship this derives from the naming of experimental prototypes during the First World War. These frameless balloons were described as 'limp'. The A-limp model was not a success. B-limp was.

blindfold The true origin is the Middle English *blindfeld* 'struck blind' from Anglo Saxon *fiellan* 'to strike'. The form 'fold' derives from the folded handkerchief tied around the eyes of the 'victim' in the old game of Blind Man's Buff.

blind pig American term for an illicit drinking establishment. When the sale of hard liquor was prohibited the ban was evaded by letting the customer pay to see some alleged curiosity, e.g. a blind pig, and then giving him the drink free.

blockbuster British name in the Second World War for what was for the time a superlarge bomb weighing eight thousand pounds. The word is now sometimes used for a decisive argument brought in to terminate a discussion.

blowed in the glass Meaning absolutely genuine this predominantly American expression derives from the practice of liquor manufacturers and others having their names 'blown' (actually moulded) in the bottle as a guarantee of the product's authenticity. Anything without the name 'blowed in the glass' was suspect. Compare the traditional British phrase 'dyed in the wool'.

blue-blooded A term of Spanish origin, associating aristocracy with paleness of skin as proved by the degree to which the veins were visible through it. In these circumstances the veins appear blue.

blue stocking A derogatory term for a learned woman. It ultimately derives from an intellectual clique in fifteenth-century Venice whose 'club badge' was the use of blue stockings. In the 1590s a group of women in Paris adopted the badge, and from there the name travelled to England.

blurb A brief and eulogistic note on the character and contents of a book printed on its paper dust-jacket. A strikingly successful example of this on a book by the American writer Gellette Burgess featured a Miss Belinda Blurb, and this name came to be associated with all such wrapper advertisements. The word entered Standard English in the 1920s.

boards, *to tread the* This phrase, now only used ironically, means simply to be an actor. In early days the stage was often a makeshift affair of boards on trestles in some temporarily converted building. See also PLATFORM for a similar usage.

Bobby Nickname for a London policeman deriving from the name of Sir Robert Peel (1788–1850) who founded the original London force. An alternative name was 'peeler' and this form was preferred in Ireland.

Bob's your uncle   The origin of this has been much disputed and an Irish origin has been suggested. This is only indirectly true. The phrase became current *c.* 1890 and has been associated with the appointment of Arthur Balfour as Secretary for Ireland by his uncle the Prime Minister, Robert Cecil, Lord Salisbury. 'Bob's your uncle' is the guarantee that things will work out to your advantage.

bogus   Most likely from the French *bagasse*, meaning 'trash' or 'rubbish'. A Boston, Massachusetts, newspaper once related the word to the activities of a notorious swindler of the 1830s called Borghese. This origin is unproven, but the word as we have it may well be an echo of both influences.

bohemian   Perhaps obsolescent, but still to be encountered as a description of the unconventional life style of artists and writers, the adjective derives from *bohémien*, the French word for 'gipsy'. (Gipsies often gave themselves a fictional origin. Our own word is in fact a corruption of Egyptian.) In French *la vie de bohème* means 'living from hand to mouth', but when Henri Murger's novel of that title was turned into opera by Puccini the 'romantic' associations of the word became irremovably established in the public mind.

bones (*to make no bones about something*)   This means to swallow or accept something without finding any difficulty or making any objection. To come straight to the point. Another eating metaphor is that of 'biting off more than one can chew'.

bone to pick (*to have a bone to pick with someone*)   To wish to discuss something with someone, with the suggestion of a complaint against them. This picturesque expression suggests the sight of two medieval diners bending their heads together over the object of their interest. A 'bone of contention', on the other hand, is something positively quarrelled over.

bone up   Student slang for intensive study, deriving from the firm of Bohn, famous for its literal versions of classical texts, which, for examinations, are notoriously studied in translation.

boondoggle Invented by an American, Robert Link, as a name for the elaborate and utterly useless leather thong worn by Boy Scouts. By transference the name was given to attempts to create work where none existed made by the Federal government of the United States during the depression.

boutique In the years after 1945 Paris couture houses began using their foyer space for a 'shop within a shop' selling accessories, etc. Such shops were called *boutiques* and the term reached Britain in the 1960s and was used by small expensive 'fashion' shops. The word itself is simply a French word for a small shop, deriving ultimately from the Greek *apotheke* – a place where goods are displayed. Ironically the English word 'shop' is now much in vogue in France.

bowdlerise To expurgate a book, usually to an unnecessary degree. Thomas Bowdler (1754–1825) was a British editor whose versions of Shakespeare and other authors were prudishly innocuous.

box the compass A sea phrase describing the feat of reciting all the thirty-two points of the compass in order. It now refers to a complete reversal of former opinions, perhaps because being able to box the compass indicated an acquaintance with too many opposite points of view.

boycott To have no dealings with someone. In the struggle between the Irish peasant and his absentee landlord in the 1880s, Captain Boycott was a landlord's agent who made himself unpopular. He was treated 'as the leper of old' and shunned by all the community. Compare 'sending to Coventry', an English equivalent.

brainwashing Translation of a Chinese phrase that became widely used after the Korean War of 1950–3. In Chinese usage it meant 'cleansing' the minds of prisoners of their capitalist ideas and making them sympathetic to communist

24

viewpoints. In English usage it has the wider and more general significance of securing mental dominance over someone. Every coin has two sides!

brand new Originally this phrase applied to metal objects only, fresh from the smith's fire. In Germanic languages, of which Old English was one, *brand* means 'fire'. Now the phrase simply means 'visibly new'.

brass In northern England a term used for money. England's 'copper' coins were officially described as 'bronze', and there has always been confusion between brass and bronze in popular usage. In the Authorised or King James version of the Old Testament what modern archaeologists describe as bronze is uniformly called brass. Brass is also 'cheek', insolence or temerity approaching, in fact, the Yiddish conception of *chutzpah*. Bold as brass never refers to standing out in any admirable way.

brassed off Totally, utterly bored, as with the mindless routine of army life. A variant is 'browned off'. A 'brown' was London slang for a penny, and to be browned off was to be given a penny to go away and not be a nuisance. We end as we began, with the coinage.

brass hats High-ranking army officers with masses of gilt insignia on their caps.

brass rags, to part A naval expression. Sailors who habitually worked together when, for example, cleaning the bright metal parts of the ship often kept their joint store of cleaning materials in one bag. Should they quarrel this common store would be split. They had 'parted brass rags'.

brass tacks In old-style drapers' shops cloth was measured against evenly spaced brass-headed nails (tacks) on the edge of the counter. When you 'got down to brass tacks' you were actually measuring off something bought by a customer.

break, *to give someone an even* To give them a fair chance. In

25

coursing, the sport in which a pair of greyhounds race to catch a hare, the dogs must receive 'an even break', an absolutely simultaneous release from the double leash in which they were brought up to the starting point. The same sport gives us the phrase 'straining at the leash'.

bridegroom This rather curious word is a straight derivation from the Anglo-Saxon *brydguma*, 'brideman' and the German *der Braütigam* keeps close to the original. In England the form 'groom' was supplied and rationalised as 'attendant'. 'Groom' is based on the Old Norse *gromr*, 'a boy'.

bridge The card game much favoured by the socially 'select' would seem to take its name from the Russian *biritsch* – a form of whist. But what wit gave 'the poor man's bridge' the name pontoon?

brief encounter 'An extra-marital affair deeply moving but unconsummated'. From a successful film of that title starring Trevor Howard and released in 1945.

brinksmanship Coined by American statesman Adlai Stevenson as a modern equivalent of 'Sabre rattling' and admittedly based on English humorist Stephen Potter's 'gamesmanship' 'lifemanship', etc.

Brodie, *to do a* An attempt at suicide. The reference is to a Steve Brodie who jumped from the old Brooklyn Bridge over the East River – and survived. His fame encouraged him to open a Bowery saloon. Brodie was portrayed by the late George Raft in the 1933 classic gangster film *The Bowery*.

Browned off See BRASSED OFF.

bucket, *to kick the* The bucket here was a wooden frame on which a pig was hung by its feet after slaughter. To 'have kicked the bucket' is therefore to have died.

Buckley's chance An Australian phrase for the most remote of chances. William Buckley was a convict who escaped and, against incredible odds, survived among the Aborigines for thirty years. By a strange coincidence, a Melbourne business with the name Buckley and Nunn became linked in the popular mind with this phrase. In a very tight corner you have two chances: Buckley's or none! Compare HOBSON'S CHOICE.

Bughouse Square This contemptuous term was bestowed on Washington Square, Chicago, Union Square, New York, and other such places which commonly witnessed mass meetings and demonstrations, especially in the 1930s. A cynical reaction to signs of distress.

bulldoze From the American South. A dose (of the whip) sufficient for a bull or from a bull-whip, hence, any coercion or overriding by brute force, and finally we get 'bulldozer', a machine that carries out just this function.

bumf At first Public School and Services slang for toilet paper the term is now widely used to mean unnecessary documentation, unsolicited publicity material or any bureaucratic 'software'. It derives from 'bum fodder' an expression used since the seventeenth century for any printed matter deemed to be of a contemptible character.

bunk, bunkum Nonsense, from Buncombe, North Carolina. When a Congressman was censured for pointless and time-wasting talk he justified it as being, not for the House, but 'for Buncombe' where he had been elected. Felix Walker of the XVIth Congress is the man usually named in the story.

Burke 'To burke the issue' is to stifle a tricky or embarrassing question. Burke was a notorious Scots murderer who smothered his victims and sold their bodies to teachers of anatomy. When he came out for execution in 1829 the waiting crowd cried out 'Burke him', thinking hanging was too humane.

Burton, *gone for a* Second World War Royal Air Force euphemism for being killed in action or, when applied to objects, being hopelessly damaged. Theories as to its origin abound. It has been variously related to a 1930s beer advertisement ('Where's Charlie?' 'Gone for a Burton'), to the inflatable 'Berthon' jackets of the old Royal Flying Corps and to the radio proficiency tests held over Burton's shop in Blackpool after rigorous training at Olympia. There are many others – some quite frivolous and a book could be written about them.

bury the hatchet This derives, it is said, from the Amerindian custom of symbolically burying weapons of war no longer needed.

busman's holiday Certain drivers of the old London horse-buses were so attached to their horses that they would spend their rest day as a passenger on their own bus to see that the horses were properly treated. A busman's holiday, then, is to spend your free time in the same way as when at work.

by and large A nautical expression now used in a metaphorical sense. To sail 'by and large' was to keep slightly off the line of the wind to reduce the risk of being suddenly 'taken aback'. To speak 'by and large', then, is to speak without meticulous exactness, perhaps as an interested amateur rather than as a professional.

by-election Not the same origin as by-law, but an extra election, out of the normal course of events.

by-law Law of local application only, from the Danish *by*, 'a town'. Plot on a map of England all the places with names ending in 'by' and you will have marked out the area of former Danish settlement.

C

cab The immediate origin of this word is the French cabriolet, a one-horse carriage of the type first licensed in London in 1823. The ultimate origin, however, is the Italian *capriola*, the playful leaping of the goat. The name derives from the speed and lightness of this type of vehicle as compared with its lumbering predecessors.

cabal This means a clique of intriguers. Ultimately derived from the Hebrew *qaballah*, the study of the secret meaning of the Jewish scriptures, the word was current in French and German as well as in English. In 1670 it was given a new lease of life when someone noticed that the initials of a group of unpopular ministers, Clifford, Ashley, Buckingham, Arlington, Lauderdale, made up CABAL. This fixed the nature of the term as one of reproach.

Cabinet This word first meant a little room and came from the Italian *cabinetto*. A small room would be most suitable for the meetings of an inner ring of confidential councillors and soon the men themselves were called after the place where they were to be found. Compare the custom of saying 'the throne' when we mean the king who sits on it.

caboodle 'The whole caboodle' means 'the whole lot', 'absolutely everything' and probably derives from the Danish *boedel*, meaning 'property' inheritance or household goods. See also LOCK, STOCK AND BARREL.

ca' canny A Scottish phrase meaning to work deliberately slowly as a form of protest. Ca' is to drive or push along. Canny is cannily or shrewdly. Working to rule, going slow, and non-co-operation are variants of the idea.

caddy This traditional word for a tea container derives from the Malay *kati*, a weight of just over a pound.

caddy (*in golf*) This word came to us from France via Scotland. *Cadet* is French for the younger of two brothers. In one direction it came to mean a trainee army officer or member of a pre-army training unit, in another it attached itself to the golfer's bag-carrier and adviser. In eighteenth-century Edinburgh 'caddies' were street loungers who made a living by providing such casual services as anyone might require, bag-carrying, showing the way, taking messages, etc. The derogatory term 'cad' is also a development of cadet or caddy. The socially humble are regularly regarded as dishonest and contemptible. See BLACKGUARDS.

cadge A cadge was once a pedlar's basket, so pedlars were said to 'cadge' for a living. Now it means to beg or borrow, or rather to make a habit of begging or borrowing.

cafeteria Originally coined in Los Angeles, California, in the 1950s this proved to be only the first of a long series of similar formations. It derives from the Spanish *cafetera*, 'coffee pot'.

cakewalk 'It's a cakewalk' means a prize easily won or something for no real effort. Negroes of the old South dressed in their best and walked in couples round a prize cake. The most elegant pair 'took the cake'.

calculate, calculation These words derive from the Latin *calculus*, a 'pebble'. Roman numerals were not intended to be used in pen-and-paper arithmetic, but for recording conveniently the 'answer' when obtained by the use of pebble counters on a board abacus.

Canary Islands, *the* According to Roman tradition these islands took their name from the dogs (Latin *canes*) which abounded there. The local yellow finches took their name from the islands and not the other way about.

candidate From the Latin *candidus*, 'white' In Ancient Rome seekers of public office wore white robes (hence, *candidatus*, 'clothed in white') perhaps to signify the purity of their intentions. See also CANVASS for more political cloth.

canoe The advice 'Paddle your own canoe' was first given by the author Captain Marryat in 1843, but the phrase only became popular when used by Sarah Bolton in a poem in *Harper's Magazine*.

canopy   The strange origin of this word is the Greek name given to the primitive mosquito nets used by fishermen on the Nile.

cant   This means hypocritical talk or argument. The Latin 'cant-' is part of the verb 'to sing' and was applied to the nasal manner of speech said to be characteristic of the Puritans. Traditionally it was a pair of Scottish brothers, Alex and Andrew Cant, who perfectly exemplified their name, who gave the old word a new lease of life.

canteen   This word of many uses originally meant a wine cellar. From this beginning it evolved into a name for a place of refreshment, and then for a bottle of wine or water carried by soldiers on the march. A canteen of cutlery is a full set in a substantial case. The name here derives from the container.

canter   Canter is derived from Canterbury and was the leisurely pace of horse-riding preferred by medieval pilgrims to that city.

canvass   The word now means to go about seeking orders, opinions or, most commonly, votes. It originally meant to make intensive enquiries or a close examination. It is from the Old French *canabasser*, 'to sift through canvas', a coarse cloth made from hemp.

caper   When we caper we leap about playfully like a young goat. The actual derivation of the word is from the Italian. See CAB. Native English uses the same image as in the phrases 'acting the goat', playing the giddy goat'. To film fans a 'caper movie' is one about an ingeniously conceived robbery plan, well exemplified by such films as *The Italian Job* or *Topkapi*.

capitalism, *the unacceptable face of*   Phrase used on 15 May 1973 by Edward Heath in a speech in the House of Commons, referring to methods of tax avoidance, etc., by large companies, which were legal yet obviously unacceptable to the ordinary public who were unable to use such loopholes even on a minor scale. It caught the imagination and was adapted to other purposes, e.g. the 'unacceptable face' of anything which was otherwise considered in itself 'acceptable' by the speaker, either genuinely or ironically.

carat This word, the name of a jeweller's weight, comes from the Arabic *qirat*, meaning 'the seed of the locust tree'. The carat was equivalent to the Roman *silequa* or one twenty-fourth of the gold *solidus*. In this way it came to be used as a measure of the purity of gold. Nine-carat gold is only nine twenty-fourths pure. Because gold is a rather soft metal twenty-two carat is the normal maximum.

cards A great many popular phrases derive from card games or from the use of cards in fortune-telling. 'It's on the cards' is an example of the latter and means 'It seems very likely that . . .' A sure card is one certain to win. A leading card is the first argument used in a debate or discussion to set the tone or test the resources of one's opponent. A trump card is one sure to win. To turn up trumps is to come in and save the situation. Trump is a corruption of triumph. Trumps must win. Which cards are trumps depends on the rules of the game being played. A queer card is one difficult to sum up. To say of someone, 'He's a card' or 'a-bit of a card' means that the card in question is 'The joker'.

careful, *if you can't be good be* Although this jocular warning only gained wide circulation in the first decades of the twentieth century it was well known to medieval preachers in a Latin version *Si non caste tamen caute*. Tradition attributed it to St Paul.

care will kill a cat First used by Ben Jonson (1573–1637) in the play *Every Man in his Humour*, and repeated verbatim by George Wither (1588–1667) in his 'Poem on Christmas': 'Hang sorrow. Care'll kill a cat.'

carpet To be on the carpet is to be called before one's superior for reprimand. In the British Civil Service attainment of a certain status carries with it the right to a piece of carpet in one's office.

carpetbaggers These were opportunist politicians owning little more than the contents of their carpet bags who set off for the conquered Confederacy after the American Civil War, hoping to exploit the newly enfranchised Negro voters.

carpet knight A knight, usually a civilian, given the honour in comfort as opposed to the traditional hero knighted on the field of battle.

Carruthers of the Foreign Office Now a stock figure in anti-establishment satire on stage or screen, the original Carruthers of the Foreign Office was a serious, indeed sympathetic character in Erskine Childers's 1903 yachting and espionage classic, *The Riddle of the Sands*.

carry coals to Newcastle This means to do a useless task. Newcastle upon Tyne was once the main source of London's coal. Notice the obsolete plural 'coals'. A country version of this sentiment talks of 'taking water to the well'.

carte, *a la* The opposite to *table d'hôte* (q.v.). French for 'according to the sheet of paper, or menu card', it originally meant a list of dishes which could be specially prepared on request, so costing more than taking whatever the host would be having in any case at his own table. Nowadays, the distinction is almost invariably one of cost only.

carte blanche In the case of a military defeat, the conquered party might have to place their signature on a *carte blanche* or 'blank piece of paper', leaving the conquerors to fill in their own terms. Hence the figurative meaning of giving someone freedom to act on behalf of others in any way they wish. The same idea is seen in 'to write a blank cheque'.

cartoon Originally a painted sketch for a tapestry or some similar art project the word derives from the Latin *charta*, 'a paper', via the Italian form *cartone* 'a big (piece of) paper'.

The modern meaning emerged when the magazine *Punch* satirised the designs for the new Victorian Houses of Parliament. Nowadays the primary sense of cartoon is 'an animated film'.

case-hardened To say of an offender that he is case-hardened means that he is impervious to reforming influences. The word comes from metallurgy, and refers to a process by which the outside only of a soft iron object could be given the hardness of steel.

cash There are two origins here which are difficult to disentangle. One root is the Old French *casse*, 'money-box', from the Latin *capsa* of the same meaning. This word has a variety of parallel forms in other languages (Serbo-Croat *kasi*, Spanish *caja*, German *Kasse*), not to mention the French *caisse*, all meaning 'cash-desk'. The other is the word *cash*, actually of southern Indian (Tamil) origin, used for a heavy square Chinese copper coin. It was the inconvenience of this metal coinage that caused the Emperor Hien Tsun *c.* A.D. 800 to devise 'flying money' made of paper.

cat (*not enough room to swing a cat in*) The cat in this case is the nine-stringed whip, the 'cat o' nine tails', once freely used to maintain discipline in the old Royal Navy.

cat (*to let the cat out of the bag*) This means to reveal a secret, usually without meaning to do so. Piglets were sometimes taken to market in a bag (the proverbial pig in a poke), and wily dealers were said to try passing off cats on to foolish buyers. Cats were not always co-operative and the trick was sometimes exposed. In similar circumstances one might also be 'sold a pup'.

cat's-paw One used as a tool by another. The allusion is to the fable in which a monkey persuades a cat to 'pull his chestnuts out of the fire' for him.

Catch 22 From the 1955 novel of that title by Joseph Heller. The story is set in a US airbase in the last days of the Second

34

World War. The colonel relentlessly increases the number of missions each man must fly before his stint is completed. Men are on the verge of cracking. Incipient insanity would be a valid reason for grounding them but a concern for one's own safety is deemed to be the act of a rational mind so they must keep flying. Use of this phrase reflects the rational man's despair when he falls into the hands of a crazy bureaucracy.

caucus An American term for a meeting of politicians to discuss the claims of candidates for party office. It originates from a Red Indian word for adviser.

causeway This old word for 'a paved way', usually across marshy ground, was once 'causey', a straight derivation from the French *chausée* 'a high way'. As the old sense of the word was forgotten, 'way' was added to rationalise it. See SLEDGEHAMMER and PEA-JACKET for other examples of this process.

cellar If a salt cellar, the word is a corruption of the French *salière*, 'salt-dish'. If it is an underground store room it is from the Latin *cellarium* via French *cellier*, 'a store room'.

Celtic Sea This term used by oilmen for the water between Wales, Ireland and South West England was coined in 1921 by marine biologist E. W. L. Holt but applied by him to an area considerably further south reaching to Brittany.

Cenotaph This famous Whitehall monument to Britain's war dead gets its name from two Greek words meaning 'empty tomb', a form of monument used for those who died far away from home and whose bodies could not be recovered.

chain reaction This phrase describing the key process in the liberation of atomic energy was coined in 1934 by Hungarian physicist Leo Szilard. According to Professor J. Bronowski the concept of this possibility, namely that if an atom could be struck by a neutron and two were released by the 'explosion' this process might continue indefinitely, came to

Szilard while standing in Southampton Row, London, waiting for a traffic light to change.

chalk, *a long* The phrase is usually negative, e.g. 'He'll never do it, not by a long chalk'. The reference seems to be to marking up the score in a game. A variant form, 'not by long chalks', is perhaps more accurate, meaning 'not by long lines of chalk marks'.

chalk it up 'Make a note of what I owe and I will pay it later.' The phrase comes from the practice of village inns where credit was readily given to well known customers. A variant is 'Put it on the slate'. See also PS AND QS.

changes, *ringing the* It means re-using the same components (e.g. items of clothing) in new combinations to create a variety of effects from a limited amount of material and is derived from English traditional bellringing where the aim is the faultless ringing of all possible combinations of a set of bells rather than the Continental 'tune playing'. In racing parlance a 'ringer' is one horse substituted for another. Ringing the changes is also the name of a petty swindle in which a shopkeeper is confused into giving too much change.

chapel As a name for a branch of a printers' trade union this word always causes surprise. The traditional, though incorrect, explanation of its origin refers to the fact that Caxton, the first English printer, set up his press within the precincts of Westminster Abbey. This is true enough, but we find the word used in a similar way in France where the site of Caxton's workshop is of no significance whatever. A possible alternative origin might be from *chapellerie*, 'a hatter's workshop', for the hatters were strongly organised from very early times. Research has yet to decide this question.

charlatan Despite the many strange stories told, this word is simply a variant of the Italian *cialatano*, a 'quack' or 'swindler'.

Charley More This is Royal Navy slang for all that is

honest, upright and reasonable. It is said to derive from the sign displayed by a publican in Malta, 'Charley More, the Fair Thing'.

Charley Paddock, *to do a* Obsolete expression in the United States for making one's escape, especially from the police by running. Paddock was a noted athlete. Compare the British 'do a Bannister'.

chauvinism This word, meaning fanatical 'patriotism', especially of a reactionary and militarist type, derives from Nicholas Chauvin, one of Napoleon's veterans and his devoted admirer. The English equivalent is jingoism. See JINGOES. Women's Lib. has popularised the cliché 'male chauvinist pig'.

cheesed off This expression which means utterly bored (compare 'browned off', 'brassed off') must have been coined by someone who knew his Dickens for in the fiftieth chapter of *The Old Curiosity Shop* Dick Swiveller, when asked 'And how is the cream of the clerkship?' replies, 'Turning rather sour, I'm afraid; almost to cheeseness.'

chestnut A chestnut is an old, oft-repeated joke well known to all. The origin of the term may be found in an early nineteenth-century melodrama, *The Broken Sword*, in which a character, Pablo, corrects a reference to a cork tree by saying, 'A chestnut! I have heard you tell the story twenty-seven times.'

chivalry A most interesting word with many linguistic relations. Chivalry today is a rather old-fashioned word for a rather old-fashioned kind of courteous conduct. The original chivalry was the code of conduct expected of the medieval knight. It derives from the French *cheval*, 'horse', which in its turn goes back to the popular Latin *caballus*. A Spanish gentleman is a *caballero*, a French knight is a *chevalier* – the letters 'b' and 'v' being near relations – and so we find in English 'cavalry' and 'cavalier', but 'cavalier conduct' is not chivalrous, it is high-handed and positively discourteous. Superior conduct was expected from a man rich enough to ride a horse and this idea has become built into our language.

chivy (chevy) Used in the sense of chasing someone about (literally or in metaphor) this word is a humorous coinage from the title of a famous ballad 'Chevy Chase'.

choice, *Hobson's* Hobson was a Cambridge horse-keeper who insisted that his horses should only be used in regular order. The would-be hirer had to take Hobson's choice, not his own. Hobson's choice is therefore no choice at all.

choke (*someone*) **off** This now means to reprimand or rebuke, but the original picture is that of a dog-fight. A dog would be gripped by the throat and choked to make him release his hold.

chowder The famous American clam-stew (which has its own chapter in Melville's *Moby Dick*) gets its name from the French *chaudière*, 'a cauldron' and this in turn comes from the Latin *caldaria* which has the same meaning.

church mouse, *as poor as a* Since there is no kitchen or larder in a church, the mouse who lives there obviously has a very thin time.

clap-trap A theatrical term for any device to induce cheap applause, it is now used to mean cant or insincere nonsense.

claque A set of people known as *claqueurs* could be hired to applaud a particular play, or even one actor or actress in it. The claque was a regular feature of the Paris theatres from the 1820s. In Britain the term is only used metaphorically.

clink, *in the* Although this semi-obsolete slang term was used to mean in any prison, 'The Clink' was once the name of a specific prison on London's Bankside. It, in turn, took its name from the district in which it stood, the Liberty of the Clink, a district of Southwark exempted from the jurisdiction of the City of London.

clover Clover is the best pasturage for cattle. To be very well content with one's situation is thus 'to be in clover'.

clue In Old English, a ball of thread. A ball of thread can help you find your way through a maze, as in the story of Theseus and the Cretan labyrinth. From this it can be easily seen how 'clues' lead to the solution of mysteries. 'I haven't a clue' means 'I have no idea at all'. To describe someone as clueless implies lack of initiative.

cobweb When we know that *coppe* was an Old English word for 'spider' this apparently odd word makes simple sense.

cock-and-bull story This phrase is a reference to the fables of old in which animals spoke. It is now used of something that simply cannot be believed.

Cocker (*it is all according to Cocker*) Cocker was the author of a popular textbook in mathematics. An American variant is 'according to Gunter', who devised the standard surveyor's chain. Both phrases mean 'correct' or 'just as it should be'.

cock-fighting 'That beats cock-fighting' is said either literally or ironically in astonishment at some spectacle. 'To live like fighting cocks' means to have the best of everything, as did valuable fighting cocks in training.

cock of the walk The dominant character of a group. When poultry was kept in a confined 'walk', one cockerel would soon emerge as dominant. See also PECKING ORDER.

cockpit The miniature arena in which the game-cocks fought, hence any scene of repeated battle, e.g. Belgium has been called 'the cockpit of Europe'. The word is also used quite independently for the control seat, into which the pilot had carefully to insert himself, in old one- or two-man aircraft.

cocktail Many weird and implausible stories are told about this word. The authentic originator of the cocktail seems to

39

have been Antoine Peychaud of New Orleans. Since *Coquetel* existed as the name of a mixed drink popular in south-west France, it is logical to see the new word as derived from this old one.

codswallop Now a general term meaning 'nonsense' the expression derives from *c.* 1870 when one Hiram Codd invented the bottle closed by a glass marble in its neck and held in place by the pressure of the gaseous lemonade within. 'Wallop' was a slang term for beer. Codswallop was far from the real thing!

cohort Increasingly, under American influence, the word cohort is being used in the sense of associate and sometimes of henchman. Its original and, until recently, its only use was as the name of a Roman military formation, the tenth part of a legion. In the generalised sense of subsection it entered the vocabulary of botany for a group of families making up a logical subdivision of a class. Sociologists also use it similarly, but as meaning 'associate' it is simply an error now established by much repetition.

cold shoulder To be given the cold shoulder is to be actively discouraged from social contact. It seems to derive from offering the unwanted visitor only left-over meat that involves no preparation, and symbolises one's lack of enthusiasm for his coming.

coloursupp. Used in a pejorative way in much the same sense as 'trendy' this expression derives from the 'colour magazines' or 'supplements' issued by some of the leading British newspapers, notably the *Sunday Times,* from the early sixties. The supplements consist largely of advertising matter and have great influence on middle-class life styles.

come up to scratch In the old bareknuckle boxing matches contestants had to start the fight with their left foot on a line scratched on the ground between them, and moreover, 'come up to scratch' at the start of each new round or forfeit the contest.

companion   From the Latin *panis*, 'bread', 'companions' are those who eat their bread together. Compare the naval 'mess mate'.

con amore   This is Italian for 'with love'. In modern English usage it means free in the sense of 'without recompense'.

constable   The English language is replete with words of 'horsy' origins (see the notes on HENCHMAN and MARSHAL). Constable also belongs to this class. It derives from the Old French *conestable*, which is the Latin *comes stabuli*, 'Count of the stable'. The line of evolution began when the 'Master of the Horse' (an equivalent English court title) became responsible for peace-keeping in the immediate vicinity of the monarch. The name then acquired its association with law enforcement.

Contemptibles, *Old*   Members of the British Expeditionary Force that went to France in 1914. The German Emperor is said to have referred to them as 'a contemptible little army'. He probably said 'contemptibly little', which is not quite the same.

contract, *a social*   Much bandied about in the Labour Movement in the mid 1970s this term was used to mean a proposed agreement between a Labour government and the Trade Union movement to work together for economic and political improvement. Its first use in this context (as opposed to the historic one by Locke and Rousseau) is variously ascribed to James Callaghan, Lord Balogh and the former Dennis Lyons, now Lord Lyons of Brighton. It all came to nothing.

copper bottomed   Where this is not merely descriptive of a saucepan, but is used to indicate a distinctly desirable investment, it derives from the insurers' preference for the faster-sailing, teredo-proofed, copper-sheathed ships of the mid eighteenth century.

corn in Egypt   A slang expression meaning abundance or

41

plenty. The brothers of Joseph, in the Biblical story, went down to Egypt for corn when their own land was starving.

corporation This is a slang term for a large paunch from the traditional picture of a city councillor, a member of the Corporation. In the old days civic life was marked by frequent banquets for those in office.

cosh From the Romany (gipsy) word for a stick. In Britain in the 1950s there was much concern about cosh-boys, young robbers who clubbed their victims into insensibility before robbing them. New Yorkers are familiar with the same sort of thing as 'mugging'.

costermonger See MONGER.

coventrate Term used in Second World War for obliteration by bombing as happened to Coventry, England on the night of 14/15 November 1940.

Coventry, *to send someone to* This means to be banned from social contact. Royalist prisoners in the English Civil War were 'sent to Coventry', as there the population would have no sympathy for them.

coward This derives from the Latin *cauda*, 'a tail' through the French *couard*. The English phrase 'to turn tail' has in it the same basic image.

cricket (*it's not cricket*) The modern game of cricket emerged in England in the latter part of the eighteenth century. In less than a century cricket and fair play had come to be interchangeable terms. 'It's not cricket' is therefore a rebuke to someone who appears to be deviating from the highest standards of conduct.

credibility gap, *the* The difference between what is claimed as fact, especially in matters of official government policy, and actuality. The phrase was first used in 1966 by Gerald Ford, then an American Republican Congressman, in connection with the discrepancy between the actual escalation of American participation in the Vietnam War, and the claim by the Johnson administration that no change had taken place in policy.

Croesus, *as rich as* Croesus was the fabulously rich King of Lydia in Asia Minor (560–546 B.C.). Lydia is said to have been the first state to use coinage.

cross (*to be cross as two sticks*) Another example of verbal confusion. One stick laid upon another is 'cross'. As a phrase implying undoubted anger, irritability, etc., it is all but pointless. Compare BELL, as clear as a.

crow's nest The look-out post at the very top of a ship's mast, named from comparison with a high-built nest. A fantastic derivation alleges that Vikings used homing ravens to search for land. This is too obviously based on the story of Noah, and a crow is not a raven, either in Old Norse or modern English.

cryonics In 1964 Professor Robert Ettlinger of Detroit published *Prospect of Immortality* in which he advocated the deep and rapid freezing of subjects at the moment of their apparent death in order to prevent, or at least arrest, the process of true cellular death, and so preserve them in a state of 'cryonic suspension' until medical science was better able to tackle the case in question. Supporters of this 'death foiling tactic' are called cryonicists from the Greek *kryos* 'cold'. Although several subjects have been deepfrozen in the way suggested, the first in 1967, no one has yet been unfrozen to verify the cryonicists' crucial claim.

curry favour, *to* To seek advancement by flattery or excessive attention to someone. To curry is a horseman's word for 'groom' or 'rub down'. The original phrase spoke of 'currying Favel', a marvellous horse in medieval romance.

Curse of Scotland This traditional name for the nine of diamonds has, it might be said, far too many origins. The standard explanation is that on this card was written the Duke of Cumberland's order to give no quarter after the Battle of Culloden (1746). The phrase, however, was in use before this time. For example, an unpopular judge, Lord Justice Clerk Ormistone, was known as the Curse of Scotland and when the nine of diamonds appeared on the card table it was called 'the Justice Clerk'. Again it has been related to the nine lozenges on the arms of Dalrymple, the Earl of Stair, who was hated not only for his link with the Glencoe Massacre but also for his part in the Act of Union with England (1707). In summary, we may say that long-standing tradition associates the name 'Curse of Scotland' with this particular card, and that although the true origin of this association has long been lost, there has been a tendency to associate the name with some currently unpopular figure.

curtains Originally United States usage only but quickly transmitted to Britain via the gangster movies, this euphemism for death is said to derive from the 'Death Rows' of American prisons where the other cells were curtained off when a man was led to execution. In England it was customary for houses to draw their curtains on the day of a neighbour's funeral so the expression would be readily understood there as well and indeed, makes better sense against this background.

D

dab To be a 'dab', or a 'dab hand', at something means to be an exceptional performer at it. The word has its origin in 'adept' from the Latin *adeptus*, 'one who has attained', that is, one who has attained skill in an art. To dab a wound, however, has a different source. This comes from the Old Dutch *dabben* and Old English *dubben*, meaning 'to strike or hit'. A man was 'dubbed a knight' in a ceremony that involved his being touched on the shoulders with a sword.

dachshund This popular breed of dog, originating in Germany, is a 'badger dog'. In German *der Dachs* is the badger. The short legged, long bodied dachshund was ideally formed to tackle the badger in its underground tunnels. In England the sealyham was used in similar fashion. The dachshund's nickname, 'sausage dog', now seems to be obsolete.

dahlia This popular garden flower takes its name from Anders Dahl (d. 1789), who introduced it into Europe from Mexico in 1784. See also FUCHSIA for a similar formation.

dairy The current association of this word with milk is quite fortuitous. It derives from the Old English *Daeg*, 'day', and was the scene of the day's work. The principal women's work on the Saxon homestead was milking the cows and the preparation of butter and cheese.

daisy The name of this flower is also from the Old English 'day'. The daisy is 'the day's eye'. It closes as the sun goes down and opens again each morning.

dam The phrase 'I don't give a dam' or 'I don't care a dam' has a disputed origin. One theory identifies the dam with an Indian coin of trivial value. The Dutch 'stiver' and the Irish 'rap' were certainly referred to in this way in similar phrases, but another suggestion is that the 'dam' was a piece of clay used by a tinker to stop a hole in a kettle or pot while he repaired it from the outside. The dam was then discarded. This dam was also known as a 'cuss', hence the low value set on 'a tinker's cuss'. Against the theory of Hindi origin is the fact that the word would be heard by English ears as pronounced 'dawm'. Oliver Goldsmith did not care 'three damns' and the Duke of Wellington (who had incidentally made his name in India) 'did not care a twopenny damn'. The debate continues.

damask Damask is one of the many textiles – muslin and lisle are other examples – that take their name from their town of origin. Originally a rich silk brocade from Damascus, damask is now usually a material with a woven design used for table linen.

damn To wish to see someone damned is to hope for their condemnation to Hell. The word comes from the Latin *damnare*, 'to condemn', and this in turn from *damnum*, 'a loss'.

Dan (*from Dan to Beersheba*) A Biblical phrase meaning from one end of the country to the other. It is used in its simple literal sense in Judges xx: i. Laurence Sterne, the eighteenth-century novelist, seems to have been the first person to use the phrase in a metaphorical sense. This was in his *A Sentimental Journey* (1768).

dance 'To dance attendance on someone' is to be at their beck and call. The reference is to an old wedding custom in which the bride was required to dance with every guest and would have given grave offence had she not done so. As a writer in 1543 put it, 'Then must the poore bryde kepe foote with a dauncer, and refuse none, how scabbed, foule, droncken soever he be.'

dandelion This word has no connection with 'dandy' but means *dent de lion*, French for 'tooth of the lion', from the jagged tooth like edges of the leaf, thought to look like the teeth of a lion.

dander 'Is your dander up?' or 'riz' means 'Are you angry?' This phrase seems to be of American origin and has been associated with the Dutch *donder*, 'thunder', but in the West Indies dander was a ferment used in the preparation of molasses, and to be in a state of ferment is a fair description of 'having one's dander up'. See also DUNDERHEAD.

dandy
This word, meaning a fop or one overconscious of his elegant appearance, came into popular use in this sense just after the Napoleonic Wars. It is usually derived from 'dandle', to play with a toy. 'Playboy' could be a modern equivalent.

darbies An old word for handcuffs. It has been derived from 'Darby and Joan' because this old couple were inseparable, but the original Darby lived till 1740 and handcuffs, it seems, were 'Father Derbie's bands' as early as 1576. It is likely that a new joke was made about a much older word. 'Johnny Darbies' was a humorous English corruption of *gendarmes*.

Darby and Joan The affectionate nickname given to old married couples in the evening of their life. The term first appeared in a ballad by Henry Woodfall in the eighteenth century. As a boy, Woodfall was apprenticed to a London printer called John Darby whose wife was called Joan. Woodfall gave his master an unlooked-for immortality.

Davy Jones's locker A sailor's term for 'under the sea', especially with reference to those drowned or buried at sea. Davy Jones was conceived as 'the fiend that presides over all the spirits of the deep' (Smollett) and has appeared as such in pantomime. There is no proven origin for this term. Jonah has been invoked and so has Duffy, a West Indian ghost. Shonee was a Celtic sea god. Perhaps Davy Jones is only the ghost of a memory of all these.

D-Day The name given by the Allied Military Command in the Second World War to the day when the long-planned landing on the Normandy coast would begin. The sequence of events was carefully timed. At H-hour on D-day the operation would begin. Appropriate stages would be reached by D-day plus two, etc. Once the attack began the pattern would fit real dates. D-day proved to be 6 June 1944.

dead (*as a dodo*) Dead here usually means extinct, long vanished, out of fashion, laughably antique. The original dodo was a large flightless bird of Mauritius, of the pigeon family, utterly unable to defend itself and killed off by sailors before the end of the seventeenth century. Its name is from the Portuguese *doudo*, 'silly'.

dead (*as a door nail*) The 'door nail' is the large-headed one on which the door-knocker falls. Anything hit on the head with such force, so regularly, must be dead.

47

deadheads This is old theatrical slang for someone given a free place at a play or concert. It is probably no more than coincidence that some Graeco-Roman theatre tickets (in the form of coin-shaped tokens) have skulls depicted on them. In the ancient world the theatre was not commercial in our sense and so the question of *deadheads* hardly arose. See also ANNIE OAKLEY.

dead horse, *flogging a* The image here, of making efforts that cannot possibly elicit any response, seems a simple and obvious one but it has a curious relation in the old sailing ship phrase 'working the dead horse'. This referred to the first month at sea which, because of advances before sailing, was being worked for nothing. When the month was up a symbolic 'dead horse' was swayed to the yardarm and dumped in the sea. The dead horse days were over and a man was working for money again.

deadline A deadline today is some absolute time limit which must not be exceeded. The original deadline was an absolute space limit. The term comes from American prison usage. Anyone crossing the 'deadline' was likely to be shot.

deaf (*as a beetle*) The beetle in this case is not the insect, but the heavy wooden instrument used to drive in wedges or to level paving stones. A variant of the phrase is 'deaf as a post'. A post stands still and unresponsive because it has not heard.

dear, dearest These apparently simple words can have distinct and opposite meanings. When taken from the Old English *derian* it means 'to hate'. It is in this sense that Shakespeare wrote in *Hamlet,* I. ii: 'Would that I had met my dearest foe in Heaven.' If, however, it means someone beloved the derivation is from the Saxon, *deore*, meaning 'rare'.

deathwatch This is the popular name given to a species of beetle (*Xestobium rufovillosum*), which bores into dead wood.

The male makes a characteristic ticking sound, which was once held to be an omen of impending death, by striking its head against the wood in order to attract the female.

début This means to make a first appearance, and is a French word now naturalised into English.

December Obviously named from the Latin *decem* meaning 'ten', this seems a very odd name for the twelfth month. Equally odd are September, October and November as the seventh, eighth and ninth months. The names once were accurate, for in earlier systems, the year began with March.

decimate This is a word regularly misused particularly in newspapers. It does not mean 'almost annihilate'. It originally referred to a Roman military punishment involving the execution of each tenth man.

deco (*art*) This 'style label' was derived from the 1925 Paris Exhibition of Decorative and Industrial Arts and indicates an art inspired by the machine age, stark and functional, in opposition to the art nouveau of the preceding period which emulated the flowing lines of nature.

delirious This word, which describes the ramblings of a person whose mind is disordered by sickness, has a Latin origin: *lira* is a 'rut' or 'furrow'. Hence, *de lire* is 'from the furrow', 'out of the proper track', and so unguided and rambling.

demise This is one of the most misused words in the language. The wrong usage is to speak of a person's death as his demise. The word is from the French *démettre* which means 'to put down'. The demise of the Crown means the 'putting down' of the royal office, normally because of death. Hence the confusion.

denarius This was a Roman coin of low value and is mentioned here as the origin of the sign for pence in the pre-decimal British system, denoted by the letters £.s.d. The pound sign was an elaborate 'L' for *libri* (Latin for pounds) and the 's' stood for *solidi*, plural of solidus, a silver coin.

denims This coarse cotton material was originally serge *de Nîmes*, the French town which was once a centre of its manufacture. Many other textiles take their names from traditional places of origin: jeans, lisle, damask and worsted are parallel examples. In mainland Europe corduroy is often called *manchester*.

Devil The Devil in one sense or another is found in a variety of phrases, most of which have quite independent origins. 'Gone to the Devil', for example, was much used in connection with a tavern that stood in Fleet Street near to the London Law Courts. A barrister was often missing because he had gone 'to the Devil', and someone whose company was not wanted was told to go there. The phrase has rarely been used as a serious wish for another's damnation. 'The devil to pay', on the other hand, comes from the shipyards, and its origin is made clear by the usually forgotten second part which adds: 'and no pitch hot'. The devil here was one of the seams of a ship and to pay it was to seal it with pitch. To be 'between the devil and the deep blue sea' has a similar reference. A person thus placed was hanging over the side and so in a precarious position. An assistant barrister was known as a devil and so classically was a printer's boy. As one old writer put it, 'They do so commonly black and bedaub themselves that the workmen do jocosely call them devils.' Another story links the word with the Negro servant of Aldo Manuzio, the famous printer of Venice. Because early printers were suspected of magical arts, and because the Devil was traditionally black, the boy was seen as 'the printer's devil'. 'Devil take the hindmost' comes from the medieval story that the Devil had a school at Toledo in Spain. When the students had completed their studies they ran through an underground room, the last one being seized by the fiend and kept as his servant for ever. 'Devil among the tailors' once referred to a variant of the game of skittles in which wooden blocks had to be knocked over with a spinning top. Diabolo was another more recent game in which a whirling piece of wood was called a devil. In modern usage, however, 'Devil among the tailors' means an uproar and is a reminiscence of a riot in eighteenth-century London when a crowd of tailors demonstrated against a play that seemed to reflect unfairly on their trade. Finally, in the American West, barbed wire was known as 'Devil's rope'.

Devil, *to outdance the*   In the Middle Ages vast assemblies of witches are said to have taken place. Dancing was a feature of these 'Sabbats' in which the neophytes sought to emulate their master in frenzied dances which often ended in their death from exhaustion. To outdance the Devil is a fatal attempt to do the impossible.

devil's advocate   In the canonisation procedure of the Roman Church the claims of a 'cause', as a candidature is called, are minutely examined in a form similar to judicial process. An official Advocatus Diaboli, 'the devil's spokesman', has the task of seeking for flaws in the promoter's case which would prevent the cause being successful.

dexterous   Originally formed from the Latin word for 'right hand', this word now means skilful. See ADROIT.

dickey   This was a shirt-front, an additional protection, though later worn by the impoverished without the shirt it was supposed to cover. In its last years it became a comic 'prop' of the old-style comedian. The name comes from the German *decken*, 'to cover'.

die (*the die is cast*)   Die is the singular form of the more usual 'dice'. This phrase is a translation of words attributed to Julius Caesar when he crossed the Rubicon (another phrase meaning to take an irrevocable decision) and invaded Italy in a bid for supreme power in the state, '*Jacta alea est*',

'The dice have been thrown; I have made my gamble'. A close modern parallel is the phrase, 'The chips are down'.

digit This word for a single number derives from the widespread habit of counting on the fingers: *digitus* is the Latin for 'finger'.

digs, diggings A colloquial name for lodgings said to derive from the 'dug-out' winter homes of the Wisconsin lead miners. The normal association of the word 'diggings' is, however, with gold mining and the California gold rush.

dilemma The picturesque phrase 'On the horns of a dilemma' is perhaps more striking than exact. Its origin is the Greek *di*- or *dis*-, meaning twofold and *lemma*, a thing taken or received. A dilemma, therefore, is a position in which one is faced with two possible courses, neither of which offers clear advantages over the other.

dirty tricks, *department of* One of the many expressions thrown up by the Watergate scandal that led to the downfall of President Richard Nixon in August 1974. The future President's alleged predilection for doubtful tactics began with the campaign against Governor Pat Brown in California in 1962.

dished This well-established and perhaps now obsolete slang term, meaning to frustrate, is a contraction of 'disherit'. A person is dished when something he expected to inherit is left elsewhere. When in 1867 the Tory party caused a political sensation by sponsoring an act to extend the franchise their leader, Disraeli, said, 'We have dished the Whigs'. The Whigs had assumed that reform could come from their party alone.

distaff (*the distaff side*) This old expression for the female line of descent (as opposed to the male 'spear side') is like 'spinster', another example of the historic connection between women and spinning. The distaff was a primitive spinning aid.

ditto This word for 'the same again' is Italian, but ultimately derives from Latin *dictum*, 'that which has been said before'. 'To say ditto' is to endorse someone's views.

ditty box, ditty bag There seems to be no clear indication of the origin of the name for the sailor's 'hold-all' for his odds and ends. An abbreviation of commodity has been suggested, as has the cloth called 'dittis'. A Scots word 'dicht', a variant of the English 'dight', meaning to refurbish or decorate, has also been invoked. Other possibilities are a corruption of the Australian *dilly bag*, 'a bag made of rushes', or from the obsolete *dutty*, a Hindu word for a type of coarse calico. This last has the support of Professor A. Weekley. *Dutty* will be more familiar to those who know India in the form *dhoti*, 'loin-cloth'.

divan A long, low backless couch of Turkish origin. Because Turkish ministers and officials reclined on couches rather than sat at desks the word divan came to signify the Council of Ministers. A variation of the word gives us *douane*, the French for 'customs'. See CABINET for a similar development.

Dixie, Dixieland This term for America's old South, roughly identifiable with the Confederacy in the War between the States, has been the subject of much discussion. As used among slaves, it is said to relate to ideal conditions on the estate of a certain Mr Dixie, but he lived in New York. A better suggestion relates it to the Mason-Dixon line dividing the slave States from the free.

dock The origin of this essential piece of British courtroom 'furniture', symbolically confining the prisoner, is obscure. The dock is not known to statutes and is rarely mentioned in official literature. Prisoners traditionally stood 'at the bar'. Was it thieves slang? Is it to do with 'dock' in the sense of 'cutting off'? As to the growth of the usage we can say it was unknown to Shakespeare but well known to Dickens. One of the minor mysteries of the Law.

doctor, *to* To 'doctor' wine was to strengthen it by the addition of brandy. To 'doctor accounts' is to falsify them, making them appear 'stronger' than they really are. To 'doctor' a tom-cat is a euphemism for castrating it.

dog, *gay* This is a slang term for a philanderer. Dog here means no more than 'chap' or 'fellow'. We also find 'sad dog', 'surly dog' in the same way. A 'dogsbody' means a general assistant, one who makes himself useful as and when required in various capacities. See FRIDAY, *girl*.

dog days Roughly the six weeks covering the month of July and the first half of August. The Romans believed that the influence of Sirius the 'Dog Star' made these the hottest days of the year. In the Royal Navy, the dog watches were the two two-hour late afternoon 'shifts' put into the normal sequence of four-hour watches to ensure that the same men did not have to do the same watch every day. It was the 'dodge watch'.

dole This was the name given to relief money during the depression of the late twenties and early thirties. A dole, from the Old English *dal*, 'a piece', is something given out in small quantities, 'doled out' in fact. There is no link with 'doleful' from the Latin *dolor*, 'sorrow'.

Dollar, *the Almighty* Several languages have satirical references to money as God. In 1837 Washington Irving, in a sketch called 'The Creole Village', wrote: 'The Almighty Dollar is the great object of devotion throughout the land.' In German one can find references to St Mark.

dolly shop An old name for a secondhand-clothes shop in the days when the trade was regarded as a somewhat squalid one. A black doll was hung out as a trade sign.

dominoes Tradition tells us that this game was invented in a French monastery and that it was the custom for the winner to repeat the first line of the service called Vespers, '*Dixit Dominus, Domino meo*'. Even today the player of the winning piece sometimes says 'Domino'. The Domino Theory is American military/political jargon for the view that, should one of the states of South-East Asia (e.g. Vietnam) be allowed to fall victim to communism, then each of the others would follow in turn.

donkey's years 'That was donkey's years ago' means that it was a very long time since it happened. Donkeys have long ears and the original phrase was a simple parallel, 'as long as donkey's ears'. A slurred pronunciation gave us the phrase we have today.

doss A slang word for sleep which seems to have come to us from 'dossel' a bundle of hay or straw. Perhaps this in its turn comes from Latin *dorsum,* 'the back'.

double, *to do at the* This was the old seaman's name for the rapid drumbeat calling all hands to action stations.

Double Dutch Speaking Double Dutch means uttering something quite incomprehensible. Dutchmen were for long regarded in England as the typical foreigner. See DUTCHMAN.

doughboy This word for an American soldier has had two explanations. An English one relates it to the large bun-like buttons on the uniform of Civil War infantrymen. An American explanation relates it to the British Army practice of whitening parts of their uniform with doughlike pipeclay.

doves American political shorthand for those who favour a pacific policy as opposed to the bellicose 'hawks'. Doves are traditional symbols of peace, while War Hawk is a well-established American term dating from the War of 1812.

doyley These small, largely ornamental pieces of table linen are named after their inventor who kept a draper's shop in the Strand, London. Doily is a variant spelling. The modern article is made of paper.

dozen, *a baker's* A baker's dozen is, in fact, thirteen. The weight of bread, rolls, etc., was very strictly regulated in the

55

Middle Ages and the fraudulent baker severely dealt with. The addition of a thirteenth item to each dozen was a protection against any accidental deficiency. The expression may also have had some use as a substitute for the ill-omened thirteen.

dozen, *going nineteen to the* This expression for high-pressure activity, without stop, is usually reserved for the compulsive talker. It was in fact originally a standard of efficiency for Watt's steam-powered pumps used in the Cornish mines from the 1770s on. We read, for example, 'This week Wheal Fortune hath gone nineteen to the dozen', that is, had raised 19,000 gallons for every twelve bushels of coal used.

Drat them! This and many similar expressions are easily seen to be euphemised oaths. In this particular case the original would have been 'God rot them'.

drawing room Until quite recently this was the 'with-drawing room' to which the ladies withdrew after a formal dinner, leaving the gentlemen to wine, cigars and stories not deemed suitable for mixed company. This phase was terminated, after some considerable time, with the host's words 'Shall we join the ladies?'

drawing the King's picture This charming phrase is very old criminal slang for the offence of making counterfeit coins.

Draw it mild! An admonition to someone inclined to use undue exaggeration or needlessly strong language. The allusion is to beer and the message here is that the mild is preferred to the strong.

draw the nail This is an old expression for releasing a person from a promise. It is said that the custom once existed of registering an oath by driving a nail into a tree-trunk. While the nail lasted, so must the oath be kept. But 'circumstances alter cases', and it was sometimes desirable that a man should be allowed 'to draw the nail'.

dreeing his weird Dree is Scots for 'perform' or 'endure'. Weird, in this context, means fate or destiny. Dreeing his weird, then, is to fulfil his destiny. The phrase is now only used facetiously.

dressing down, *to give a good* This means a 'tongue-lashing' and is a butcher's term for the initial cutting into the animal's carcass. The recipient of a dressing down ends up (metaphorically) lacerated.

drink, *in the* Originally 'the drink' was a humorous American expression for any large stretch of water. The expression was taken up in the Second World War by the Royal Air Force for use with reference to any forced 'landing' in the sea. Incidentally the ancient Greek word for river, *potamos*, means 'the drink'.

drongo This 'Australianism' for a consistent failure and predictable flop is a memorial to a racehorse of that name well known at Melbourne for his consistent lack of success. In his own unlikely way Drongo made his name not only in the racing world but now far beyond it.

drum An eighteenth-century term for a big social occasion, an allusion, perhaps, to the drumming noise made by hundreds of voices? By analogy, a kettle drum was an afternoon tea party.

dry goods From the 1770s this term has been used in the United States for linen and woollen drapery. It would seem to derive from transport considerations. English barrel makers made similar distinctions in their work, dividing it all into 'wet' and 'dry', the latter being made to less exacting standards.

dud The expression 'It's a dud' is most commonly used for new bulbs that fail to light, fireworks that do not go off, etc. The word had strong military associations (dud shells, for example) and may have an origin in the Dutch *dood* or 'dead'.

dudgeon This word for resentment or ill-feeling derives directly from the Welsh *dygen*, 'evil feeling'. The customary phrase is 'in high dudgeon'.

dukes This is old slang for 'fists', as in the command 'Put up your dukes' when someone is urging another to fight. The origin is obscure. One suggestion argues that noses were 'dukes' because of the Duke of Wellington's famous nose and that fists were therefore 'duke-busters'. It is certainly not derived from the Romany *duk*, for this means 'palm', not fist.

dumps To be 'down in the dumps' is to be in low spirits, and the word would seem to have a natural association with the Dutch *dompig*, meaning 'dull and low'.

dun To 'dun' a person is to pursue him for a debt and the expression derives from the activities of one Joe Dun, a London bailiff with a great reputation for the successful apprehension of defaulting debtors. 'You had better Dun him for the money' was the original phrase.

dunce Traditionally the name for a slow or incapable learner, this word is a relic of the theological controversies of the Middle Ages. It is derived from the philosopher Duns Scotus, himself named from his birthplace, Dunse, in Scotland. Scotus lived *c*. 1300 and became associated with the defence of older ways of thought as against the new learning that was replacing former orthodoxy. His battle was lost and his name became a by-word for ignorance.

dunderhead A stupid blockhead, one lacking in active intellect. Dunder is a name for the overflow of fermenting liquors. See also BALMY and DANDER.

Dunkirk, *to do a* The allusion is to the withdrawal of the British Expeditionary Force from France in 1940. The position of the British forces was desperate and Dunkirk was the only point suitable for a mass evacuation. Despite incessant bombing by hundreds of German planes, something like three hundred thousand British and Allied troops were taken off and brought to Britain between 26 May and 3 June. Thousands of little ships, many of them yachts and pleasure cruisers, carried out the operation which was movingly described by Sir Winston Churchill as 'a miracle of deliverance'.

Dutch, *my old* This phrase from a song made famous by Albert Chevalier, the cockney comedian, has been accepted as a piece of London slang of the nineteenth century. Chevalier himself had in mind the round face of an old Dutch clock, but cockney rhyming slang 'Duchess of Fife' (=wife) must have played a part in helping the phrase become so widespread.

Dutchman There are a variety of phrases in English which turn on references to certain imagined characteristics of Dutch people. They all derive from the seventeenth century when the Dutch and the English fought for control of maritime trade. Here are some examples. To declare that something is as the speaker says or '. . . I am a Dutchman', expresses the strongest possible confidence as the acceptance of the name of Dutchman would be the ultimate disgrace. 'Dutch courage' is that derived solely from drinking. 'Dutch Gleek' also means drinking, gleek being the name of a popular card game. The implication is that drinking is the Dutchman's only game. A 'Dutch wife' was a name given to a large bolster. Comment seems superfluous. 'Talking like a Dutch uncle' is the giving of unsolicited and unappreciated good advice. In the United States 'going Dutch' or 'Dutch treat' means to share the expenses, that is, no 'treat' at all.

D V These letters are an abbreviation of the Latin words *Deo volente*, 'God (being) willing'. They are usually found in notices of religious services, etc., e.g. 'A service will be held (D V) at eleven o'clock . . .'.

dyed in the wool This phrase, meaning 'through and through', the total reverse of superficial, derives from the old textile industry. Cloth dyed in the wool, that is before weaving, kept its colour far better than that 'dyed in the piece'. A dyed-in-the-wool criminal, then, was one not likely to change his character. See BLOWED IN THE GLASS.

E

earmarked This word, meaning set aside for a particular purpose, derives from the old custom of indicating ownership of an animal by notching or otherwise marking one of its ears. The custom in Biblical times extended to human property. In Exodus xxi, 6, it is written of a servant: '. . . his master shall bore his ear through with an awl; and he shall serve him for ever.'

earn (*to earn one's living*)   The basic fact of economic life, the necessity for a surplus of food before workers may engage in non-agricultural activities, provides the background of this word's development. It is connected with the German word for harvest, *die Ernte*. The Dutch have a similar word.

earwig Popular belief is that this insect is so called because of its habit of crawling into the ears of sleeping human beings and penetrating the brain. None of this is true, neither the account of the insect nor the origin of its name. The ear is derived from the Old English *eor*, a 'bud', and *wic*, a 'hiding place'. The favourite hiding place of this creature is in an undeveloped bud and this is the reason for its name. The false origin, however, gave rise to a secondary meaning. In old slang an earwig was a flatterer always close to the ear of his prey.

Easter It is an astonishing paradox that the principal feast of the Christian Church derives its name from a pagan goddess, Eostre. She was a goddess of the dawn and her festival was celebrated at the spring equinox. It was the declared policy of the early Church to smooth the transition from paganism to Christianity by making use of existing institutions and giving them new functions. The fact of the Resurrection being commemorated at this time is not surprising. The retention of the old name is.

eavesdropper   An eavesdropper is one who listens, unnoticed, to the conversations of others. The expression has an Old English origin. The eaves of a house (Anglo-Saxon *efes*) are those parts of the roof that overhang the walls in order to deflect water from them. Eavesdrop is the water that falls from the eaves, so an eavesdropper is someone who stands close to the house 'within eavesdrop' to listen to what the people inside are saying.

eccentric   In normal usage this word suggests that someone is a little odd. Its correct meaning is simply 'off centre' and its original application was to descriptions of the orbits of planets which were at one time thought of as being circular, with the earth as their common centre.

ecology   Derived from the Greek and meaning 'the study of organisms in their surroundings, this once obscure scientific term has now become something of a cliché. It had to wait a long time for its popularity, having made its first appearance in English scientific literature in 1873 when it was used in an English version of the German Ernst Haeckel's *History of Creation*.

ecstasy   A state in which the mind is exalted or is liberated from the body. The word comes from the Greek *ek*, 'out', and *stasis*, 'a standing'; ecstasy, then, is a displacement of consciousness, a 'going out of this world'.

egg on   To egg someone on, meaning to urge or incite them, is not slang but derives from an Old English word *eggian*, which meant 'to spur', 'to incite'.

eggs (*as sure as eggs is eggs*)   There seems to be general agreement that the origin of this phrase must be sought in mathematics. It should be 'As sure as x is x'.

ego   This is simply the Latin for 'I'. Egoists push themselves forward on every possible occasion, thinking there is no one to compare to themselves.

egotism   This is the habit of continually speaking about oneself. Those in authority often conceal this tendency by identifying themselves with their organisation and saying 'we'. In editors of journals this is perhaps justified and in reigning monarchs traditional. Others, with mock modesty, prefer to say 'one'. It is said of General de Gaulle that he rarely used the word 'I' in his political speeches. He said 'France'.

eisteddfod   This word is now often used for a festival of the arts and particularly music. It is properly the gathering of the Welsh bards and derives from the Welsh *eistodd*, meaning 'session'.

elephant, *to see the*   Meaning to have seen everything or all there is to see, this American phrase has been in circulation since the 1830s. The original form was ' "That's sufficient," as Tom Haynes said when he saw the elephant.' Who Tom Haynes was we do not know, but he has British relations as, for example, in the phrase ' "I don't believe it" as the farmer said when he saw the giraffe.' Tom's elephant is also related to British lions. See LIONISE.

elephant, *white*   This expression is now used for some expensive, though useless, object, not easily disposed of. The name originates in Siam, where the white elephant was venerated. The King of Siam, wishing to get rid of a courtier no longer in favour, used the device of giving him a white elephant. The cost of upkeep of such a gift was ruinous.

Eli, sons of   The alumni of Yale are sometimes referred to in this way. On the surface a straight reference to Elihu Yale their founder, it also recalls I Sam. ii: 12, 'Now the sons of Eli were sons of Belial; they knew not the Lord.'

ell   An old measure of length encountered in the proverb,

'Give him an inch and he'll take an ell'. It is Anglo-Saxon *eln* and is the same as the Biblical cubit, the distance from the elbow to the tip of the outstretched fore-finger.

emmy, *see* OSCAR.

encore   This plea to a performer for a repetition is of French origin but used in a way unknown to that language. If a French audience desires a thing to be repeated they shout '*Bis*' (twice). Encore means 'another', as in '*Encore une tasse*', 'Another cup'.

endorse   To say 'I endorse that' means literally to back it. It derives from the Latin *in dorsum*, 'on the back'. The original and literal use of the word was when a person endorsed a promissory note and in this way accepted responsibility for it.

ends-a-wagging   A term of naval slang meaning that the end of a job is in sight. In the old sailing-ship days much time was spent in hauling in ropes and cables, and the sight of the loose end was a welcome one.

enfant terrible   A French expression adopted into English. It means literally an embarrassing child, and is often used with reference to newcomers, especially young ones who pay little respect to conventional reticences.

English sickness   Coined in Germany after the Second World War for the combination of industrial anarchy and inflation which caused stagnation in Britain, as compared with the 'economic miracle' achieved in the Fatherland. It later became evident as a world-wide trend, even in Germany itself.

entail   This word derives from French *entailer*, 'to cut into'. An entail is a legal device that limits the rights of inheritance so that an heir, for example, may only profit from the income of an estate which he must hand on intact to his own successor. The use of the word to mean 'logically lead on to' is only indirectly linked to the legal term.

erk Royal Air Force slang for an aircraftsman of the ground staff, this word seems to have been created, in the form of 'airc' or 'airk', by Wing Commander Heading in 1920.
'While Jack is on the quarterdeck and Tommy rules the
 square,
We look to you, the boys in blue, to guard us in the air.
You fear no foe when up you go to keep the country free,
Give me an airk who does not shirk; he's the boy for me.'
The word found favour at Uxbridge where it evolved into 'erk' and by 1944 'Joe Erk' had come to represent the lowest though not least valuable rank of the service.

esquire Without doubt one of the most misused words in the English language. From the Latin *scutarius*, it was originally applied to one who carried the shield or *scutum* of a knight. The Richmond Herald, C. H. Athill, Esquire, compiled the following list of those legally entitled to be called esquires: 'The sons of Peers, Baronets and Knights; the eldest sons of the young sons of Peers and the eldest sons in perpetuity; the eldest son of the eldest son of a Knight, and his eldest son in perpetuity; the Kings of Arms, the Heralds of Arms; Officers of the Navy and Army of the rank of captain and upwards, Sheriffs, J Ps while they are in commission, Serjeants-at-Law, King's Counsel, Companions of Knighthood, certain Officers of the Royal Household, Deputy Lieutenants, Commissioners of the Court of Bankruptcy, Masters of the Supreme Court, and those whom the King in any Commission styles Esquires.' And nobody else – legally. However, the complexities of this were too great to master, and the modern use is widespread and ill-defined. Its commercial use is sometimes characteristically English, and cases have been known in which all clients doing business above a certain level have been addressed as Esq. and lesser ones have had their letters sent with the indignity of Mr.

et cetera This is not a word but a Latin phrase meaning 'and the other things'. It should therefore not be applied to people, nor, being plural already, does it ever require an 's' on the end.

etiquette This is a French word meaning a ticket or label. It is in fact the origin of our word 'ticket'. At some formal functions an 'etiquette' would indicate what procedures should be followed, what dress would be worn and similar matters. From this the word came to mean a code of social conduct.

eureka A Greek word (properly 'heureka') meaning 'I have found it'. Tradition tells us it was first uttered by Archimedes of Syracuse when, on stepping into a brimming bath, he noticed the displacement of an amount of water, which, he perceived, must be equal to his own bulk, This observation suggested a solution to a problem he had been asked to solve and so excited was he that he ran naked through the streets crying 'Heureka'. The problem concerned a crown said to have been made up from a certain quantity of gold. The king suspected that some alloy had been used. Archimedes realised that if a metal lighter than gold had been used the mixture would have to be bulkier than the original quantity of gold. Testing the displacement of the crown against that of the right quantity of gold he found the king's fears were justified. 'Eureka' was adopted as the motto of the State of California in allusion to the discovery of gold there.

Exchequer This name for the British 'Ministry of Finance' derives from the custom of receiving payments into the king's treasury at a chequered table, the squares of which were used as a calculating device.

excuse The saying 'A bad excuse is better than none' is first recorded in Udall's comedy *Ralph Roister Doister* of *c.* 1534.

expletive deleted When, in the summer of 1974, President Nixon finally released edited transcripts of his hitherto closely guarded White House tapes, 'middle America' was much shaken by what was then revealed about the atmosphere in which the President's circle conducted the business of the State. In an attempt to soften the inevitable blow the editorial euphemism 'expletive deleted' was employed in place of the profane or obscene expressions frequently used.

eye-opener This American word originally described a mixed drink taken as a cure for drowsiness. Now it is most commonly used for some astonishing revelation, some new light thrown upon the situation.

eye-teeth This traditional word for the 'canines' derives from the belief that the roots of these teeth extended as far as the sockets of the eyes.

F

Fabian Society A socialist group founded in 1884 by Sidney Webb and Bernard Shaw. Its methods were evolutionary and educational and its aim was the gradual penetration of all aspects of political and social life by socialist ideas without any need for direct confrontation with its opponents. The *Daily News* in 1894 said: 'Fabian tactics lie in stealing inches not in grasping leagues.' Like Fabius of old, they hoped to win their 'war' by 'wariness and caution, not by violence and defiance'. The Society still exists as a constituent body of the Labour Party.

Fabian tactics This expression derives from Quintus Fabius Maximus (275–203 B.C.), appointed dictator of the Roman state in order to avert the total defeat threatened by Hannibal of Carthage. The policy adopted by Fabius was one of avoiding any direct clash, preferring instead to pursue a course of pinpricks and harassment. In this way he avoided further disasters until such time as Rome was in a stronger position to take further measures. Fabius was given the surname Cunctator, 'the delayer'.

face, socialism with a human In January 1968 the Czech communist leader Novotny was replaced by Alexander Dubcek who inaugurated the more liberal policies epitomised in this phrase and proclaimed to the world in the Party Action Programme in April of the same year. This 'Prague Spring' soon attracted the hostility of the USSR though it had itself known a similar phase in the 'thaw' that followed the death of Stalin. Dubcek and his associates were brutally overthrown but the phrase, essence of the Prague Programme, lives on and is the basis of many similar formations not all of them humorous or sarcastic.

factoid Facts which have no existence before their publication, were dubbed factoids by Norman Mailer in his biography of Marilyn Monroe, *Marilyn* (1973). He had in mind particularly the sort of item which appears in film publicity handouts, and then continues to be repeated in the media as accepted fact, never being checked, and often being uncheckable. An earlier phrase for a similar phenomenon was 'pseudo-event'.

factotum A 'general factotum' is expected to do everything and that is the simple, literal meaning of this Latin word, which derives from *facere*, 'to do', and *totum*, 'everything'.

fag, fag end These slang words for a cigarette and its stub, respectively, originate from the textile industry. The fag was the end piece, generally of coarser material than the rest, of a piece of cloth. Small boys in the weaving towns called out to smokers 'Give us the fag, mister', using the word they knew for 'the end'. A fag was also the untwisted end of a rope, hence perhaps the term 'fagged out' to mean total exhaustion.

fake This word, meaning 'to falsify', is Germanic in origin and belongs to the world of thieves' slang. Its earliest form was 'feague' and its usual association was with 'faking' unfit horses to make them worth more in the market. 'Coping' was another word for horse faking. When it specifically applied to the horse's teeth it was known as 'bishoping'.

fall As a word for autumn, this is not an American coinage but one of the many cases in which American speech has preserved an old English term since forgotten in its own land. The falling of the leaves is an unmistakable indication of the change of season.

fall foul of To fall foul of someone is to become on bad terms with them. The phrase, like so many others in English, comes from the world of ships. A ship falls foul of another when it impedes her progress. A foul anchor is one with its own cable twisted round it, so preventing it from lying as it should. In sport a 'foul' also has this same idea of impeding the proper progress of the game.

fan As a twentieth-century term for an enthusiastic supporter of some usually recreational activity 'fan' came to Britain from the United States but, as with so many 'Americanisms', it was no more than an old British term coming home again after a holiday abroad. It started life, in fact, as a jocular abbreviation of fanatic and occurs as early as 1682 in a religious satire called *News from Bedlam* as 'fanns' or 'phans'.

fanatic Strictly speaking this word should be confined to uses connected with religion. It derives from the Latin *fanum*, 'a temple', and was applied to those while at the temple fell into a state of religious ecstasy.

Fanny Adams Fanny Adams was a young woman who was murdered in 1810. Her body was dismembered and the pieces thrown into the river at Alton in Hampshire. The Royal Navy, with grim humour, began calling their rations of tinned meat 'Fanny Adams'. Meanwhile, in cockney rhyming slang, 'nothing at all' had been transmuted into 'f . . . all', abbreviated into F.A. and then re-expanded by men familiar with the earlier usage. And why 'sweet' Fanny Adams? I am convinced it is associated with the Italian *dolce far niente* which means 'sweet idleness' the pleasure of doing nothing at all.

68

fare This word ultimately derives from the Old English *faran*, 'to go'. It came to mean a journey for which passage money was paid, then the person who paid it, then the money itself. These last two uses still survive. 'How did you fare?' is quite simply 'How did you get on?' or 'How did it go with you?' The origin of fare as meaning food and provisions is uncertain.

farm This word for 'agricultural land holding' has a curious origin. The fact that gives a farmer his distinctive name is the fact that he rents his land. Farm ultimately derives from the Old English word for 'rent', *feorm*. This, in turn, originally meant a feast or night's entertainment. Primitive 'rent' was often in the form of so many nights' entertainment of the Lord of the Manor and his retinue.

feather, *to show the white* This is an old cockfighting term and means to show signs of cowardice. The pure-bred game-cock had no white feathers in its plumage. If it did then it was not pure bred and would not display the highest qualities of its kind. In Britain in the First World War 'patriotic' women often presented white feathers to men who in their opinion should have been in the Army.

feather in his cap If something is said to be 'a feather in someone's cap' it is an honour or distinction. The phrase is often said to derive from the Red Indians on the assumption that the many-feathered 'war bonnet' represented an accumulation of honours. This origin is suspect. Oliver Cromwell disparagingly referred to a title of honour as 'but a feather in the hat' and this would seem a far more probable origin.

feather one's nest To feather one's nest is to take advantage of opportunities for corruption. The allusion is to the habit of birds lining their nests with down to make them comfortable.

feature film This expression, still sometimes found, no longer has either point or purpose. It goes back to the days when cinema performances often included 'a full supporting programme' and possibly even vaudeville acts. The 'feature' was the major item, 'top of the bill' as it were.

fee This is one of that huge class of words that are rooted in the primitive agricultural life of our ancestors. The Saxon (Old English) *feoh* meant 'cattle', the main form of property and principal means of payment. In Latin a similar development occurred, *pecunia*, 'money', being derived from *pecus*, meaning 'cattle'. Capital also derives from *capita*, 'head' of cattle).

fetish The ultimate origin of this word is the Latin *facticius*, 'made by art'. Its immediate origin is a Portuguese form of that word, *feitiço*, which was applied to African cult objects sold to the Westerners as curiosities. They imagined that the Africans worshipped these things as gods or idols. When we say a person 'makes a fetish of something' we mean they have an obsessive concern with it. Fetishism is a sexual deviation in which sexual interest is focussed on an object or class of objects, rather than on another human being. In all meanings a fetish is 'a thing of power'.

fettle This word has a number of meanings but they are linked by the common theme of processing or, more exactly, of preparation. Fettled ale has been seasoned with ginger and nutmeg. To be 'in fine fettle' means to be in good condition and ready for anything. The origin is to be found in *fetel*, an Old English word for 'girdle'. There is a parallel with the Biblical idea of 'girding up the loins', which was tucking the end of one's long robes into the belt so as to leave the legs free for activity.

fiasco This word, meaning an utter failure, is of Italian and specifically Venetian origin. In Italian it means simply 'flask'. Two stories exist that purport to explain its evolution. One concerns a Harlequin who, failing to raise the expected laughs, loudly blamed the flask he was using as part of his stage 'business'. The other suggests an origin in the glass

70

factories of Venice where any fine piece that went wrong was likely to end up as a cheap flask. The word seems to be an 'escape' from the theatrical world, which perhaps favours the first suggestion rather than the second.

fib This child's word for a lie is a contraction of 'fable'.

fiddle Used in the sense of a swindle or confidence trick, the terms 'fiddling' or 'on the fiddle' have a long history behind them. The original, classic 'fiddle' was a real one. The story is that a tramp, or other passing stranger in obviously poor circumstances, would leave his fiddle at an inn as security for money owed and to be repaid when he next came by. Another stranger, then coming in, would see the fiddle, declare it to be valuable and offer fifty pounds for it. The landlord thereupon explains he cannot sell it, as it is not his, but offers to see what can be done. The tramp returns and is persuaded to part with his fiddle for twenty pounds. The interested purchaser is never seen again.

Fifth Columnist This term used in the Second World War for a concealed traitor derives from the Civil War in Spain, 1936–9. 'Columns' were the organisational units of the Spanish Army and the fascist general outside Madrid said he had four columns attacking the city from the outside and a fifth fighting for him within the ranks of the defenders.

fifty cards in the pack American metaphor/euphemism for mental deficiency. The sense is 'something lacking'. A British equivalent was 'ninepence in the shilling'.

fig In 'full fig' means in full official dress and perhaps comes from the Italian *bella figura*, 'a fine outward appearance'. On the other hand, 'not to care a fig' is from the Spanish *fico*, a traditional gesture of contempt made by putting the thumb between the first and second fingers.

finger, *to lift the little* This, like 'bending the elbow' is said of a man known to be a heavy drinker. It is very difficult to drink without making the movements alluded to.

flak Another wartime popularisation, this is a contraction of the German word for anti-aircraft gun, '*Fl*ugzeug*a*bwehr-*k*anone'. The German language tends to develop excessively long words and counteracts this awkward trend by compressing them again. Radar is an English example of the same process. The word sometimes has a metaphorical usage in the sense of 'severe adverse criticism', for example, 'He had to take a good deal of flak over that decision'.

flame As a word for a lover, flame is plainly related to the well-established usage of French and, before that, Latin literature in which 'flame' is the symbol of love. We often speak of 'ardent' lovers and ardent has a Latin origin in the verb *ardere*, 'to burn'.

flogging a dead horse This striking metaphor which describes efforts to stir some long dead cause into life goes back to the Victorian politician John Bright and was used by him with reference to Lord John Russell's attempt to promote a second reform of Parliament in the 1860s.

foolscap A sheet of paper measuring 13½ by 17 inches. The name is derived from an old watermark, the first example of which dates from 1540. Now obsolete, its nearest metric equivalent is the sheet known as A4.

footing 'On a good footing' means to have an assured place in some institution. It comes from the custom of paying one's footing. This phrase was born in the days of trade apprenticeships when a newcomer, on the first day of his job, was expected to pay for drinks for all. Generosity on this occasion would be long remembered.

fop This word has a German and Dutch root in the word *foppen*, 'to jeer'. The idea is implicit in Vanbrugh's character Lord Foppingham in a play of 1697.

fork out This expression, meaning to pay over money due, comes from old thieves' slang in which fingers were known as forks. These two ideas are also associated in the phrase 'Fingers were made before forks', used as a form of mock apology when anyone finds certain essential cutlery is missing and proceeds without it.

four hundred, the The élite of the American social scene. Ward McAllister, when it was discovered in 1892 that Mrs William Astor's ballroom would hold only 400 guests, cut the list of invitations for her to the four hundred who really counted.

Fourth Estate This description of the Press was first used by the eighteenth-century statesman Edmund Burke. The three traditional 'Estates of the Realm' or significant classes, as they would be called today, were the Lords Spiritual, the Lords Temporal and the Commons.

fragging The morale of the American Army suffered very badly during the long-drawn-out and indecisive war in Vietnam, reaching its nadir when enlisted men began expressing their discontent by sporadic attacks upon their own officers. Fragmenting anti-personnel bombs tossed into billets or clubrooms were the preferred method, hence the term 'fragging'.

Franglais This semi-humorous post-war coinage refers to the massive invasion of the French language by English and American words. Obvious examples are the names of characteristic imports such as tweed, whisky, twinsets, fair play, westerns, hot dogs and sex appeal. The *Petit Larousse*, France's most influential dictionary, first admitted such words in 1971 and the floodgates are now open. The same tendency is at work in German.

freelance In modern usage this word describes a writer, artist or indeed any skilled person who works for no regular employer, but who takes his talents to the market that pays best. Originally the word referred to the mercenary soldiers of the Middle Ages.

French, *pardon my* A mock apology used by those who have resorted to indelicate language in the company of those who might be offended by it. The tendency to blame unpleasant or embarrassing things on to a neighbouring people is a universal one. In English the French have their name attached to a number of things for which they have no particular responsibility, for example, French letter for the common rubber contraceptive. 'To take French leave' is to slip away unnoticed, or sometimes to take something without permission. 'Leave' here is permission, so 'French permission' is no permission at all. It must be pointed out that the equivalent French expression, *'s'en filer à l'anglaise'*, refers the habit to the English.

Friday, *Girl* An advertiser's euphemism for a general assistant. See also DOGSBODY. In Daniel Defoe's novel *Robinson Crusoe* Crusoe's native companion is called Friday, and becomes the castaway's faithful and willing servant ready to do anything required of him.

frisbees These popular 'throwing discs' are said to be named after a (surely legendary) Mother Frisbee's pies; 'they throw better than they eat'.

frog in the throat, *a* Sometimes, in making an attempt to speak, the words seem to fade away in the speaker's very mouth, and he might be referred to humorously as having 'a frog in the throat'. In earlier centuries this would have been no laughing matter. When so many people drank from springs, ponds and wells, there was a lively fear of swallowing scraps of frog-spawn or fish eggs, and folk tradition told gruesome tales of people unwittingly nourishing frogs, newts, etc., in their stomachs. This would continue until either the 'guest' was lured out or the 'host' died a horrible death.

fub To 'fub (or fob) someone off' is to placate them with some plausible story. The word has the same root as 'fop' on which we have written above.

fuchsia The common pronunciation of this flower name 'fewshia' conceals its origin. The name was coined in 1703 for certain South American shrublike plants and is based on the name of Leonard Fuchs (1501–66), an early German botanist.

funnybone No doubt this was originally a medical student's joke, for the correct name of the bone of the upper arm is the humerus. The 'funnybone' itself is a spot at the elbow where the ulnar nerve is very near the surface and unprotected hence its liability to be affected by a knock.

furbelow This very old-fashioned word is a corruption of the Spanish *falbala* which means a flounce or frill on a woman's dress.

future shock This phrase is the title of a book by Alvin Toffler and describes the state of those overwhelmed by the ever increasing pace of social and technological change.

G

gab 'The gift of the gab' is the power of fluent and persuasive speech or at least the ability to maintain a ready flow of words. It seems to be no more than coincidence that the primitive Celtic word for 'mouth' was *gab*. Our word has its origin in the Middle English *gabbe* meaning 'idle talk' which in turn has a Danish origin. The Celtic word, however, has made its influence felt through French, where it is the root of such words as *gobet* (English 'gobbet') 'a morsel', *gobelet* (English 'goblet') 'a drinking glass' and *gobe-mouche*, an expression meaning 'someone who catches flies with their ever-open mouth', in other words a gossip or compulsive talker. These are the sources from which we derive our English 'gob', as in the vulgar 'Shut your gob', meaning 'Be quiet', or in the name of the huge sweet once known as a 'gobstopper'. By extension 'gob' has a vulgar usage as a verb 'to spit' or as a noun 'spittle'.

gadget This is a widely used but loosely defined word. A gadget might be described as any small but useful fitment or device, and the term first appeared in R.A.F. circles but has no generally agreed origin. The Scots 'gadge', a variant of gauge, has been suggested. So too has the French *gâchette* a small metal part in the mechanism of a clock or gun. The word certainly is attested as having been in existence since the 1860s among sailors, but it does not appear in print before 1886 and the *Oxford English Dictionary* did not see fit to admit it before 1933. Obviously it had to bide its time until sufficient 'gadgetry' existed to justify its claim to recognition.

gaff This word is most likely to be encountered in the slang phrase 'to blow the gaff', meaning to let out the truth of some concealed matter, perhaps even 'to expose the deceit'. The origin of this slang usage is uncertain, but it may well be connected with another 'gaff'. This, the 'penny gaff', was the lowest form of nineteenth-century theatrical performance. The root idea here must be the German *gaffen*, 'to stare', to look on. The phrase 'as crooked as a gaff' is from a common European word for boat-hook, or hook used by fishermen for landing heavy catches. *'Gaffe'* is also a French slang term for a social error and this usage has been adopted into English.

gaffer The word crops up in two contexts. Sometimes it is simply a disrespectful term for an old man, 'a toothless old gaffer', or, in industry, it is a popular term for the 'boss'. Both usages have a common origin. Gaffer is a corruption of grandfather. The parallel 'gammer', from 'grandmother', is no longer used.

gag In the entertainment world a gag is now a joke or witticism. It gained this sense by certain well-defined stages. The first gagging was the disconcerting of a fellow actor by suddenly speaking words not in the script. It then became 'filling in' with extempore words when someone had missed his entrance cue or forgotten his words. The gag today is a carefully contrived piece of verbal humour, frequently the work of a professional writer (gagman) who sells his work to the comedian.

gallivanting This curious word is a contraction of 'gallant', in this context meaning a philanderer, and 'vaunting', making a vain display. Gallivanting then was attempting to catch the eye (and perhaps more) of the opposite sex by activity and display.

galvanise To galvanise something is to submit it to galvanism, and galvanism, the production of current electricity by chemical action, takes its name from the scientist Luigi Galvani (1737–98) of Bologna, Italy. The verb 'to galvanise' has two separate meanings. In technology it is the process of giving sheet iron a zinc coating by electro-chemical means, in order to prevent rusting. In ordinary speech we talk of someone being 'galvanised into action' and mean shocked or stimulated as though by electricity. This was in fact the essence of Galvani's most famous experiment in which the legs of dead frogs twitched when touched by electric current.

gamesmanship In 1947 Stephen Potter gave a new word to the language when he published *The Theory and Practice of Gamesmanship*, gamesmanship being defined as 'the art of winning games without actually cheating'. Numbers of parallel formations have since appeared, such as 'one-up-manship' in the social field. Potter also revived the virtually lost word 'ploy'. A ploy is to the gamesman what the gambit is to the chess player.

gamey The traditional game birds, pheasant, partridge, etc., were not eaten until they had been 'hung' for some considerable time. People not brought up to this usage considered them undesirable as being too near to rottenness. The word 'gamey' used metaphorically, conveys this whiff of aristocratic corruption.

gammon This is Dickensian slang for fraud or deception. Tony Weller says in *The Pickwick Papers*, 'They're the

wictims of gammon, Samivel, they're the wictims of gammon.'
In this sense the word derives from an Old English original
meaning a game. Game and gamble have the same origin and
we also see this word in the name backgammon. Gammon,
as the cured thigh of a pig, has a French origin and is *jambon*
from *gambe* (modern *jambe*) meaning 'a leg'.

gammy 'To have a gammy leg' is a popular expression
meaning to have suffered a leg injury, or to have a deformed
leg or to limp. It derives from the Celtic *kam* which means
'crooked'. A more literary form of the word is 'game'.

gamp Obsolete or facetious slang for an umbrella. Its origin
is from Sarah Gamp, the disreputable and drunken 'nurse' in
Dickens' *Martin Chuzzlewit*. She carried her umbrella with
her everywhere she went.

gamut This word will be found in some such phrase as 'to
run the gamut of emotions', meaning to go through the whole
range or scale. Guido d'Arezzo in the tenth century denoted
the 'steps' of the musical scale by letters. Gamma was the
first or lowest note, and ut the first word of a mnemonic verse
that recorded the old names used in singing (ut, re, mi, fa, so,
la, si). Gamma ut became 'gamut' and the name was later
applied to the whole scale.

gang The origin of this word is the Old English *gangan*, 'to
travel together'. A gang is therefore a company of 'fellow
travellers' presumably on the road to retribution! A ganger
is the leader of a gang in the sense of 'work team', an industrial usage.

gardenia This flower takes its name from Dr Alexander
Garden (1752–82) a physician of Charleston, South Carolina,
who first popularised it. It has since become a symbol of
sophistication.

gargantuan This adjective, meaning large beyond belief,
derives from a character in the medieval satire *Gargantua and
Pantagruel* by François Rabelais. Gargantua, a giant of in-

conceivable size, could drink a river dry and once ate five pilgrims (with their staves!) in a salad. The name comes from the Spanish *garganta*, 'a gullet'. Gurgle and gargle also have the same 'throat' associations as has the next entry.

gargoyle This object, a feature of the Gothic period of architecture, was really no more than a 'throat' or spout to carry rainwater from a roof so it fell clear of the wall. Its immediate origin is the Old French *gargouille*, 'throat'. It was also the custom to decorate churches with hideous devil-frightening faces or masks. These were combined with the water-spouts in one feature, a grotesque creature peering over the edge of the roof, and this is now the essential meaning of the word gargoyle.

garret This word now means no more than the topmost small room of a house. It was originally a watch-tower (*garite* in Old French) and the word 'garrison' has a similar origin.

gas This is a word fabricated by the pioneer chemist J. B. van Helmont (1577–1644) who first identified this class of substance. It is said to be a variant of the Greek 'chaos'. An alternative view is that the German *Geist*, 'spirit', contributed to the word. Gassing is a slang term for talking at excessive length.

gat This American slang term for a gun was originally short for 'Gatling', the early machine gun invented by R. J. Gatling and first used in the American Civil War.

gauche See ADROIT.

gauntlet, *to run the* This expression has no connection with the following one at all. It is of Swedish origin and describes a military punishment in which the victim ran between two lines of men carrying sticks who struck at him as he passed. Its first form was 'gantlope', from the Swedish *gata*, a passage, and *lope* which meant 'leap'.

79

gauntlet, *to throw down the* The gauntlet here was the armoured glove of the knights of old and to throw it down was to issue a challenge to combat. It is simply the French word for glove (*le gant* today, in the Middle Ages *le gantelet*). A modern gauntlet is a glove that extends over the wrist.

gazette This name for a newspaper has a Venetian origin. In the sixteenth century, during the wars between Venice and the Turks, one paid a *gazetta*, the smallest coin of the day, to hear the official news read. An interesting alternative theory that may, however, be no more than a happy chance reminds us that *gazetta* was also the chattering of the magpie (*gazza*).

gazumping In December 1971 the House of Commons considered a bill for the abolition of 'Gazumping and Kindred Practices', gazumping being defined as altering the price of a house after a buyer's offer has already been accepted. The word came to the notice of Parliament in the context of house-buying but it has a long history behind it in the motor trade. Its ultimate origin is the Yiddish *gezumph*, and it seems to have had its first currency among stallholders and showmen in New York. It means exactly what it is: swindle.

geewhiz An obsolete American expression of surprise. It is a distortion of Jesus.

gen This well-used little word was Second World War and specifically Royal Air Force slang for 'vital information' and derives from 'intelli*gen*ce'. It occurs in such phrases as 'Give us the gen' or 'You had better get yourself genned up on this'.

gerrymander The periodic redrawing of the boundaries of electoral districts to ensure the continuation in power of the governing party. (No opposition party is, of course, in a position to do this sort of thing.) The story of the name is said to go back to Elbridge Gerry (1744–1814), a Massachusetts politician who was involved with an electoral redistribution scheme. The weird though purposeful shape reminded someone of a salamander. The name 'Gerrymander' was suggested as an improvement. A new word was born.

ghost (*the ghost walks on Friday*) This curious phrase, meaning 'Friday is payday', has a theatrical origin. The story goes that a small theatrical company playing *Hamlet* was having difficulty in extracting regular wages from the manager, who always pleaded poor takings and heavy expenses. The actor playing the ghost (incidentally the part in which Shakespeare made his name as an actor), when he heard that no wages were being paid, simply said, 'Then the ghost doesn't walk tonight.' He was paid. After that the enquiry as to whether the ghost would be walking or not was reminder enough of the threat.

GI A GI or 'GI Joe' was slang for the American private soldier of the Second World War. GI meant 'Government Issue'. Everything that Joe ate or wore or used had been issued by the government. He was, in fact, in his capacity as soldier GI himself.

gibberish At first Gibberish was the obscure mystical jargon of Geber, the eleventh-century Arab alchemist. To the unsympathetic this was equated with nonsense. The word dunce shows a similar history of changed estimation. Oddly enough, the word gibber does not seem to be a formation from gibberish but a variant of jabber.

gilt off the gingerbread, *to knock the* Meaning to show something up as worth far less than was imagined or, more generally, to destroy an illusion, the expression goes back to the old country fairs of the last century and earlier, where gingerbread cakes were sold covered with gold leaf, sometimes real but more often imitation. To knock the gilt off the gingerbread would show it as it was. At sea the carved woodwork at the stem and the stern of the old sailing ships was sometimes called 'the gingerbread', perhaps because it was so often gilded.

gipsy The gipsies appeared in England early in the sixteenth century, alleging they had come from 'Little Egypt'. The story was taken at its face value and gipsy is a corruption of Egyptian. The French called and call them Bohemians. Most other nations in Europe use a name derived from Atzigan, a major tribal group. The gipsies call themselves Romani from their own word *rom*, 'a man'.

give beans The threat 'to give someone beans' meaning 'more than he bargained for' is in fact half a French proverbial saying, 'If he gives me peas, I will give him beans'. 'I will not only repay him in his own coin, but give him something extra too.'

glamour A loosely used word for attractive, seductive, etc. Its first meaning was 'bewitchment', especially the deception of the sight by magical means. It derives from the medieval English 'gramarye', magic, but came into the modern language with Highland associations via the novels of Sir Walter Scott.

global village This striking phrase which sums up the concept of the new world community created by the mass communications media was coined and launched by the American thinker Marshall McLuhan.

gnomes (*of Zurich*) When, in the autumn of 1964, it was felt that the Swiss bankers were active against Britain's financial interests, Labour leader George Brown (now Lord George Brown) certainly popularised, if he did not actually invent this striking phrase which evokes images of little men toiling away underground, amidst heaps of treasure.

gods, *up in the or among the* This old phrase means sitting in the topmost gallery of the theatre. The traditional English explanation is that at Drury Lane Theatre the roof was decorated with paintings of the Olympians. Perhaps so, but in France the occupants of the gallery are *les enfants du Paradis*, the children of Paradise. The gods sit 'on high', watching and judging the performances of those below.

gold, *all that glitters is not* Although Shakespeare put the sentiment into its most quoted form (*Merchant of Venice*, II. vii), we can trace it back some two hundred years earlier to Chaucer's 'Canon's Yeoman's Tale' as follows: 'All thing which shineth as the gold/Ne is no gold as I have herd it told!'

Goldberg (*Rube*) This mythical gentleman is the US equivalent of the English Heath Robinson and is held responsible for all those precarious devices of elastic bands and string that are sometimes botched together to serve serious mechanical purposes. The phrase was used for example in the US Government report on a Turkish Airlines jumbo DC10 crash outside Paris in March 1974.

Goldwynisms Samuel Goldwyn (1882–1974), who became Hollywood's greatest independent film producer, had a second reputation as 'the Great American Malaprop'. Too deeply immersed in his many enterprises to bother about the finer points of English usage he coined many a magnificently mixed metaphor. In later days others were attributed to him and even, it is said, written for him. Among the best known of his creations are, 'Include me out'; 'In two words, impossible'; 'A verbal promise is not worth the paper it is written on'; 'They are always biting the hand that lays the golden eggs'; 'The trouble with this business is the dearth of bad pictures' and finally, looking back over a long career, 'We have all passed a lot of water since then.' For an English parallel see NEWTONISM.

Goodman's croft This phrase is a good example of euphemism. The croft was a small corner of a field deliberately left untilled as a concession to the spirit of the place who would otherwise be driven out and therefore liable to take counteractions. He or it was referred to as 'Goodman' because he was feared to be the opposite.

goody An obsolete polite but rather patronising expression for an elderly woman of the poorer classes. It is a corruption of 'good wife'.

goose   Current US and intellectual usage for what has been neatly defined as 'erotically motivated digital probing'. It is almost certainly derived from the old London rhyming slang 'to have a goose and duck'.

gooseberry   The name of this fruit is derived from neither goose nor gorse, as has sometimes been suggested, but from the French *groseille*, and this in turn is from the German *kraus*, meaning 'crisp'. Old Gooseberry is one of the many euphemisms for the Devil as in 'He played "Old Gooseberry" when he found out'. 'Playing gooseberry' can also mean being the unwanted third, a *de facto* chaperone, with a pair of lovers. The origin of this is utterly obscure, though not beyond conjecture.

Gordon *Bennet*   This name, often invoked by those too shy to call upon God direct, belonged to a once famous proprietor of the *New York Herald*, who also made a name by his sponsorship of balloon races. I do not accept the view that Bennet was chosen for anything other than his forename. Others who also believe in moderating their swearing prefer to exclaim the name of that famous Scots regiment The Gordon Highlanders.

gossip   This word is of Saxon origin and was once *god sib*, *sib* meaning 'relation'. Gossips were then people related to each other as godparents of the same child, and therefore having much of common interest to chat about.

graffiti   Anonymous writings or drawings on walls: from the Italian *graffio*, 'a scratch'. They may be expressive of unsatisfied sexual desire, political protest, thwarted ambition, or philosophical reflection, and have a long history. One of the earliest is the supernatural example recorded in the Old Testament Book of Daniel, when a detached hand inscribed the words *Mene, mene, tekel, upharsin* on the wall at Belshazzar's feast. Daniel interpreted the words to mean the fall of the ruler and his kingdom. The great ages of the graffito have been those of the Roman Empire, Rome and Pompeii being rich in such remains, and the modern era when they have become a cult and collections have been published. See KILROY.

grass London criminal slang for an informer this word has a disputed origin. Certainly it is relatively modern for the eighteenth century equivalent of 'to grass was 'to peach'. One theory begins with the hint or 'whisper' passed on by a whisperer. It is then alleged that the 1940s Inkspots hit song *Whispering grass* created the new expression. An alternative theory begins with London's 'copper shop' meaning police station, notes the derivative 'shop him', i.e. denounce him to the police, turns the habitual 'shopper' by rhyming slang into 'grasshopper' and then abbreviates this to 'grass'. Neither is yet proven.

grass widow This was an expression originally used in British India for a woman separated from her husband by the custom that caused wives and families to be sent up to the cool hill country (where grass grew) during the hottest season of the year. The expression is little used now, but we do hear of golf widows, etc. 'Company or corporation widow' might be predicted as a term likely to emerge.

graveyard shift, *the* The midnight shift at a mill or factory working 'round the clock'. The term became common during the First World War and reflects the higher accident rate during these 'unnatural' hours. British locomen talked of 'the birth control shift' for certain long distance night journeys.

green light, *to get the* Meaning 'permission to proceed' this derives from the railway signalling system which was also taken up for urban traffic lights. To see the red light is to get warning to stop. Modern rocketry is putting newer equivalents into circulation – the final command 'All systems go!' and the phrase 'to have lift-off'.

gremlin This word originated in the Second World War among the men of the Royal Air Force. A gremlin was an (imaginary) imp or goblin who caused otherwise inexplicable mechanical failures. The word has become part of the language but is now often used with the general sense of minor technical problems as in the odd sentence 'A few gremlins remain to be ironed out'. The gremlin idea is not a new one. The first German printers in the fifteenth century blamed some of their misfortunes on a *Druckfehlerteufel*, 'the misprint demon'.

groat The value and origin of this coin have often been enquired about. It was a fourpenny piece and was named from the Dutch *groot*, meaning 'great' or 'large' as it was substantially bigger than the other low-value coins.

grocer A grocer was, in the first place, a wholesale dealer, one who dealt in the gross. The English development of this word is an odd one. The French *épicier*, 'spice dealer' and the German *Kolonialwarenhandler*, 'dealer in colonial goods', are both more logical.

Grocer, *The* This nickname for British politican Edward Heath was, in his own view, awarded to him for the technical expertise he displayed in Britain's Common Market membership negotiations. One suspects, however, a jibe at his non-aristocratic origins. Many professional politicians, on one side at least, still 'dearly love a lord'.

grog Until 1971 every sailor in the Royal Navy was issued with a ration of diluted rum known as grog. The practice was introduced by Admiral Vernon, known as Old Grog from his preference for a grogram cloak. Growing from this root we have grog shops, an old term for a cheap drinking house, and grog blossoms, the red patches on the face of the man who drinks too much. Feeling groggy is another result of overindulgence.

grotesque The artistic and architectural meaning of this

86

word is distorted, bizarre. Its origin lies in the Italian *grotto*, a picturesque artificial cave much in vogue in the eighteenth century and a 'romantic' feature of many a landscaped estate. In contemporary slang grotesque evolved into 'grotty' perhaps best defined as absurdly inadequate and below legitimate expectations.

grouse This word, meaning to grumble and complain, seems to have emerged in military circles and was well established by the 1890s. One thing is certain, it has no connection with the gamebird.

growlers These were four-wheeled cabs once common in London at the beginning of this century. They got their name from the surly nature of their drivers. The conductors of the first horse buses also had a similarly bad name and were known as 'cads'.

Grundy The character Mrs Grundy is first mentioned in Thomas Morton's comedy *Speed the Plough*, first produced at London's Covent Garden Theatre in 1800. She has since become the symbol of a rather narrow-minded propriety. In the play there is constant reference to what Mrs Grundy will think or say, though she herself never actually appears. It may well be that the name of this fictional character will yield place to that of the real-life Mrs Mary Whitehouse whose moral strictures on the content of radio and television programmes have in recent years attracted so much notice.

G-string The minuscule covering for the crotch used by near-nude female dancers. The name was originally applied to the waist cord and narrow strip of cloth between the legs worn by North American Indians, and is thought to derive from the G string as the lowest of the four strings of the violin.

Guinea-fowl These birds have nothing to do with the coinage in any direct sense but both the fowl and the metal that became the 'Guinea gold' coin both came from that part of West Africa.

Guinea-pigs Guinea-pigs have no connection with Africa at all. Like the turkeys that do not come from Turkey, they come from South America. There are, in the world of business, titled people who are paid to let their name be used on a company prospectus in order to create confidence. In another sense a guinea-pig is anyone subjected to some experimental procedure, as the guinea-pig was once the animal most commonly used in laboratories for this purpose. The Guinea Pig Club described those servicemen who, during and after the Second World War, had undergone massive facial reconstruction under the care of the famous plastic surgeon Sir Archibald Macindoe at East Grinstead Hospital, Sussex.

Gunter The expression 'according to Gunter' is an American equivalent of 'according to Cocker'. Surveyors traditionally used 'Gunter's chain', twenty-two yards long and divided into one hundred links. Edmund Gunter (1581–1626) was an eminent mathematician, whose name will no doubt live in the phrase when his chain has long been 'metricated' out of existence.

guralnikism David Guralnik, editor in chief of the 1970 college edition of Webster's *New World Dictionary*, deleted as offensive several such terms as 'dago', 'wop', etc., notwithstanding their widespread use in society. An Oxford lexicographer, R. W. Burchfield, coined the word guralnikism in 1973 to describe this new form of bowdlerisation. See BOWDLERISE.

Gutter Lane 'It all goes down Gutter Lane.' Gutter (once Guthrum's) Lane was, in medieval London, the street of the silversmiths, and *gutter* was the Latin for 'throat'. This punning phrase was used when a man ate and drank his wealth away. Gutter Lane still runs from Cheapside to Gresham Street.

H

Habeas Corpus These are the opening words of a Latin legal formula. They mean 'thou [shalt] have the body'. The 'Habeas Corpus' procedure is an important element in the maintenance of civil rights in Britain, because if anyone is arrested, apparently without definite charges being made against him, his friends or family may apply to a magistrate for a 'writ of Habeas Corpus'. This is an order from the magistrate to the appropriate law officer ordering him to make definite charges in order that their validity may be determined by normal process of law. This method of guarding the citizen against arbitrary arrest, though known in the Middle Ages, was confirmed and redefined in an Act of 1679. In time of war or of political unrest the Act has sometimes been suspended.

haberdasher Like the mercer, the haberdasher deals in small articles of clothing. The name derives from *hapertus*, a mixture of silk and wool. Here a specialist name has been generalised. It is the exact opposite of the process we see in connection with the word grocer.

hack Short for 'hackney', a horse let out for hire, hence 'hackney carriages', the first public-hire vehicles of London and Westminster, which date back to 1637 in the reign of Charles I. Hence also 'hack' journalists, song writers, etc., who are to be distinguished from those colleagues who choose what they will produce, confident that they will find a buyer for it. Hence also a 'hackneyed theme', one that has been very well used by a great number of people and distinctly shows its age. 'Hack' is also a rather technical term for simply riding on an ordinary horse. 'It was only a short hack home.'

hag-ridden Today we call a person hag-ridden when they are obsessed with doubts and fears. Originally the expression was meant quite literally. The hag-ridden person had suffered from the 'nightmare', a female monster who crushed and suffocated her victims as they slept. (The entry on INCUBUS explains a classical and more explicitly sexual variant of this fantasy.) Animals were also hag-ridden. Witches were believed to ride furiously through the night on borrowed horses which were found sweating and exhausted in the morning, their manes tangled with 'hag-knots'. There are bizarre variants of these stories in which human beings are actually ridden by witches sitting on their shoulders. In this way the gods 'ride' on Voodoo cultists in Haiti.

ha-ha A ha-ha is a device of the landscape gardener for making a boundary to an estate or to part of one without in any way spoiling the view. Sometimes described as a sunken fence, the ha-ha takes the form of a sudden vertical drop, as it were a small cliff, which when approached from the other direction appears as a steep unclimbable wall. According to the eighteenth-century writer Horace Walpole in his book upon gardening the name was derived from the expressions of surprise uttered when people found such a 'sudden and unperceived check to their walk'.

Hail As a greeting this word or some variant was common in the Norse and Teutonic world, e.g. Icelandic *heill*, Anglo-Saxon *hal* and modern German *Heil*. It simply means 'health'. Compare the Modern English 'hale', as in 'hale and hearty'.

hair (*of the dog*) An invitation to take 'a hair of the dog' means to have yet another drink. The full phrase should be 'a hair of the dog that bit you' and refers to the ancient belief that a hair of the dog in question was an antidote against the bad effects of dog bite. Likewise an alcoholic 'hangover' was thought to be best treated by more drinking.

hake 'To lose in hake but gain in herring' was a fisherman's equivalent of the fairground saying, 'What you lose on the roundabouts you gain on the swings'. Hake were thought to feed on herring, so were driven from the fishing grounds, though they were saleable fish themselves.

halcyon days Nowadays this expression is a metaphor only for times of peace and contentment. The Greek name for the kingfisher was *halcyon*, and the bird was believed to lay and hatch its egg in a nest that floated on the sea. The seven days before and the seven after the year's shortest day were believed to be regularly calm ones. It was then that the halcyon made its nest and brooded. These were the halcyon days.

half seas over When a sailing ship had all her sails set, a sudden change in the wind would often lay her over on her side and bring the sea swishing halfway up the slant of the deck. Walking across such a deck was perilous in the extreme. Drunken sailors, reeling and staggering along the street, had the expression 'half seas over' aptly applied to them by onlookers.

Halifax Gibbet Law In the days of the medieval woollen manufacture Halifax in Yorkshire was famed for the sharp and summary justice executed there. For all who stole goods to the value of thirteen and a half pence, or more, the death penalty was inflicted on the same day by a type of guillotine. Taylor, the seventeenth-century poet, described it thus: 'At Halifax, the Lawe so sharpe doth deale / That whoso more than thirteen pence doth steal, / They have a jyn that wondrous quick and well / Sends thieves all headless into Heaven or Hell.'

hallmark To bear a hallmark is to carry the best possible guarantee of quality. The phrase derives from the British practice, instituted at Goldsmiths' Hall, London, in 1300 under a statute of Edward I, of requiring all gold and silver articles to bear a stamp, eventually consisting of a maker's mark, assay office mark, standard mark and date letter. Other assay offices are at Birmingham, Edinburgh and Sheffield. Similar marking is practised in many other countries, usually after assay by government analysts.

ham actor A contemptuous expression for a poor or incompetent actor, this term is said to derive from 'ham-fatter'. The old-style black-face comedian first covered his face with ham fat and then applied his burnt cork. A ham-fatter or ham was considered to be the lowest form of theatrical life. 'Ham' is also a contemporary word for the operator of an amateur radio transmitter, though the reasons for its usage in this field are not obvious.

hammer and tongs An expression suggesting forcefulness and vigour, whether in action or argument. The blacksmith holds the hot iron with his tongs and beats it with the hammer.

hammer cloth This oddly named article was the cloth hanging off the driver's seat or box on the old coaches or carriages. It is most probably 'hammock cloth', some of these seats being slung in the manner of a hammock.

hammock One of the few words we have adopted from the language of the Caribs, the pre-Columbian natives of the West Indies. Columbus himself noted the word and used it for 'the nets in which they sleep'. In modern Spanish its equivalent *hamaca* is used for a 'deckchair'.

handicap This word, originally exclusively sporting in context, is a corruption of 'hand in cap' and refers to the drawing of lots out of a hat or cap. In modern usage the word is often a euphemism for a physical or mental defect.

hand in glove This vivid phrase describes the closest possible association between two people, usually with some suggestion of disapproval, for example 'The detective and the thief were subsequently found to have been hand in glove with each other'.

hand in your checks An Americanism meaning to die, this phrase originated from the practice of accumulating a number of bills (checks) before settling up an account. To hand in one's checks and to pay the bill is therefore to terminate one's business at the establishment. Another possibility is a reference to cashing one's chips or tokens at the end of a gambling session.

handkerchief The origin of this word is 'kerchief', meaning a head covering from the French *couvrir*, 'to cover', and *chef*, an old word for 'head'. Worn as a scarf it becomes a neckerchief and carried for general utility is known as a handkerchief. There is an element of euphemism.

hands (*to wash one's hands of something*) This phrase meaning to disclaim responsibility for any further developments derives from the action of Pontius Pilate, the Roman Governor at the trial of Jesus Christ. The incident is recounted in the Gospel of Matthew xxvii: 24.

hands down, *to win* One of the many sporting expressions of the English language. A jockey who is so far ahead as to be without any fear of being overtaken can drop his hands and let the horse complete the course without any further urging.

'hand that rocks the cradle' This long-established cliché comes from the poem 'What rules the world?' by the American William Ross Wallace (1819–91). It opens with 'They say that Man is mighty . . .' and concludes with the lines 'But a mightier power and stronger / Man from his throne has hurled / And the hand that rocks the cradle / Is the hand that rules the world.'

hang out The question 'Where do you hang out?' is rather dated slang for 'Where do you live?' It seems to derive from the custom of displaying trade signs outside one's premises. This custom was never given up by English pubs. Recently some British banks have resumed the practice of displaying a symbol, and many publishers have a distinctive colophon.

hansom cab This was a public-hire carriage of a type popular in London until the First World War. The driver was perched high above the vehicle at its back. The hansom cab was patented by Joseph A. Hansom in 1834, though he was not the actual inventor.

harbinger Nowadays this word has the sense of a bearer of glad tidings. Its original sense was very different. The first harbingers were officials who went ahead of the army to requisition food and lodgings. The name derives from the Old German *hari*, 'army', and *bergan*, 'to lodge'. These harbingers were certainly forerunners, though not of anything very welcome.

hard up The normal meaning of these words today is short of money, in financial difficulties, though one can also be hard up for new ideas, etc. The term, like so many others in English, comes from the sea. To put the helm of a ship 'hard up' was to put it as far as possible to windward, thus turning the ship's head away from the wind.

hare, *mad as a March* March is the breeding season for the hare and the traditional reference is thought to derive from the hare's courtship displays. A rarer variant of the phrase prefers marsh hare, arguing that the lack of cover on this terrain made the hares there especially wild, but hares are not creatures of the marshes.

harlequinade This was a type of dramatic entertainment deriving from the *commedia dell'arte* of Italy and later evolving into the English pantomime. The characters were stereotyped. The clown loves beautiful Columbine and she alone can see the sprite Harlequin who uses magical powers to frustrate the crude and oafish clown. The role is not dissimilar to that of Ariel in Shakespeare's *Tempest*. The magic of Harlequin is the origin of the 'transformation scenes' that characterised the traditional pantomime. Greatest of all Harlequins was John Rich, once part owner of Drury Lane.

hat, *to hang up one's* This domestic image is symbolic of becoming master of the house. Visitors usually held their hat in their hands. In ordinary speech, however, the phrase is often used ironically when someone seems to be acting a little too independently on someone else's premises.

hat-trick Properly this should refer only to the taking of three wickets at cricket with successive balls. It is, however, often used for any triple achievement. At one time the bowler performing this feat was given a new hat at the expense of the club. A batsman scoring the 'century' of a hundred runs acknowledges the applause of the crowd by touching his cap.

hawker This word is of German origin and the variant form, huckster, preserves the older form. In Low German *hukke* meant a 'bent back' and *hukkester* came to be the name for a travelling packman or pedlar. In modern economic conditions the hawker is of little importance, and the line between hawking and virtual begging is a narrow one. The word has offensive implications as when, almost on the eve of the war against Hitler, the forthright Labour leader Ernest Bevin accused the pacifistically inclined George Lansbury of 'hawking his conscience around Europe'.

hearse The first form of this word was 'herce', which in Old French meant a harrow. Shaped like a harrow, the 'herce' was a framework, holding candles, which was placed over the coffin. Later such a frame with candles was used for carrying the coffin from house to church. By logical extension the name came to be used for the specialised vehicle used in funerals, whether horse-drawn or, as now, in the shape of a motor-car.

heathen This Christian term for a non-believer is an interesting example of parallel developments in different languages. A heathen was a dweller on the heath (one might almost say a backwoodsman), isolated from and ignorant of the Christianity of the larger settlements and towns. The Roman word *paganus*, meaning 'villager' or 'countryman', had a similar usage and when the Empire became officially Christian was adopted as the standard term for those who were not believers in the new faith.

Heath Robinson William Heath Robinson (1872–1944) was an English cartoonist who specialised in drawings of elaborately and ingeniously improvised machinery. Emergency repairs carried out with pieces of string, tin cans, bent nails, etc., will result in the job being condemned as a Heath Robinson affair. The American *haywire* has something of the same implication.

heavy man This is the traditional name for the unsympathetic character who plays as foil to the hero. The 'heavy' was so called because of the robust physique usual in these characters and because of their ponderous 'hammy' style of acting. The 'heavy' is perfectly illustrated in the early Chaplin films and, to go back even further, one might see the archetypal pattern in Jack the Giant Killer and David and Goliath. In contemporary drug and pop scene idiom 'heavy' means 'unfriendly', 'menacing'. There is some continuity of thought here.

heel, *to bring to* A well-trained dog walks at its master's heel, i.e. just behind him and sits there when ordered as well. By metaphor, to bring someone to heel is to impress upon them their inferior status. When used of human beings the phrase has unpleasant implications.

hell bent for election Used to mean 'moving with incredible speed or alacrity', this phrase was originally a theological one. In the religious system associated with Calvin it was conceived that the mass of mankind was doomed to destruction. They were 'hell bent'. A remnant only were 'the elect' chosen by God for salvation. To imagine the hell bent, given the chance, opting for 'election' gives the phrase its meaning.

henchman This is yet another term of Anglo-Saxon origin, being a compound of their word *hengst*, 'horse', and man. Henchman was therefore originally a word for groom or horseman. It evolved into a more general sense of page or servant and has finally sunk to discreditable associations in the same way as blackguard and villain.

hick This word, a rather patronising diminutive of the proper name Richard, came to be associated with the simple-minded countryman. The English language still has a number of such expressions disparaging the country; other examples are clodhopper, chaw-bacon, country bumpkin, and swede-basher. Hick became obsolete in England but survived in the United States whence it has returned to its country of origin. A parallel American term is 'hayseed'.

high old time The phrase means a thoroughly enjoyable time (whatever the consequences might be) and, though its history is obscure, must have some connection with the German *Hochzeit*, meaning 'wedding', which is literally 'high time'. The Jews speak of High Holy Days and standard English has the expression 'high days and holidays'.

Hip hip hurrah! All that can be said for certain about this phrase is that 'Hep hep' was the traditional cry of the Jew-baiters of medieval Germany. This cry is said to derive from the initials of *Hierosolyma est perdita* or 'Jerusalem is lost'. Hurrah is again said to derive from the Slavonic *hu-raj*, 'to Paradise'. In English, however, hurrah seems to have replaced an earlier Huzza!

hipped To be hipped is to be in low spirits and the word is a variant of the first syllable of hypochondria which the *Oxford English Dictionary* defines as 'a morbid state of causeless depression'. To hype, however, is American slang for deceive or delude.

hippies The word first appeared in the San Francisco *Examiner* in 1965 as a slick jibe at some aspects of the 'beatnik' cult, in particular their claim to be 'hip' i.e. up to date or 'with it'. Like Quaker and Methodist, or for that matter Whig and Tory, it was taken up and used by those against whom it was directed. The hippy stands for an alternative lifestyle, aesthetic rather than economic in interest. They have much in common with the old 'simple lifers'.

hippodrome The older generation will think of this word as the name of a music hall or cinema. It is in fact the Greek word for a racecourse, from *hippos*, 'horse', and *dromos*, 'course'.

hippopotamus This means 'horse of the river'. No river in Greece was navigable and the Greeks logically called their rivers after their chief use, which was for drinking. The modern words potion, potations, potable all preserve the same root meaning. American service slang revived the same idea. An airman 'down in the drink' had crashed in the sea.

hoax This is most plausibly derived from *hocus pocus* which in turn is a corruption of '*Hoc est corpus*', key words of the Roman Catholic Mass, which was derided by the Protestant reformers as the very epitome of superstition. See the entry on MUMPSISMUS for a human story on the subject of the clerical ignorance so brutally derided by the reformers.

hobbit In 1937 Professor J. R. R. Tolkien published his story *The Hobbit*, which was reissued in slightly expanded form in 1951. *The Hobbit* foreshadowed the great *Lord of the Rings* trilogy of 1954–5, which has since become the object of a cult in student and what might be called psychedelic circles. Hobbits, as the first line of the story tells, live in holes. The word is a coinage from *hob* (dialectal dwarf or peasant) and rabbit.

hobnob This is a corruption of hab-nab, 'have or have not', which can be interpreted as the spirit of give and take or share and share alike which characterises our closest friendships, hence 'to hobnob together'. Incidentally, Hobnob is the name of the old processional dragon kept in the city of Salisbury.

Hobson's choice See CHOICE, *Hobson's*.

hold the fort The phrase is immortalised from its use by General Sherman in 1864 during the American Civil War. He signalled the message to General Corse from the top of Kenesaw. The line was utilised in a hymn by the American evangelists Sankey and Moody, 'Hold the fort for I am coming, Jesus signals still.'

holocaust Though often applied to any great loss of life, this term should be restricted to fire disasters. It derives from the

Greek *holos*, 'whole', and *kaio* 'I burn'. It meant a sacrifice completely consumed by fire. Its current and rapidly extending usage is with reference to the mass murder of Jews in Nazi dominated wartime Europe.

'Home Sweet Home' This, formerly one of the best-loved sentimental songs in the English language, was first heard in the opera *The Maid of Milan* produced at Covent Garden in 1823. John Howard Payne, writer of the words, was an American and the music by Sir Henry Bishop is based on a Sicilian air. In fact this 'typically British song' has very little that is British about it. Moreover, J. H. Payne seems never to have had a home in his life, but was a wanderer living in hotels. Perhaps the words in his song were a heartcry?

honeymoon This word is derived from the old Germanic custom of drinking hydromel or diluted honey for thirty days following the wedding feast.

hoo ha This word, meaning fuss and bother, is a straight adoption from Yiddish.

hoodlum This word, introduced into England via American gangster films, has a curious origin. A San Francisco reporter wishing to write about some local delinquents decided to disguise his subject-matter slightly by reversing the name of the gang leader Muldoon into 'Noodlum'. This perhaps intentionally ludicrous coinage was lost to posterity when the compositor set the word up as hoodlum and added a word to the language. By a curious parallel, the English *hooligan* is said to derive from a delinquent family in the Lambeth district of London. The Russians have added this word to their vocabulary of political abuse, but a vagary of their language, the absence of an initial 'h', has turned it into *gooligan*.

hook (*by hook or by crook*) One of the rights of the medieval villager was to gather firewood where he could cut it with his hook or pull it down with a crook without inflicting any permanent damage to the tree, a drawing of interest without, as it were, breaking into the capital. This, despite many fanciful suggestions, is the obvious origin of the phrase.

hooker One of the many US terms for a prostitute, this is traditionally derived from the women who followed the division of General Joseph Hooker in the Civil War.

hook, line and sinker, *to swallow* This phrase, derived from the art of the fisherman, is used to express someone's quite improbable acceptance of an implausible story. Not only has the bait been taken but the hook, too, and the line and lead weight attached to them. A more complete swallowing cannot be expected.

hoosegow Americans got this word, like so many others, from the Spanish-speaking south-west. It is a near enough accurate reproduction of the Mexican pronunciation of *juzgado* (the 'j' and 'd' are silent), a word meaning 'sentenced', 'judged'. Perhaps because it was so often used in explanation of a worker's absence it was adopted as effectively meaning jail.

horse-play This term for boisterous conduct derives from the antics of the hobby horse that accompanied morris dancers and other traditional performers.

hose This term for stockings (men's socks being strictly half-hose) derives from the Saxon *hosa*, which meant any leg-covering, including breeches. This explains the description of Elizabethan costume as 'doublet and hose', without any apparent mention of breeches.

hour, *at the eleventh* This phrase is derived from the New Testament parable of the vineyard, in which the lord of the vineyard pays the same penny to those only employed 'at the eleventh hour' as he did to those who had been working for the whole day. In modern usage the phrase has about it suggestions of last-minute rescue, as in the old film cliché of the United States cavalry, which have no place in the original.

100

house, *to bring down the* This phrase, descriptive of thunderous applause, has its origins in the old days of travelling theatre companies who performed in barns (hence barnstormers) or tents or any ramshackle building that would accommodate them. Too much violent approbation might indeed 'bring down the house'.

humble pie, *to eat* This expression takes us back to the world of the medieval feast. The great folk dined off the venison whilst the lower orders had to be content with the entrails and offal, which were baked in pies. The entrails were then known as 'umbles'. Humble pie is a pun. The humble fed off umbles. Compare the note on BEEFEATERS.

humbug This emerged as a slang term by 1735 and has been plausibly interpreted as a compound of hum, to hoax and bug, a false alarm. The Irish *uim boig*, a 'false coin', cannot be the origin of humbug, but may well have helped its spread.

hung in the bell-ropes A betrothed couple are said to be hanging in the bell-ropes during the three weeks required by law to elapse while their intended marriage is announced on three successive Sundays at the church. This is 'calling the banns'. If the marriage is called off, the deserted one is said to be 'hung in the bell-ropes'. The phrase is now a rare one.

Huns Originally the Asiatic nomads who invaded Europe *c.* A.D. 375, and under their King Attila, 'the scourge of God', ravaged great areas in the fifth century with unparalleled ferocity. In the First World War, the name was revived in Britain as a propaganda designation for the German enemy, without any 'racial' foundation whatever.

hurry (*don't hurry Hopkins*) This ironic Americanism goes back to a certain Hopkins from Kentucky who wrote on his promissory note, 'The said Hopkins is not to be hurried in paying the above.'

husband This is an Anglo-Saxon word and meant a man who derived his status from being a householder (*hus-bonda*).

This rank was logically attained on marriage. Since most householders were farmers, 'husbandry' has come to mean the art of farming. Since householders must be prudent, we still speak of 'husbanding one's resources'. In origin the word is clearly one of economic and not marital status.

hussar This word for a cavalryman is from the Hungarian *huszar*, 'twentieth'. King Matthias Corvinus when he ascended the throne raised an army by decreeing that each twenty families should choose, equip and maintain a man for service. In Serbia, however, *husar*, is a 'robber'!

hussif A derivation of housewife, this word has come to mean a little 'holdall' of sewing and repairing material, a regular part of the soldier's equipment. The line of thought is obvious.

hussy Another uncomplimentary derivation. A hussy is a flirt, a gossip and an idler, compounding all these offences with insolence and failure to respect the proper housewife from whom her name is corrupted.

hustler Of Dutch origin, this word passed into English in American colonial days. A hustler was at first simply someone who went about his work briskly. Later it developed the suggestion of the, stop at nothing', 'go-getter' type of person and in a professional sportsman has some of the implications of 'gamesmanship'. In the United States the term currently describes a homosexual prostitute.

I

ibid. This is a contraction of the Latin *ibidem*, 'in the same place', and is most commonly found in footnotes or works of reference. It means that the fact or quotation referred to may be found in the same place as something referred to just above it.

iceberg The name means 'ice mountain', *berg* being a common Germanic word for this.

ice blink This is a peculiar appearance of the air caused by the reflection of light from land covered in ice or by pack-ice floating on the sea. Ice blink was a natural navigational aid for early explorers in Arctic waters. Blink is from the Anglo-Saxon *blican*, 'to gleam'.

ice-brook temper This almost obsolete expression derives from the technique of the Spanish sword-smiths who hardened the steel of their blades by plunging them, white-hot, into the ice-cold water of the Salo rivulet in Aragon. To be 'of ice-brook temper' was to be of the highest quality, of superb strength and toughness.

iconoclast This is the Greek word for 'image-breaker'. It originally referred to a party in early medieval Constantinople (Byzantium) who opposed all use of images in worship. Emperor Leo the Isaurian began this movement and his dynasty continued it until their extinction. In modern usage an iconoclast is one who systematically attacks widely accepted beliefs.

id. Like IBID. above this is another word most often found in footnotes which refer to sources. It abbreviates the Latin *idem*, 'the same', and directs the reader to the same author as in the immediately previous reference.

idiot Modern English has a wide range of words indicating varying degrees of mental incapacity. Idiot comes from the Greek *idios*, meaning 'private' or 'of one's own'. In Greek *idiotes* signified a man in private life as opposed to one holding public office and from there the word continued to degenerate until today, in English usage, it implies positive mental incapacity. Idiosyncrasy preserves the original meaning.

ignoramus This is a piece of legal jargon that has escaped into the outside world where it has gained a new meaning.

Grand Juries wrote *ignoramus*, meaning 'we ignore it', on the backs of rejected proposals for indictments. The implication of 'we wish to hear nothing of this' is perhaps responsible for its development into a description of someone who knows nothing of anything.

ilk, *of that*   This must be one of the most misused expressions in the language. Ilk itself is from the Saxon *ilca*, meaning 'the same', and is only used correctly when the surname of the person spoken of is the same as the name of his estate, for example Kinloch of that ilk, meaning Kinloch of Kinloch. It should not be used to mean 'of that same name or character'. It has little if any modern usage outside Scotland.

ill-starred   Nowadays this word simply means unlucky or, more specifically, doomed to failure. It is a survival from the days when belief in astrological influence was general.

imbecile   Here we have another example of a radically changed meaning. The origin must be the Latin *bacillus*, 'staff' or 'stick', and so 'depending on a stick' and thence 'physically weak'. The word came into English via Old French and in the seventeenth century was being used as a verb. Jeremy Taylor wrote in his *Holy Dying*: 'It is a sad calamity that the fear of death shall so imbecile a man's courage . . .' Later on the word assumed the sense of weak in mind only.

imp   Now this word is a rather patronising one for a mischievous child. Originally it meant 'offshoot', in Anglo-Saxon *impe*. As a verb, 'to imp' meant to graft on new shoots or just to extend something. 'Offshoot' to mean child is an obvious metaphor. The suggestion of mischief derives from the stereotyped phrase 'imps of Satan'.

incubus   The word comes from the Latin *incumbere*, 'to lie upon', and in medieval times the incubus was conceived as an evil spirit which had intercourse with women while they slept. The incubus was both an exculpatory interpretation of sexual dreams and an acceptable explanation of the birth of deformed children. Men were visited by the *succubus* or 'under-lier'. In modern usage an incubus may be any oppressive influence on the mind. We also say that duties are 'incumbent' upon us.

Indian file This descriptive term simply means walking in a line one behind the other. It takes its adjective from the Red Indian custom of a warrior band walking each in the man ahead's footprints. The last man in the file obliterated the line of footprints, thus leaving no trace of how many men had passed or indeed of whether any men had passed at all.

Indian giving This expression from the United States means to make a gift and then want it back again. The meaning derives from a misunderstanding which goes back to the first white contact with the Red Indians, whose social system required ceremonial exchanges of gifts on state and diplomatic occasions. To the simple European settler to make a gift and then immediately expect something back again was at best naive or at worst perverse. Hence this disparaging expression.

infantry The origin of this term for footsoldier is the Latin *infans*, 'a child'. In the United Kingdom, until the Family Law Reform Act of 1969, all were held to be infants until reaching the age of majority, but this law both reduced the age of majority from twenty-one to eighteen, and replaced the term 'infant' by the less confusing 'minor'. Younger men would fight on foot in support of the mounted knights who were their seniors and superiors.

infra dig. A clipping of the Latin *infra*, 'below', and *dignitatem*, 'dignity', thus beneath one's dignity and something one cannot do without losing status and self-respect.

in loco This is short for the fuller Latin phrase *in loco parentis* and means 'in the place of a parent'.

insult This word literally means 'to leap on' in the sense of 'to treat with contempt'. It is the Latin *insultare* from *saltus*, 'a leap'.

in the straw This is a vulgarism that means a woman is ready to give birth. It takes its origin from the ancient custom of using straw for bedding. A wild flower has the folk name 'lady's bed straw' and the sailor called his mattress a 'donkey's breakfast' because it was stuffed with straw.

in the swim River fish keep together in a group called a swim. A fisherman who is 'in the swim' will catch plenty of fish, hence the use of the term to mean 'well in with the right people' or 'in the right circles to do well for one's self'.

iota See JOT.

iron (*the Iron Chancellor, the Iron Duke*) The name of the metal is conventionally used to indicate strength of will and firmness of purpose as in these examples of Bismarck, founder of the German Empire in 1871, and Wellington, who vanquished Napoleon.

iron curtain These words were originally included in two of Sir Winston Churchill's telegrams to President Truman in 1945, but it was in 1946 at Fulton, Missouri, that he first used the phrase in a speech similarly referring to the ideological divisions of the times, saying 'An iron curtain has descended upon Europe.' From that time on 'behind the iron curtain' has been a standard phrase for the situation of the Soviet Union and its associated states in Eastern Europe. Churchill possibly half remembered the phrase from Lord D'Abernon's use of it (in a precisely opposite sense as a kind of 'safety curtain') with reference to the proposed security pact of 1925, the subsequent Locarno Treaties. The phrase 'bamboo curtain' was later coined to characterise what was seen as the parallel political intransigence of China.

iron rations This traditional name for an emergency food supply derives from the iron box in which they were stored to keep them from the air.

irons in the fire The phrase means to have more than one project in hand and usually occurs in a stereotyped warning against having 'too many irons in the fire'. It is said to derive from the practice of laundresses who kept two or three flat irons heating in the fire when ironing clothes. Too many irons in the fire might mean that some would become overheated and make burn marks. The phrase could be equally apt for a blacksmith who tried to keep too many jobs 'on the go' at the same time.

i's, *to dot the*   The phrase is completed by 'and cross the t's'. It means to complete a job thoroughly, to put the finishing touches to it. The 'i' and the 't' are two of the few letters in English which require additions after the word containing them has been written. Hence this phrase.

it   In 1927 the romantic novelist Elinor Glyn began to use 'it' to denote the quality of 'sex appeal' which itself, often abbreviated to 's.a.', became something of a catchword. Film star Clara Bow, held to exemplify the quality to a superlative degree, was called 'the "it" girl'. In cocktail bars the old order 'Gin and Italian (vermouth)' became 'Gin and It' and gained a new shade of meaning. To pursue this theme into strange places, see VAMP and VERMOUTH.

Ivy League   The old-established universities of the United States, where the buildings have had time to become ivy-clad; the equivalent of Oxbridge in Britain, as opposed to the raw bareness of the 'redbrick' newer universities.

J

Jack   This is the English language's 'word of all work' and is used in a wide variety of phrases. Firstly it is commonly used as a substitute for John, the most popular of all masculine forenames, though strictly speaking this is incorrect, as Jack, like its French parallel *Jacques*, must derive from the Latin *Jacobus*, which evolved into James. In France *Jacques Bon-homme* is the ordinary peasant and *Jacquerie* was the name given to a French peasant uprising. It has been suggested that

107

the name derives from the characteristic artisan's jacket on which there is a note below. Whatever the origin of his name, Jack in English is the common man and so we hear 'Jack will never be a gentleman', the contemptuous 'Jack of all trades, master of none', the usually ironical 'Jack's as good as his master' and the all-embracing 'every man Jack of them'. The knave in a suit of cards is commonly called the Jack. Sometimes the word merely implies masculinity as in jack-hare, jack-rabbit and jack-ass, though this last has once again implications of stupidity, the universal allegation against the peasant. Jack then was humble, though undeniably useful, and so we get 'boot jack', a device for pulling off one's own long boots without assistance and the modern 'car jack' which is a mechanic's lifting device.

Jackanapes This now obsolete term for an insolent or pushing young man derives from 'Jack (monkey) of Napes', Napes being a form of Naples. Traditionally it was first applied to a Duke of Suffolk whose crest was the log and chain of a tame ape.

jack-boots The name is derived from French *jacque*, 'a leather jerkin or jacket'. They were jack-boots because they too were made of leather. A (black)jack was a leather drinking vessel. In current usage 'jack-boot' is associated with political repression as exemplified by the uniformed supporters of the German Nazis and the Italian Fascists of the 1930s. By a strange coincidence blackjack has shifted its meaning in a similar direction and now commonly means a small club or 'cosh' originally made of leather, or, in the US, is the usual name for the card game vingt-et-un.

jacket This is from the French *jacquette*, a diminutive of the *jacque* referred to above.

Jack Downing 'Major Jack Downing' was the creation of Seba Smith (1792–1869), founder of the Portland *Courier* in whose columns the Major first appeared in 1830. Downing was the first of a long line of American 'homespun philosophers'. The character was much imitated and the costume devised for him by cartoonists was later inherited by the new figure of Uncle Sam who by mid-century had ousted Downing as the national symbol.

Jack Robinson, *before you can say* There is an old story that this phrase which expresses the idea of extreme speed or suddenness derives from the habit of a certain volatile gentleman of that name who frequently changed his mind and often abandoned an intended social call before the servant had had time to announce his name. The story is most improbable. An even less likely French version exists. *Robinson* (from Robinson Crusoe) was formerly a popular term for a gingham umbrella. When these articles were newly in vogue the proud owner anxious to impress would call for his umbrella on the slightest excuse and the cry, 'Jacques, Robinson' came readily to the lips. Note the use of Jacques as the typical servant. The reader may take his choice or offer a better story.

Jack-tar This name for the ordinary sailor must derive from the essentially tarry nature of the sailor's work in the days before steam. Ropes and timbers were tarred as a means of waterproofing, as was canvas, in which case it was known as 'tarpaulin', which became another term for 'Jack Tar' himself.

jail-bird The implication here is one of regular or repeated imprisonment, a haunter of jails. The term has nothing to do with cages for the analogous 'gallows-bird' exists and is a much older term. Ravens traditionally sat on the gallows to peck out the eyes of the hanged man and in German *der Rabenstein* 'ravens' stone' means 'place of execution'. In modern slang a prison sentence is known as 'bird', but this has quite a different origin. Serving a sentence is known as 'doing time' and in London's rhyming slang time is 'bird lime' which is abbreviated to 'bird'. That bird lime was used to catch birds is sheer coincidence. See the note on STIR for other prison slang terms.

Jamie Duff A Scots term for a mourner at a funeral from a certain legendary character of that name who looked forward to a funeral because he enjoyed the ride in the coach. A famous (and authentic) lover of funerals was the English Member of Parliament George Selwyn (1719–91). When his friend Lord Holland lay dying he said he would like Selwyn to visit him and added: 'I shall be glad to see him if I am alive and he will be glad to see me if I am not.'

janissaries This word for a famous regiment of Turkish troops is not surprisingly of Turkish origin, deriving from *jeni cheri*, 'new troops'. The new troops in question were originally Christian boys seized by the Turkish overlords at an early age and trained as an élite army corps which came to occupy a position similar to that of the Roman Praetorian Guard. The janissaries were disbanded in 1826 at a time when the Turks were adopting a more westernised military outlook.

jarvey This old nickname for a coach or cab driver was once derived from an original Jarvis, presumed surname of some early driver. A better origin is from the French St Gervais, a patron of coachmen whose symbol was a whip. Another saint with like associations was St Fiacre. In 1650 the first Paris cab rank was established outside the Hôtel de St Fiacre, hence the use of the saint's name for the cabs themselves.

jazey This is a traditional theatrical name for a wig. The allusion is to the fact that wigs were once commonly made of Jersey flax and fine wool.

jazz New Orleans was the cradle of jazz and the word is ultimately of Creole French origin. A New Orleans dandy was a *chasse beaux*, a beau who cleared the field of all rivals, for the word means 'beau chaser'. The *chasse beaux*, transformed into Jazzbo, became a character at the cakewalk and the minstrel show, and his name stuck to the improvisations practised wherever the Negroes gathered and made music.

jeans Jean was originally a cotton twill cloth of very great strength and first introduced into Britain as *jene fustian* from

110

Gênes, the French form of Genoa, its point of origin. The Liverpool firm of Lybro first manufactured jeans as working clothes in Britain *c.* 1850. At the same time in the United States, Levi Strauss, a Bavarian immigrant to California, a sail-maker with little business, turned to making his jean sailcloth into working trousers for miners. In this way the name 'levis' was born.

jeep During the Second World War the American forces brought with them a small, high, exceedingly powerful open car of general utility type and officially described as a quarter-ton reconnaissance car. Its popular name of jeep seems to have a double origin, firstly from the letters G P (General Purposes) painted on the side and secondly with reference to the well-established character 'Eugene the Jeep' in E. C. Segar's comic strip 'Popeye the Sailor'. In 1945 the Dublin Industrial and Commercial Property Registration Office refused an application to use the word 'jeep' as a trade mark on the ground that, by common usage, the word 'had fallen into the public domain'.

Jekyll and Hyde From R. L. Stevenson's 1886 story, *The Strange Case of Dr Jekyll and Mr Hyde,* the phrase is used when a person seems to reveal differing, indeed violently opposed, aspects of personality. Dr Jekyll, seeking by chemical means to extirpate the evil aspects of his own character only succeeded in concentrating them to such an extent that from time to time they took him over and he became openly what had previously been hidden – Mr Hyde.

jerry builder There is no undisputed origin for this word but it seems reasonable to associate it with the nautical 'jury' (as in jury-rigging, jury-mast) meaning temporary, for the time being, and deriving from the French *jour*, 'a day'. Jerry-built houses were meant to stand up long enough to be sold and not much longer. The story of the falling walls of Jericho perhaps reinforced the usage.

111

jib (*I know him by the cut of his jib*)   A jib is a triangular sail borne in front of the foremast and sailors could often recognise a vessel at sea by the shape of its jib. The phrase is now used of people and means 'I knew who [or what] he was by his manner'.

Jiminy   This explanation of surprise or of assertion is, like many such, a vestige of medieval religion, being a contraction of *Jesu Domine* 'Jesus Lord'. A far less likely possibility is that it is *Gemini*, the Zodiac sign depicting the twin gods of Ancient Rome.

Jingoes   This was a name given to the pro-war, anti-Russian party in the Balkan crisis of 1877–8 when Turkey seemed at the mercy of Russia and a body of opinion was urging British intervention. A music-hall song of the day declared: 'We don't want to fight but, by jingo, if we do / We've got the ships, we've got the men, we've got the money too.' Jingoism is now used for a bellicose patriotism. 'By jingo' is much more likely to relate to such abbreviations as 'By G— and by J—' (for God and Jesus) than to the Basque '*Jinko*', meaning God.

jockey   The name for a rider of racehorses comes from Scotland and is a diminutive of the typical 'servant' name Jock (= John or Jack). The first jockeys engaged in racing were often boys as well as lightweights, hence the 'patronising' form. By an interesting analogy, stable attendants, whatever their actual age, are still called 'lads'.

Joe Miller   This name is traditionally called out, especially among theatrical people, when the beginning of an old familiar joke is recognised. Miller was an early comedian and a book of his material was compiled in the reign of James II and for many years was virtually the only joke book available. See also CHESTNUT.

Joey   As the worldwide name for a clown this description honours the famous and unsurpassed clown and pantomime artiste Joseph Grimaldi (1779–1837). He is also remembered

112

at the annual 'Clown's Service' held each year at a church in Dalston, London. As a small silver coin (at first a fourpenny piece but later a threepence) the joey comes from Joseph Hume (1777–1855) an MP who pressed the case for coining these pieces. The new name 'Joey' soon replaced the ancient term 'groat'.

John Audley   The travelling, or fairground, players depended for their income on the number of shows they could put on each day. If while a performance was proceeding a queue gathered outside which would fill another 'house' the showman called out from the door 'Is John Audley here?' This was a signal to the people 'on stage' to finish off quickly to make room for the new audience waiting outside. The trick is said to have been invented by an old showman called Shorter. To 'John Audley' something is therefore to cut it short or abbreviate it.

John Bull   This long-established name for the typical Englishman was first used in a satire written by Dr Arbuthnot in 1712 and called *Law in a Bottomless Pit*. The Dutchman was called Nicholas Frog and the Frenchman Lewis Baboon.

John Doe   In legal proceedings in the United States directed to the discovery of the real person guilty of an offence, the fictitious name John Doe is initially used, hence the name has come to be synonymous with the ordinary American – likely to be blamed for everything.

John Hancock   As an American synonym for signature this derives from John Hancock, Boston merchant and revolutionary patriot, who put an especially large first signature to the Declaration of Independence, 'so the King of England could read it without spectacles'.

John Roberts   This gentleman was a Member of Parliament of the 1880s who secured the closing of Welsh public houses on Sundays. A large-sized tankard, designed to hold sufficient beer to last a frustrated drinker from Saturday night till

Monday morning, was named after the advocate of Sunday closing.

jolly boat The small boat often hoisted at the stern of the ship gets its name from the Danish *jolle* or the Dutch *jol*, which also give us our own word 'yawl'.

joss This pidgin-English word derives from the Portuguese *dios*, 'God', and was applied to the religious images of the Chinese. A joss-house was a temple and joss-sticks (of incense) were burnt there.

jot, *I don't give a* The jot one neither gives nor cares in this phrase is the Greek letter *iota* which is sometimes referred to directly under its own name. It signifies the smallest, most inconsiderable of things. The Hebrew character *yod* was referred to in a similar way as in Matthew v: 18, where it is translated as jot.

journeyman After an apprentice had served his time and was qualified in his trade he became a journeyman, the name deriving from the French *journée*, 'a day', for he was now paid wages for each day's work and not merely the pocket money of an apprentice. The fact that such a workman would often travel about seeking experience in other towns has led to a false derivation of this word from 'journey'. The union-encouraged practice of workers 'tramping' in times of unemployment reinforced this error.

jug It is a strange fact that this simple everyday word has no obvious origin. Jugge, however, was a pet name for Joan or Jane and it could be that jug has its origin in the use of this word for a daintier version of the leather vessel known as a jack. In the circumstances one might expect a jug to have been called a Jill, Jack's more usual partner. Jug as 'prison' derives from *joug*, which was French for 'yoke' and originally meant 'the pillory'.

Juggernaut This term is often used to evoke images of some monstrous thing rolling relentlessly forward and crushing all those in its path. The original Juggernaut was the Hindu god Vishnu, 'Lord of the World' (which is what the Hindi *Jagganatha* means), whose image was placed in a cart forty-five feet high with sixteen wheels each nearly seven feet across. As this huge structure rolled past, devotees would fling themselves beneath its wheels believing that such a death would ensure them eternal bliss. This, like several other Hindu religious practices, was suppressed by the British government during its rule in India. The word is currently applied to the oversize lorries entering Britain from the Continent.

Juggins   In the 1880s a Mr Juggins is said to have squandered his fortune by reckless gambling at the racecourses. The popular verdict of 'Silly Juggins' has survived.

jumbo   The original Jumbo was a very large African elephant exhibited at the London Zoo 1865–82, when he was sold to the Barnum and Bailey 'Greatest Show on Earth' in the United States. Jumbo died in 1885 after being hit by a railway engine. He weighed six and a half tons and his name has lived on in the commercial and catering world in such expressions as 'the jumbo-sized pack (or portion)'.

jumper   Although the name is now given to any kind of loose, knitted, slip-on outer garment, it originally described a kind of long loose jacket with sleeves worn by seamen, etc. It was buttoned for the whole of its length and ultimately derives from the French *jupe*, 'skirt'. The modern jump suit is an all-in-one garment which owes little to its nominal ancestry.

jump over the broomstick   This means to marry very informally and quite without ceremony. Marriage by a ritual which involved a quite literal jump over a broomstick has been associated with the gipsies in England, but it does not seem to be a real Romany custom. It was practised by the railway navvies, the tinkers and in similar marginal communities as well.

junk   This term for any unwanted material really belongs to the sea. Junk was the sailor's name for old rope ends and derives from the Latin *juncus*, 'rush', from which fibre ropes were formerly made. When the sailor called his beef 'salt junk' he meant it was as tough as old rope.

junket This substance gets its name because it was originally prepared in rush baskets. We have the original Latin *juncus*, which gave the Italian *giunco*, and, for the associated cheese or curd, *giuncata*. Hence, junket.

jury-mast For this derivation see the article on JERRY. The Old French *ajurie* meaning 'relief' is also a likely root of this use of 'jury'.

juvenile lead This is the traditional term for the men who play the leading roles as lovers in dramatic or light comedy productions. They need not be and indeed seldom are juvenile in years. See also HEAVY.

K

Kaaba This Arabic word meaning 'square house' is the name of the central shrine of Mecca, chief centre of Muslim pilgrimage. The Kaaba is associated with Ishmael, ancestor of the Arab people, and is said to be built on the spot where Adam first offered worship after being expelled from Paradise.

Kaffir This rather contemptuous term for the native peoples of South Africa has in fact a Muslim origin. It is Arabic for 'unbeliever' and was originally applied to those southern peoples who did not accept the Muslim faith which had captured so much of northern and equatorial Africa.

Kailyard School This is the 'label' given to a group of Scottish writers whose work had a strongly provincial, sentimental and simplistic character. Sir James Barrie was the best known of them. Others were J. J. Bell and S. R. Crockett. The name derives from the phrase, 'There grows a bonnie brier bush in our Kailyard'. A Kailyard is a cabbage patch.

Kaiser This German word for Emperor is a direct derivative of the Latin *Caesar*, the letter C in Latin having a hard 'k' sound. The Russian *Czar* has the same origin. Caesar is a rare example of a personal name that evolved into a general, descriptive title.

kaleidoscope Any gay and colourful spectacle, particularly one involving a variety of scenes, may find itself described as a kaleidoscope but the term properly belongs to an optical instrument which by means of two mirrors set at an angle to each other can show a seemingly endless variety of symmetrical coloured patterns. The instrument was pioneered in sixteenth-century Italy, but perfected by Sir David Brewster in 1817. The name is constructed from three Greek words, *kal*, 'beautiful',*eidos*, 'appearance' and *skopein*, 'to behold'.

kangaroo court The first kangaroo courts were held among the convicts of Australia when one of their fellows had infringed their code of conduct. The term is currently used for self-appointed groups of trade unionists who sit in illegal judgement on their fellow workers who have gone against prevailing opinion. Why 'kangaroo'? An authoritative answer is not easy to find – perhaps because the 'court' had no more legal or moral authority than a mob of kangaroos, that it came and went as easily?

kangaroo election An expression that had some usage in the 1980 American presidential election it refers to the situation in which the Vice Presidential candidate is deemed more attractive than the major figure who is carrying him but you cannot vote for one without the other!

keel-hauling Nowadays this means little more than a severe and protracted reprimand, but originally it was one of the more savage punishments used in the old Royal Navy. The unfortunate victim was tied to a rope and literally hauled from one side of the ship to the other beneath the keel. Near drowning was combined with severe laceration and death frequently resulted.

kennel As a dog house this word comes immediately from the Old French *chenil*, which means just that, and ultimately from the Latin *canis*, 'dog'. Where it means gutter or watercourse it is still Latin, this time from *canalis*, 'water pipe'. Canal and channel are really the same word.

Kentish fire This term for thunderous applause accompanied by the stamping of feet is said to go back to the political controversy about full civil rights for Roman Catholics in the late 1820s. Kentish audiences were hostile to the reform. In the theatre Kentish fire is usually ironic in character.

Kersey This traditional woollen cloth takes its name from the Suffolk village where it was first manufactured.

kettledrum In nineteenth-century Indian Army circles this was a slang term for a tea party and derives from the eighteenth-century usage of 'drum' for a big social occasion.

keys, *the king's* Crowbars, hammers and other instruments used to force entrance into a building so that a warrant might be executed were sometimes referred to in this way. One is reminded of the traditional inscription on cannons. It is *Ultima ratio regum,* 'The final argument of kings'.

khaki The word itself derives from the Hindustani *khak*, meaning 'dust colour', and the origin of the British soldier's khaki uniform is as follows. In 1883 a Mr Leeman was travelling in India on behalf of a Manchester textile firm. An army colonel stressed the need for a cotton-drill cloth, khaki-coloured as a means of concealment which, would be fast to the sun and to washing. The successful product resulted from the collaboration of Leeman with a dyer called Gatty. It was, however, not until a sample had been boiled in an old rusty pan that a sufficiently fast dye was found, the oxide of chromium having been 'fixed' by the iron oxide of the pan. A private company, F. A. Gatty and Co. Ltd, was established to market the new product and khaki became the standard wear of British troops.

kick There is an old and a new usage of this word. In the nineteenth century the phrase 'quite a kick' was derived from the Italian *chic*, meaning 'dandy'. After the Second World War 'kick' became a slang term for what we may clumsily call 'immediately satisfying sensations' and 'living for kicks' a philosophy of life. The first use of 'kick' in this way was American in such phrases as 'I get a kick out of . . .'

kickshaws Now a very old term meaning 'odds and ends' or 'bits and pieces', usually with implications of contempt. The word is mangled French based upon *quelque-chose*, 'something'.

kidnap The word kidnap is an old one, being established as early as the seventeenth century. It meant child-stealing, nap being a variant of 'nab'. The word travelled to America and came back into general English usage from there, with reference to the 'gangster subculture' of the twenties and thirties. Strictly speaking, the word should be restricted to the abduction of children in order to extort money from their parents. In the 1970s 'kidnapping' of public officials or prominent foreigners has become a standard tactic of the 'urban guerrilla' groups in Latin America and elsewhere.

Kilroy was here In the Second World War and after this phrase was frequently written on walls and elsewhere as a kind of ironic memorial to someone's presence at that place. It came with the American forces and has no proven origin though a United States shipyard inspector who signified his presence thus has been suggested.

king This simple word is the Saxon *cyning* somewhat contracted. *Cyn* was the 'people' or 'nation' and *ing* 'son of', 'descendant of'. Far from being 'Father of his country' (the Roman *Pater Patriae*) the Saxon king was 'son of the nation'. *Cyn* survives as our modern 'kin'.

king's picture, *to paint the* Another piece of criminal slang that indicates the crime of coining or forgery, for coins normally have on them the king's image.

kinky   This short word provides a curious footnote to the social history of modern Britain. For more than a thousand years this common Germanic/Scandinavian word remained unchanged, and meant the twist in a rope or thread that has turned back on itself. Between the two world wars, when psychoanalysis seeped out of the consulting room into the popular Press, 'kink' was given a new metaphorical meaning, for example 'There's a kink in him somewhere', a rather more sophisticated usage than the older, mechanical image, 'He's got a screw loose'. In the 1960s commercial interests began the mass indoctrination of the British public with new standards of permissiveness, and aspects of sexuality hitherto concealed here emerged into the full light of day. Kinky now specifically suggests sexual deviations of the sado-masochistic variety considered as supplementary allurements, and 'kinky boots' for a time were in vogue and considered to be something more than mere leg coverings.

kiosk   The present wooden hut from which one purchases newspapers or cigarettes is an embarrassed descendant of the original kiosk which was a Turkish summer-house or pavilion, often raised on legs entwined with flowering creepers.

kit   As essential equipment, kit derives from the Dutch *kitte*, which was a wooden container made of hooped staves in which tools, etc., were kept. In the sense of a common fund 'kitty' presumably has the same origin: the box could contain money as well as tools.

kit-cat   This is the name given by artists to a three-quarter-length portrait usually on a canvas measuring twenty-eight by thirty-six inches. The term originated in the eighteenth century when a number of prominent Whigs formed a club which met at the house of one Christopher Catt in Shire Lane where the Law Courts now stand. Sir Godfrey Kneller undertook to paint portraits of the forty-two members of the Kit-Cat Club, as it had come to be called. Since the rooms where the pictures would be displayed were rather low, a reduced canvas was used. Steele, Addison and Congreve were among those painted.

kite, *to fly a* This has two meanings, one commercial, one general. In the Stock Exchange world 'flying a kite' was raising money by means of worthless bills. The Americans talk of 'kiting a check' when a cheque is issued without sufficient funds to meet it should it 'land' too soon. In general usage 'flying a kite' is the very tentative, unofficial, half-suggestion of a change in policy to see how the idea is received.

kith and kin The English language is full of these alliterative phrases and this one is now little more than a cliché for blood relations. Old English, however, was not an inexact language and there was originally a distinction, *kith* meaning an acquaintance or friend (from *cunnan*, 'to know') and *kin* being one's own people. In the late sixties the phrase was bandied about – sometimes seriously, sometimes ironically – with reference to the white Rhodesians who unilaterally broke their link with Britain and became de facto independent.

kleptomania This word was one of the first fruits of the psychological approach to crime. It is, like so many scientific terms, a combination of Greek elements to express a new idea. *Klept* expresses the root idea of thief and *mania* is madness. The plea of kleptomania has sometimes been advanced in cases of shoplifting, but is often received with scepticism by magistrate and public. The word *klept* or *klepht* had another interesting development. When the Greeks were finally overrun by the Turks in the fifteenth century, resistance or 'partisan' forces took to the mountains to carry on the fight. The ballads of their heroic exploits are an important part of Greek popular literature and folksong. The roles of partisan and bandit easily blend into each other (witness Giuliano in Sicily after the Second World War), hence the name *klephts* for these Greek partisan forces.

knacker In its rural sense of 'horseslaughterer' this word derives from the Icelandic *knakkr*, 'a saddle'. 'Sent to the knacker's yard' can mean 'brutally disposed of', perhaps in the sense of elderly workers being dismissed as useless. 'I'm fair knackered' is a northern slang term for being utterly worn out by unremitting effort. Knackers is also a vulgarism for testicles, probably from the original saddle connection.

knapsack A knapsack was usually a small bag in which provisions were carried such as a soldier might carry. The operative word here is from the Danish *knappen*, 'to eat'.

knave In the Old English or Anglo-Saxon speech *cnapa* or *cnafa* was the normal word for boy. Later it took the meaning of servant and so was sent on its downward path. In a society dominated by aristocrats all the servant world was disparaged and 'knave' gained its associations on villainy. In German *der Knabe* remains the word for boy.

knickerbockers Originally a loose, knee-length type of trousers, this word derives from George Cruikshank's illustrations to Washington Irving's *Knickerbocker's History of New York* (1809), Knickerbocker being what was considered a typically Dutch name. It is often forgotten that New York was once New Amsterdam and that the original Harlem is in Holland. The word had an odd future before it. Abbreviated to 'knickers', the word in America indicated the wide trousers gathered just below the knee that were once worn when playing golf. In England the major use of the word was for the woman's trouserlike undergarment, replacing 'drawers', which came to be considered vulgar. In current usage knickers now has comic/erotic associations. In 1970 knickerbockers made a brief comeback as a high-fashion style from Paris.

knight In Anglo-Saxon days a *cniht* was a youth, attendant or servant even, in a Biblical context, 'a disciple'. Because a great man in those days always had a large retinue of young men in training for the profession of arms the word began its 'upward' move towards its association with chivalry. In German the opposite has happened and *der Knecht* is an inferior servant.

122

knowing the ropes   Once we associate this term with the world of the sailing ship, its aptness for someone who knows what to do and understands the business in hand is obvious.

knives, *night of the long*   On the night of 29/30 June 1933 Hitler adjusted the balance of power within his Nazi Party by commencing a massacre of suspected 'unsound elements' of whom Ernst Roehm, the S A (Storm Troops) leader, was the most eminent. How many were killed has never been really settled, but the political aim was achieved and a new, vividly descriptive phrase came into circulation. It has often been used of milder political upheavals as for example when the British Prime Minister, Harold Macmillan, sacked one-third of his Cabinet in 1962.

knuckle under, *to*   This phrase is a euphemism for kneeling in the sense of accepting and acknowledging an inferior position. 'To knuckle down', on the other hand, means to get to grips with a job of work and tackle it efficiently. In modern English we restrict knuckle to the finger joints. This was not always so.

kudos   This is simply the Greek for 'glory'.

Ku Klux Klan   The most famous, though by no means the only, secret society founded after the American Civil War with a view to protecting white supremacy in the territory of the defeated Confederacy. Its methods were those of terror and its costume of white robes and hoods suggested the ghosts of the Confederate dead. Two accounts of the origin of the name exist. One sees it as onomatopoeic and representing the cocking of a rifle, another associates it with the Greek for a circle which would be pronounced *kuklos*. It was active from 1865 till the withdrawal of the occupational forces in the South in 1877, and from 1915 was re-formed on an anti-Jewish-Catholic-Negro basis, declining again from 1928 until the flaring of racial violence after the Second World War.

Kursaal   The name given to the famous amusement centre at Southend-on-Sea is simply a transplanting of the word from

Germany, where it indicated the main assembly hall at a spa town. (Compare the Pump Room at Bath.) One went to the spa to 'take the cure'. The 'Cure Hall' was for such visitors. *Saal* 'hall' is itself a borrowing from the French *salle* which means 'hall'.

L

labyrinth Often used today with the general meaning of a maze this word takes its origin from one particular maze, that constructed, according to tradition, at Knossos in Crete by the master craftsman Daedalus for King Minos. It was from the Labyrinth that Theseus, having killed the minotaur, escaped by means of the clew of thread given him by Ariadne as a means of marking his way through the passages. The Labyrinth has been identified with the vast complex of rooms and passages beneath the palace at Knossos excavated by Sir Arthur Evans. The symbol of the *labrys* or double axe can be seen in the palace and gives us a clue to the origin of the word labyrinth itself: 'the house of the axe'.

lackadaisical This word now means 'in half-hearted fashion'. It has no clearly proven origin but would seem to be a formation from the old, bewailing cry, 'Lack-a-day'. Does one who is always bewailing his unfortunate situation simply give up and become 'lackadaisical'? It seems probable.

laconic This means 'given to expressing much in very few words' and derives from Laconia, an alternative for Sparta, that land of stoicism and simplicity. The classic example of the laconic style is the retort of the Spartan magistrates to Philip of Macedon when he said, 'If I enter Laconia, I will level Lacedaemon [another name for Sparta] to the ground.' The magistrates replied simply, 'If.' In lighter vein is the famous *Punch* admonition. 'Advice to those about to marry – *don't*.'

lacrosse This Red Indian hockey-type game was named by an early French missionary in Canada, François-Xavier de

124

Charlevoix (1682–1761), who explored the St Lawrence region. He called it *le jeu de la crosse, crosse* being a shepherd's crook or bishop's crozier, the French word having both meanings.

lady This word has a Saxon origin and is literally 'bread-giver', *hlaef-dige*. The lord was *hlaef-weard*, 'loaf of bread guarder', an interesting division of role reflecting typical views of the idealised male and female.

lager beer Lager is a German word for storehouse and lager beer is supposed to mature in the barrel before consumption.

lagniappe This Creole word for a small 'free gift' from a shop to a customer is a compound of the Indian *ñapa*, 'a gift', with the French definite article *la* added to it. The word was originally coined in New Orleans.

laisser-faire This French phrase is used to describe a policy of 'masterly inactivity'. The eighteenth-century French economist Vincent de Gournay, when asked how best the government might promote prosperity, replied, '*Laissez-faire, laissez-passer*,' 'Let things alone, don't stand in the way.' In Britain the same idea is associated with Adam Smith.

lampblack This chemical substance is in fact a fine soot and was originally made by burning resinous substances over the flame of a lamp.

lampoon Properly speaking to lampoon someone is to attack them with brutal personal satire. The word derives from the French *lampon*, 'a drinking song', a natural vehicle for such verbal assaults on unpopular characters.

landlubber The *lubber* of this word is Danish and means 'clown' or 'yokel'. Life on shipboard soon distinguished the experienced from the inexperienced and so exposed the 'land-lubbers'.

larder An odd word this and an example of the special becoming the general, for larder is from the Old French *lardoir*, which meant a store place for bacon. *Le lard* is still the word for bacon in French today. The use of this word for our general food store reflects the importance of the pig in the domestic life of our ancestors. Certain more gruesome 'larders' are written about in medieval history. In 1307 Lord James Douglas recaptured his castle from its English occupiers and destroyed all their stores, which he caused to be mixed into a great heap on the floor, then poured on all the ale and wine, and finally flung on to the pile the bodies of the slaughtered prisoners. This they called, in derision of the English, 'the Douglas Larder'. William Wallace also had a similar 'larder' at Ardrossan in Ayrshire.

lark When used in the sense of playful merrymaking this word derives from the medieval *laik*, meaning 'to play', and this in turn derives from the Anglo-Saxon *lac*, meaning a contest. 'Laking' still survives as a regional word, for example in Yorkshire. Larking is a relatively modern variant and 'skylarking' a nineteenth-century form. 'Dance and skylark' was a naval command authorising general recreation. This larking has nothing to do with the bird of the same name, though the phrase 'happy as a lark' may have encouraged an association of ideas and the ambiguity is exploited in the story of the robin who asked his wife about the strange egg that had appeared in the nest. She admitted that she had 'done it for a lark'.

larrikin Yet another derivative of lark is this Australian word for a young street hooligan. A plausible story ascribes its origin to the Irish brogue of Melbourne police sergeant James Dalton, who described a number of rowdy youths as (with excessively rolled r's) 'a-larrikin' down the strate'. The word caught the public fancy and spread into general Australian usage.

lateral thinking Concept of thinking round and about a problem, rather than making a direct approach along a single conventional channel. It was coined by Dr Edward de Bono in his *The Use of Lateral Thinking* (1967), and further explored in later works.

laudanum   In modern times this word indicates a tincture of opium, but the word has had a chequered history. In Latin, *ladanum* was a resinous substance, exuded from a shrub in Syria and valued in the ancient world for its healing properties. When opium was first brought from the East it was confused with this substance and named accordingly. The actual form laudanum was devised by the alchemist Paracelsus who applied it to one of his elixirs. It probably recalls the Latin root *laud*, meaning 'praise', in allusion to the curative properties claimed for it.

laugh, *the last*   The proverb 'He laughs best who laughs last' is first found in the dramatist Vanbrugh (1706), but it also seems to have a French parallel, '*Rira bien qui rira le dernier*'.

laugh up your sleeve   In the days when this phrase was coined the sleeves of outer garments were very wide. A person covering his or her face with their sleeve was suspected of hiding a smile at someone else's expense.

Laureate, *Poet*   In classical times the poet who won greatest acclaim was publicly crowned with a wreath of sweet bay, for which the Latin name is *Laurus nobilis*, hence the title 'Laureate' for the court poet in modern times. Homer, Vergil, Tasso and other great poets are all represented in sculpture with their heads crowned in this way and the ancients believed that laurel communicated the spirit of prophecy and poetry.

lavender   It was until quite recently the custom to put sprigs of this plant in with the household bedlinen to scent it, and this association was not only pleasant but very appropriate, for the name comes from the Latin *lavendula*, which derives from *lavare*, 'to wash'. Our word laundress and its French equivalent *lavandière* have the same origin. Laundered was in fact 'lavendered'.

lawyer's treat   A lawyer in fact never treats his clients at a place of refreshment. They defray the cost between them. A lawyer's treat is therefore no treat at all. See DUTCHMAN.

lead, *swinging the*   At sea the leadsman had the responsible task of ascertaining the depth of water in which the ship was sailing by casting his lead ahead to find bottom and then noting the amount of line below water level. If he merely swung the lead he was 'going through the motions' only, hence the use of this term for malingerer or shirker.

leading article (*leader*)   In some prominent position in a newspaper there is normally an article which, as distinct from the news, expresses the opinions of the newspaper on questions of importance. It designed to *lead* the opinions of the readers into the line of thought supported by the paper in much the same way as the lawyer's 'leading question' is designed to suggest a certain answer to the person being examined.

leap year   In the traditional Western calendar a year is deemed to have 365 days, which is fractionally too short to correspond exactly with the 'astronomical year' in which the earth makes one complete circuit round the sun. Every fourth year an extra day is added to February and in this way the relation of the year and its days is regulated. Because of this, any day of a month falling on Monday in one year will fall on Tuesday in the next and on Wednesday in the third, but when the fourth year comes with its interpolated day it will 'leap' over the Thursday to fall on Friday. There is a tradition that in leap years ladies may take the initiative in proposing marriage. Such permission is now superfluous.

leather, *there's nothing like*   The second half of the full saying is usually left unspoken, but when it is supplied the phrase explains itself. The missing words are 'for administering a thrashing'. There is, however, an apocryphal story of a town council soliciting ideas from its citizens as to how their defences might be strengthened. The mason advocated more stone, the carpenter thought timber was the thing and when they asked the currier (a curer of skins) he replied, 'There's nothing like leather.'

leathernecks This nickname for the United States Marine Corps goes back to a feature of their uniform of the early nineteenth century which had a strong leather collar as a defence against sabre cuts. Incidentally, French civil servants were at one time nicknamed 'leather bottoms', *ronds de cuir*, from an alleged consequence of their 'chair-borne' working lives.

leave some for manners The custom long prevailed of leaving a portion of wine in the bottom of the glass and indeed in the bottom of the bottle. The same applied to food. To do otherwise would reveal an unseemly greed as well as depriving the servants of a traditional perquisite. The custom was certainly taught to children in the nursery by means of the phrase quoted above. Perhaps this usage was reinforced by the words of Ecclesiasticus, 'Leave off first for manners' sake and be not insatiable.' Certainly the sentiment is the same.

left From the earliest times most human beings have displayed a preference for the use of the right hand. All forms of salutation are normally made with the right hand. A left-handed compliment is a reproach, a morganatic marriage is a 'left-hand' marriage, a left-handed oath is one not considered binding. Although left would now normally be defined as the opposite of right, this is not the origin of the word. In Anglo-Saxon *lef* is 'weak' and *lefan* is 'to weaken'. It would seem that the left hand was so named as the weaker hand. See also ADROIT.

left in the lurch This expression was borrowed from the game of cribbage. One is left in the lurch if before thirty-one has been scored one's opponent has already reached sixty-one. The general meaning of the phrase is that one has been left in a difficult situation.

legend Here we have a word which, if it has not changed its meaning, has certainly changed its implications. Today a legend is a story with an element of the marvellous, told about a character for whom there is usually a basis in historical fact, such as King Arthur, as distinguished from a myth or story of the gods. In medieval days *legenda*, a Latin word which means 'things for reading' or 'to be read' were the narratives of saints' lives, etc., which were specifically offered as approved narratives for the faithful. It was, however, the miraculous element that caused the word to assume its present meaning.

lemon sole The name of this fish has nothing to do with lemons but derives from the French equivalent *limande*, which in turn was so called because *limande* means a board. The allusion is to the flatness of the fish. It is 'flat as a board'.

lens This name for a magnifying glass simply means 'a bean' and is of Latin origin. The standard double convex magnifier is bean-like in section. French has the same word in even more explicit form and calls a lens *une lentille*.

Lent This traditional name for the fast of forty days observed by the Church in commemoration of Christ's time in the wilderness derives from the Anglo-Saxon *lencten* 'spring', the time when the days lengthen. The name itself has no religious implication.

leopard This jungle cat's name arose from the medieval belief that it was a cross between a lion (*leo*) and a pard, the name given to the white, unspotted panther.

levant, *to* Used to mean 'decamp', this word is a quite unnecessary borrowing from the Spanish, where, as *levantar*, it means just that. Ingenious minds have speculated about a connection with the Levant, a name for the Eastern Mediterranean region. Though it would not be impossible to levant to the Levant, it can never have been a general enough practice to have led to the use of this word.

levée Now used as a general term for a royal reception, the word was once simply the French for 'getting up' or 'arising', in this case the king's getting up in the morning, which was, oddly enough, a ceremonial occasion when His Majesty received courtiers and, indeed, any one with whom he might have business.

levis (*trousers*) See JEANS.

lewd Here is another of that vast class of words that has reached its current meaning by a long process of evolution. It comes from the Anglo-Saxon *loewede*, which meant 'unlearned', and referred to the mass of the people as opposed to the clergy, just as we now talk of laymen in this sense. From 'unlearned' it came to mean base, coarse and vulgar, especially with reference to sexual talk and behaviour.

'Liars should have good memories' Many versions of this sentiment have been used through the centuries but the very first seems to have been the Roman Quintilian who wrote: '*Mendacem memorem esse oportet*,' 'It is fitting that a liar should be a man of good memory.'

libel, *the greater the truth, the greater the* This maxim, enunciated by the English judge Lord Ellenborough (1750–1818), means that the more truth there is in the type of damaging publication called libel, the greater the harm the person libelled will suffer. Truth can be a complete defence in a libel action if the truth of the statement can be proved, if it was made without malice, and it is in the public interest the facts should be known. The word libel derives from Latin *libellus*, 'a little book', and gained its present meaning from the habit of hiring a journalist to publish offensive articles or pamphlets about a man's enemies. It differs from 'slander', which derives from the same source in ecclesiastical Latin as 'scandal', meaning a cause of offence, by being permanent, i.e. written rather than spoken. However, radio and television, because of their wide audience and such factors as recordings and scripts, come into the category of libel.

liberate This Second World War euphemism for simple theft provides a cynical comment on the activities of some members of the invading forces after D-day, 6 June 1944

lick into shape It was once a fallacious belief that bear cubs first saw the light of day as shapeless masses of flesh which had to be literally licked into shape by the mother.

lieutenant This is an exact French equivalent of the Latin *locum tenens* which means, literally, 'place holding'. The Latin form is most familiar in connection with the 'locum' who takes the place of an absent doctor whilst the French form now has an almost exclusively military usage as the name of the lowest commissioned rank. Here too it originally meant a deputy for the officer next above, in this case the captain.

limb of the law This rather hackneyed term for a policeman has behind it a well-established and traditional image of an institution, in this case the law, as a person. As the limbs of the human body are directed by and obey the head, so the limbs of the law, police, lawyers, etc., carry out and obey the directions of what is above them all – the law. 'The long arm of the law' derives from the same image. The phrase 'a limb of Satan' is an analogous formation.

Limbo According to traditional Catholic theology an infant dead before baptism is debarred from Paradise, but equally unqualified for Purgatory or Hell. Its soul is therefore deemed to inhabit the *Limbus puerorum*, a borderland between these states, *limbus* meaning the 'edge', and *puerorum* 'of the children'. Limbo is the Italian form and the word is now used to describe people or things who find themselves in neither one condition nor another, perhaps overlooked in some institutional reorganisation.

Limehouse A now obsolete political term for the violent abuse of an opponent. On 30 July 1909 Lloyd George attacked bitterly, and with considerable invective, dukes, landlords, capitalists, in fact the whole of the upper classes. The speech was delivered at Limehouse in the East End of London and the place gave its name to the style.

limelight, *in the* At one time calcium (or lime) was an essential element in the spotlights used in theatres. The man on the stage was the one 'in the limelight'. Now the phrase is used for anyone who finds himself the focus of public attention.

limerick This five-lined 'nonsense verse', with the first and second lines rhyming with the fifth, and the third with the fourth, was not called a limerick until long after it had been popularised by Edward Lear in his *Book of Nonsense* (1846). There is some suggestion of a corruption of 'Lear-ic'. English people like to suggest an Irish origin for absurdities and perhaps this is the clue to the word's evolution.

limey This old American term for an Englishman was first only applied to British sailors who were issued by the Admiralty with rations of lime juice as a measure against the dreaded disease scurvy. At first 'limejuicers', the term was abbreviated to limeys. It will be remembered that in R. L. Stevenson's *Treasure Island* the apple barrel plays some part in the plot. In merchant ships an issue of fresh fruit served the same pur-pose as the Navy's lime-juice.

limousine Early motor-cars were normally open. *Limousine* was a French word for a cloak. Covered-in cars were therefore said to be 'cloaked' if they are described as being limousines.

lingo This word for language is not the slang it perhaps sounds. It is a modern popular version of the Latin *lingua*, which meant 'tongue' or 'language'.

lining the pocket This historic term for the taking of bribes has several stories told of its origin, all of them of doubtful veracity. One of them relates how a tailor wishing to obtain the great man's patronage sent Beau Brummell a fashionable coat the pockets of which were lined with banknotes. The Beau is said to have replied that he very much approved of the coat and especially of the lining. In the opposite sense a similar story is told of Sir Thomas More who, when a judge, was sent a pair of gloves filled with money. More rejected the gift because of his 'dislike for such linings'.

link-men   Link-men were torch-bearers who could be hired to lead people through old London's unilluminated streets. The word link, used for the torches made of tow and pitch, derives from the Latin *linum*, meaning 'flax' or 'linen' which is made from flax. The Dutch *lont*, 'a match', has a similar derivation.

lionise, *to*   One of the great sights of London until the early nineteenth century was the royal menagerie at the Tower. The lions were the most admired spectacle and were much gaped at by visiting 'country cousins'. If a lady of literary aspirations persuaded some distinguished writer to accept one of her invitations he might well be referred to as 'the lion of the party', there to be gaped at and to reflect glory on his captor. Readers may recall the Dickens character Mrs Leo Hunter in *The Pickwick Papers*.

little one, *but only a*   This traditional plea in mitigation of an illegitimate child gained wide circulation by its use in Captain Marryat's *Midshipman Easy*, (1836) but it has been traced back, in almost identical words to a jest book, *Gratiae Ludentes* of 1638 and may well be even older.

-livered, *white, lily, yellow*   All these colourful expressions imply cowardice on the part of the possessor of this abnormal organ. The ancients believed that the liver of a coward was deficient in blood. We know more of anatomy now but the phrase survives.

loafer   Attempts have been made to find a Spanish American origin for this word in the Mexican *galofo*, 'a vagrant'. This possibly is one root of this well-established term for an idler. Another possibility is the German *laufen*, which among other things can mean to idle away the time. The Dutch *loopen*, for strolling idly, may also be involved.

lobbying   Pressure groups, anxious to represent their particular cases to legislators, would haunt the entrance halls or lobbies of public buildings so they might never be far away from those they sought to influence. In fact the name 'lobby' has now become a term for the groups themselves and we talk of 'the China lobby', 'the armaments lobby', etc.

lobster This very old expression for a recently enlisted British soldier came into use because on joining the Army a man would don the red tunic and thus, like a lobster, assume a new colouring. In the seventeenth century, however, lobsters were those who wore the lobster-tail helmets so called from the overlapping plates that protected the wearer's neck.

loco This old American expression for crazy or insane is of direct Spanish origin. *La locura* is 'madness' and *loco* is simply 'insane'.

lock, stock and barrel This very old expression simply indicates totality. One might say, 'He took it all, lock, stock and barrel.' The phrase derives from the three principal parts of a gun. See the note on 'hook, line and sinker' for a similar phrase with a rather different implication.

lode star In medieval English *lode* or *lod* meant 'way, course or path' and a lode star was quite simply one used to guide the traveller on this correct way. The man who 'hitches his wagon to a star' is also using a lode star. The advice 'Follow your star' employs the same image.

loggerheads, *to be at* The origin of this, it must be confessed, is something of a mystery. To be at loggerheads with someone is to be quarrelling with them, almost indeed to be at blows with them. A loggerhead is a blockhead. Does it refer to stupid quarrelling as opposed to some other kind? A 'logger' was the heavy piece of wood to which grazing horses were tethered to prevent them straying too far. If two ropes were tangled and the loggers banged together one can imagine the resultant struggling. So far so good, but the only place where the actual phrase seems to have been used in any sense other than that of quarrelling was on whaleboats. There, a loggerhead was the channel in the bow of the boat through which ran the rope attached to the harpoon. This rope sometimes ran so fast that water had to be continually poured on to it to prevent it catching fire by its own friction. When such an eventuality seemed likely the cry was raised 'At loggerheads'. Important as the whale fishery was, it seems odd that such a technicality should have 'escaped' into wider usage, but the fact remains that this explanation supplies the element of friction suggested in the metaphor.

log-rolling In one sense this means no more than mutual aid but there is always the suggestion of corruption and underhand practice. Its origin, which must be sought in North America, perhaps derives from the pioneers who certainly needed any help they could get when trees had to be felled and sites cleared for settlements. Loggers too knew the work if not the phrase. Gradually it acquired its present rather derogatory sense, and Bryce in his *American Commonwealth* referred to it as a 'milder form of reciprocal jobbing'.

Lombard loan This American expression means a loan bearing an unusually high rate of interest because it involves an unusual degree of risk. The Lombards were the shrewdest bankers of Italy and London's Lombard Street still has financial associations. The Lombards would never turn business away, but reserved the right to demand appropriate interest.

loo This, the latest of a long line of substitute terms for what the eighteenth century logically called 'the necessary', was certainly known in the 1890s, outcropped among the novelists (Evelyn Waugh for example) in the 1950s and in the 1970s ran riot. Upper class in origin, it must ultimately derive from the French *l'eau* (water), but it is not a French usage. Perhaps the Scots 'Gardy-loo' the traditional warning cry when slops were flung out into the Edinburgh streets provides one root. Since the Public Schools often scorned to attempt correct French pronunciation (as Winston Churchill witnessed) it could be just a deformed *l'eau*. The influence of French *lieu*, 'place', is another possibility since it, too, is vulgarly pronounced 'loo'.

Lothario, *a gay* This now antiquated term for a practised seducer of women was originally the name of a character in a play *The Cruel Brother* written in 1630 by Robert Davenport.

lotus eater This exotic phrase for one who lives in carefree luxury derives from Homer's *Odyssey*, where we are told that all who ate the fruit of the lotus tree forgot their home and friends and only desired to live in 'Lotus land' in idleness. In classic mythology Lotis, daughter of Neptune, flying from Priapus, was changed into the lotus tree.

love As the 'nil' score in tennis, 'love' is an old French witticism and comes from *l'œuf*, 'the egg'. English cricket says the batsman with no score is 'out for a duck' and Americans sometimes call zero a 'goose egg'.

love *making* This phrase originally referred to the whole social process once known as courtship. At some time, one suspects in wartime, when words were at a discount and action everything it became a euphemism. The original activity of course persists, though in cruelly truncated form, and is now described as 'chatting up'. An exact date has yet to be set on the crucial transformation.

'Love me little, love me long' This oft-repeated phrase has been ascribed to the Elizabethan playwright Christopher Marlowe (1564–93).

lucre This term, meaning gain or profit, usually carries with it the adjective 'filthy' and the expression is used three times in the Epistles of the New Testament. The adjective is most apt when we consider the word's background. It comes in the first instance from the Latin *lucrum*, 'gain', and is linked with the Greek *leia*, 'booty'. Akin to it is the Sanscrit *lotra*, 'stolen goods', and the Hindi *loot*, which has passed into the English vocabulary. Filthy lucre is dirty gain.

Lucullus, *the feast of* Lucullus was a Roman gourmand, not to say glutton, who earned his place in the hall of fame by the enormous sums he spent on feasting. On one occasion, having prepared an especially magnificent meal, he was asked who his guests would be. He answered: 'Lucullus will feast with Lucullus tonight.' A Lucullan feast is now used as a term for any superb meal.

luggage   Luggage is essentially that which is pulled, for in medieval English *luggen* meant 'to pull by the hair'. This verb, or something very similar, was also found in the Norse languages. The noun *lug* was a Norse word for 'ear' and by extension anything that projects. Although we can 'lug' a sack 'by the ears', the two 'lugs' are quite separate and 'luggage' derives from the first one.

lukewarm   The 'warm' here is quite redundant, for *lewk* is an Old English word which means 'tepid'. Luke water makes perfect sense by itself.

lumber   It has been suggested that lumber in the sense of unwanted oddments is a derivative of the name Lombard for the Lombards, as well as being bankers, were also pawnbrokers. This may be so, but lumber as timber is likely to have another origin. The traditional London street-cry, 'Old iron and lumber', refers essentially to portable things. The verb 'to lumber' in the sense of ungainly progress must be connected with the Swedish *lomra*, 'to rumble'. Might it be considered to suggest the sound of falling timber? In contemporary English slang 'to be lumbered' is to be given some unwanted but not easily disposed-of duty or object. See ELEPHANT, *white*.

lump, *the*   Method of building industry sub-contraction in Britain under which men work in gangs and receive lump payments for their work, and so are said to be 'on the lump'. It came into use from *c.* 1960 as a device for tax evasion, and such workers are not insured. Attempts to end the practice have been made by both the government and the trade unions, but it persists for economic reasons.

lunatic   A simple origin here. From primitive times insanity in man has been associated with the dire influence of the moon. Luna was the Roman moon goddess.

lush, lushington This term for a drunkard, perhaps more common in the United States than in Britain, has a simple origin in the fact that *lush* was a slang term for 'beer'. An actors' drinking club, calling itself 'The City of Lushington', was long associated with the Harp Tavern in Great Russell Street, London. The society claimed an eighteenth-century origin and lasted into the 1890s. Whether the beer was named from the club or the club from the beer is not certain. It seems probable that behind both stands Dr Thomas Lushington (1590–1661), chaplain and drinking companion of Bishop Richard Corbet. They were both heroic drinkers encouraging each other with 'Here's to thee, Corbet' and 'Here's to thee, Lushington'.

Lydford law The meaning of this now obsolete phrase is 'Punishment first, trial afterwards'. The dungeons at Lydford in Devon, where offenders against the Duchy of Cornwall were kept, were so foul that prisoners frequently died before they ever came to trial.

lynch law This term, for 'mob justice' or executions by unauthorised and self-appointed bodies, is of American origin and is first recorded in 1817. It has never been successfully traced back to any person called Lynch and in cases where such candidates have been found, for example, Charles Lynch of Virginia (1736–96), they never seem to have been involved with what we mean by lynch law. An English dialect word *linch* is recorded and meant 'to beat' or 'to handle roughly'. The question requires further investigation.

M

macabre The origin of the word has been widely discussed but never clearly established. Its original context is that of the

Danse Macabre, translated as 'Dance of Death', a favourite subject of late medieval artists in which people of all types and classes are shown being surprised and led away by a skeleton representing Death. The ultimate source of the word may be the Apocrypha, for a fifteenth-century form of the name is *Chorea Machabaeorum*, Latin for 'Dance of the Maccabees'. A French authority suggests that *macabre* might derive from the name of the artist who first represented this 'macabre' subject.

Macadam The Macadam system of road-making was named after its Scottish inventor, John Macadam, who introduced the method in the 1820s. Macadamised roads consist of granite chips converted into a smooth hard surface by the action of a heavy roller. A modern development was to cover this surface with tar, hence the term 'tarmac'. Even our contemporary concrete roads have a macadamised base.

macaroni Nowadays the primary association of this word is with that type of *pasta* that comes in the form of long tubes or pipes. This Italian dish was first popularised by the young men who in the eighteenth century made the grand tour to Italy and who in the 1760s flaunted their sophistication at the Macaroni Club in London. The word came to mean a dandy, and later was applied to the flashy and vicious idlers who infested London's Vauxhall Gardens. An American regiment raised during the War of Independence, more smartly dressed than most, was nicknamed 'the Macaronies', and has an enduring monument in a line from 'Yankee Doodle'.

macaronic verse The derivation of this name which is given to verse, usually comic, in which words and phrases from different languages are intermingled, goes back behind that of the word we have discussed above. *Macheroni* was originally a mixed dish of flour, eggs and cheese and it is the idea of mixture that gives the name to the verse form. Macaronic verse appeared, not surprisingly, in Italy in the fifteenth century.

McCoy, *the real* This phrase, which implies indisputable

140

authenticity, seems to have emerged in the late 1920s and is traditionally associated with Kid McCoy, the boxer. A famous anecdote tells of a drunk who picked a quarrel with the champion who did all he could to avoid the inevitable result. Bystanders told the drunk the name of the man he was provoking. They were not believed. At last McCoy punched his challenger and knocked him out. When consciousness returned the drunk made his rueful admission: 'You're right, it's the real McCoy.' In another derivation the spelling Mackay is preferred, when it is dated to the 1880s and is said to refer to a brand of whisky. It must be conceded that the phrase is regularly used to praise the quality of a drink.

Macfarlane's geese   The Macfarlanes of Loch Lomond never returned to their home there after their house had been destroyed, but the wild geese of the loch were still called Macfarlane's geese and proverbially said 'to like their play better than their meat'. The phrase had been coined by King James VI (the future James I of England) who, though amused by the antics of the geese when he first saw them, found one of them impossibly tough at the dining table.

Macgirdle's mare   This unfortunate creature is a Scottish descendant of an ancient Greek beast. Macgirdle is the man who is said to have fed his mare less and less each day until, when reduced to a diet of one straw a day, it died. The oldest version of the story is found in the *Analecta Minora*, formerly a standard text for schools.

machiavellian   This opprobrious epithet derives directly from the name of Niccolo Machiavelli (1469–1527), Florentine statesman, author and political theorist. Machiavelli's reputation as an advocate of political unscrupulousness derives from his pamphlet *The Prince*, which he himself described as a whim or fantasy. The cynicism of the writer's advice to the would-be ruler has rebounded in an unexpected way. His major works reveal Machiavelli as a patriot and republican who hoped to win fame with his poetry and dramatic works. Fate was un-

141

kind to him. It is even possible that his evil reputation contributed to making 'Nick' a popular synonym for the Devil!

Mackenzie man   This piece of legal slang was coined in 1970 when, after a divorce case in London (*Mackenzie* v. *Mackenzie*), the court ruled that a person conducting his or her own case was entitled to have a 'friend' present in the court-room with whom he might confer. Such a 'friend' is now nicknamed 'a Mackenzie man'.

mad as a hatter   Hatters are no more likely to be mad than members of any other trade or profession, though Lewis Carroll's realisation of the phrase in *Alice in Wonderland* has done much to give the idea currency. Originally it was mad as an *atter* and *atter* was Saxon for 'adder' or 'viper', England's only poisonous snake. The madness in question has changed its sense too. When first coined the words meant 'poisonous as a viper'.

mad as a tup   This phrase of the English Midlands was first seen in print in 1883, but obviously has a long history behind it. In full it says 'mad as a tup in a halter'. A tup is a ram, and in English folk speech a ram is a symbol of unbridled lust. 'A tup in a halter' is a vivid picture of the rage of frustration!

mafficking   This word for extravagant rejoicing and uninhibited celebration derives from an episode in the South African War of 1899–1902. The town of Mafeking had been besieged by the Boers from 11 October 1899 until 18 May 1900. When the news that the town had been relieved was received in London uproarious rejoicing broke out. 'Mafeking Night' was long remembered and the verb 'to maffick' was humorously coined.

magazine   A curious word this. Its original was the Arabic *makhzon*, 'a store house', and it entered the English language as a word for the place where arms and munitions were stored by the Army. In 1731 it assumed the new meaning of a periodical containing stories and articles. The first of these periodicals was *The Gentleman's Magazine* described in its first number as 'A monthly collection to treasure up as in a magazine the most remarkable *pieces* on the subjects above mentioned'. (Arms in the military magazine were described as pieces.) In French *le magasin* became the word for 'shop'.

magi The original magi (singular form *magus*) were the sacred caste of priests and wise men among the ancient Medes and Persians, though the name as we use it is Latin in form. 'Magic' and 'magician' have the same origin. The Three Wise Men who visited the infant Christ were originally called the magi. They only become three kings in later legend.

magnum opus This term for someone's principal literary, dramatic or musical achievement is simply the Latin for 'great work'.

magpie In shooting this term is used for a shot striking the outermost division but one of the target. It was signalled from the butt by a black and white flag. Hence the name. The bird with characteristic black and white colouring was originally just a 'pie' for anything 'pied' is two-coloured. 'Mag' (Margaret) was an affectionate nickname in the manner of Jack daw and Robin redbreast.

mahogany, *under the* A florid Dickensian phrase for 'under the table'. 'To have your feet under the mahogany' meant to be sitting as an invited guest at the table for mahogany was a favourite wood for this major piece of furniture. Perhaps because domestic matters were discussed 'at the mahogany' the northern counties evolved a new usage by which a man would use the term to mean his wife!

maiden Several established phrases employ this word as a euphemism for 'virgin'. We may note 'maiden stakes' in racing, an event for horses which have never raced before; a 'maiden over' in cricket, one in which no runs are scored, and a 'maiden assize', at which no cases are presented for hearing. A further group extends the idea to that of a first occasion, for example the 'maiden speech' of an M P or the 'maiden voyage' of a new ship. The last handful of corn cut by the harvesters was formerly referred to as 'the maiden' and made up into a crude simulacrum of a human body to be used in certain end-of-harvest ceremonies. Here maiden is a term of cautious respect, for the last corn was supposed to embody a powerful and possibly dangerous power which was sometimes more openly called 'the hag'. Perhaps euphemism, too, explains the use of 'maiden' for a type of guillotine used in Scotland in the sixteenth and seventeenth centuries though the idea of 'useful servant' may be present as well. In the north the common clothes-horse was called a maiden.

mailed fist, *the*   This common expression for aggressive military power goes back to 1897, the occasion being a visit to China by Prince Henry of Prussia who was urged by the Kaiser, 'Should anyone essay to detract from our just rights, then up and at him with your mailed fist.' As the confrontation of 1915 grew closer, this and similar phrases used by the Kaiser came to be considered as typical expressions of 'Prussianism'. See also HUNS.

mainbrace, *to splice the*   This order when formerly given in the Royal Navy meant the issue of an extra tot of rum to all hands, usually to celebrate some special occasion. There actually is a rope called the mainbrace in the rigging of a ship, but the logic of saying 'Splice it' to indicate a celebratory drink has been lost to knowledge.

main chance, *to have an eye to the*   This phrase, meaning 'to be mindful of possible profit', seems to derive from the dice game called hazard in which players threw twice, the first throw being 'the main' and the second, determining, throw 'the chance'.

Majesty   Henry VIII was the first English monarch to be addressed as 'Your Majesty'. Previously the normal style was 'Your Highness'.

make and mend   Another piece of naval terminology still sometimes heard in civilian life. These words were used to indicate time allocated each week for the purpose of carrying out repairs to clothing and kit. Now they indicate an afternoon off without involving any specific task.

make a pile, *to* Originally the pile in question was of gold from the Californian workings.

make things hum A metaphor from the age of industry. It means to set the machinery in motion in such a way as to leave no doubt that someone is busy.

make tracks for The phrase means to set out for a destination and derives from the wagons of the American pioneers. The wheels 'made tracks' which showed the direction taken.

make-up Applied to facial cosmetics this word derives from the theatre. To make up is to create a fiction. To make up *as* someone is to assume their outward characteristics.

mandarin It is usually taken for granted that this word is Chinese. In fact it derives from the Portuguese *mandar*, 'to command', and was a word applied by the Portuguese in Macao to the Chinese officials they encountered. From there it has entered into other European languages.

man of Kent A traditional distinction is made between the men of Kent, born east of the Medway river, and the Kentish men born to the west of it. The men of Kent insist they were never conquered by William the Norman, accepting his rule on their own terms.

man of straw This expression now means a mere 'front' man whose involvement in the business in question is nominal and who has nothing to lose because he is in no real sense a principal in the matter. The term was derived from the men who once hung about the Law Courts ready to swear to anything for a suitable fee. They identified themselves by a wisp of straw in their shoes.

mansion The origin of this word which comes to us via Old French is the Latin *mansio*, 'a resting place'. Manor has the

145

same origin and provides the clue to the word's changed meaning. The estates of a medieval lord were scattered over the country and with his retinue he visited each in turn and consumed its produce. Each 'mansio' was expected to provide a suitable lodging hence a mere 'resting place' began its evolution into manor and mansion. A variant form of 'manse' is used for the residence of a Protestant clergyman. The Roman Catholic priest has his 'presbytery' and the Anglican (or Episcopalian) his vicarage or rectory.

mantelpiece   However ornate the carved mantelpiece became in the course of its evolution, it was originally no more than a shelf above the fireplace with pegs from which wet mantles or other garments could hang to dry.

manure   This is a contraction of the Old French *manœuvrer*, 'to work with the hands', which developed the meaning of 'cultivate', and then, in abbreviated form, came to signify one particular aid to cultivation. There is an element of euphemism here. The native English expression was 'to dung the fields'.

Marianne   The embodiment of the French Republic in the same way as John Bull or Uncle Sam represent their countries. There is no satisfactory explanation of her existence, and her name is said simply to have been that of the model who sat for the first portrait busts. These are part of the official furnishings in each town hall in France, and some of the more recent ones are modelled with the features of Brigitte Bardot.

marines, *tell it to the*   This phrase today suggests some incredulity on the part of the speaker. The story told about the saying is that King Charles II when told by a naval officer that he had seen flying fish remarked, 'Tell that to my marines.' A marine officer present took offence at the remark, but the king apologised for any offence unwillingly given and explained that as the marines had travelled in every part of the world they could speak for the truth or otherwise of such a

146

story. If they believed it, so would he. This is the traditional story of the phrase, but one must admit it does not impress. The phrase is certainly naval in origin and more plausibly suggests the scorn of the real sailor for those hybrid creatures 'soldiers at sea', otherwise known as marines. The king's words could then be seen as an example of his characteristic tact.

mark, *up to the* The mark in this sense is the standard of fineness fixed by the Assay Office for gold and silver articles. Articles of approved quality would carry the hallmark. Inferior work was 'not up to the mark'.

marmalade Many apocryphal tales are told about the origin of marmalade, but there is no real mystery. *Marmelo* is the Portuguese word for 'quince' and quince jam was *marmelada*. When oranges became a common fruit the name was transferred in English to what in fact is orange jam, though in continental Europe the word *marmelade* is used for jam in general. The first modern 'marmalade' was made in Dundee in 1797.

maroon To maroon a person is to put him ashore in some inhospitable place. The word has a Caribbean background, but its origin is uncertain. The Spanish *cimarron* means 'wild' or 'unruly', rather as the Hindi 'jungly' does. The Maroons of Jamaica and elsewhere were a free community made up of the descendants of escaped slaves and other refugees of all races. They lived in the most inaccessible places. *Cimarron* meant literally 'an inhabitant of the peaks'. The Marouini River in French Guiana has also been involved in the question. The colour maroon, a brownish crimson, derives from the French *marron*, 'a chestnut'.

'Marriage is a lottery' We do not know who first said this but Samuel Smiles in his *Thrift*, published in 1875, refers to it as a current maxim.

'Marry in haste . . .' Today's form of this saying appears to be a contraction of words first appearing in Painter's *Palace of*

147

Pleasure in 1652. He wrote: '. . . leaste in making hastye choice, leisure for repentaunce shuld folow.'

marshal This, like henchman and chivalry, is another of our language's many 'horse' words. However, while henchman has come down in the world, marshal has distinctly come up. Now applied to the highest-ranking military officer or to the official who directs the order of procession on state occasions, it originally meant no more than blacksmith. Old German had the word *Marschalk* meaning 'horse-fellow' which in medieval French became *maréchal*, from which our marshal ultimately derives.

martinet In English this name is given to a strict disciplinarian and is said to be derived from the name of a French general who reformed the infantry in the reign of Louis XIV. If so it is odd to note that the French do not use the word in this sense. On the other hand they do use *martinet* as the name of the whip we call the cat o' nine tails and which in monastic circles was simply known as 'the discipline'.

masher This now obsolete slang word for a man who seeks to impress women with his personality and style is a variant of the Romany (gipsy) word *masha*, 'a fascinator'.

Mason-Dixon line See DIXIE.

mast, *before the* To 'serve before the mast' meant to be an ordinary member of the ship's crew as opposed to being an officer. The crew's quarters were customarily in the forward part of the ship, 'before the mast'. The phrase is sometimes used to indicate any service in a subordinate capacity.

masterly inactivity This phrase, perhaps best known in the context of late-nineteenth-century politics, in fact goes back to the *Vindiciae Gallicae*, a work in defence of the French Revolution written by Sir James Mackintosh (1765–1831). In another work, *The Causes of the Revolution*, he uses the similar phrase 'disciplined inaction'.

maudlin Now meaning tearful and morbidly sentimental, this

148

word derives from the popular pronunciation of Mary Magdalene, traditionally shown by painters with eyes filled with tears and swollen by penitential weeping.

Maundy Thursday, maundy money On the day before his crucifixion Christ washed the disciples' feet as a sign of humility and said, 'A new commandment I give unto you, that you love one another.' In the Latin version the sentence begins '*Mandatum novum* . . .' and these words open the service for the day. '*Mandatum* Thursday', the day before Good Friday, became under French influence *mandé* and on this day the King of England was accustomed to wash the feet of certain poor people. After the reign of James II (1658–88) the custom was replaced by the distribution of 'Maundy money', specially coined silver pence given to as many poor people as the monarch is years old. In Old English another development of *mandatum* was *maund*, which became the name given to an alms basket from which bread was given to the needy.

mausoleum This name now given to any large or imposing tomb is properly only applied to one original, the splendid tomb built at Halicarnassus *c.* A.D. 350 by Queen Artemisia for her husband Mausolus, hence the name 'mausoleum.' The original Mausoleum became one of the seven wonders of the ancient world.

Mayday Distress call used over the radio-telephone, corresponding to the SOS (q.v.) of the Morse code. It has been popularly derived from French *m'aidez*, 'help me', which might be convincing if it were not that the correct French for the phrase would be *aidez-moi*.

mayonnaise This dressing made from oil, vinegar, egg yolks, etc., takes its name from the port of Mahón, Menorca, where it was confected for the Duc de Richelieu after the French occupation of the island in 1756.

mealy-mouthed The origin here is the Greek *melimuthus*, 'honey-speech', and implied 'sweetness' in speech in order to

149

avoid giving offence or in order to obtain a favour. The anglicised form of the word, however, has stronger implications of conscious hypocrisy.

meander Now used as a verb, this word, meaning to follow a slow and winding course, comes from the winding river Meander in what was once Phrygia and now Turkey. The river today is known as the Menderes.

meat, *one man's* . . . The truism that 'One man's meat is another man's poison' was first expressed in Latin by Lucretius in his *De Rerum Natura,* iv, 638, as follows: 'What to some would be food was to others the deadliest poison.'

Mecca The Arabian city where the Prophet Mohammed was born later became the object of pilgrimage for all true Muslims. The word is now used metaphorically of any 'holy city', cult headquarters or honoured place which attracts tourists.

Mediterranean This is a Roman name and means 'in the middle of the land'. It was the sea that lay at the centre of the then known world and precariously kept this distinction until the discovery of the 'New World' of the Americas.

melancholy The Greeks believed that bodily health and state of mind depended on the proportions of four fluids (or humours) in the body. Mental depression they blamed on *melas chole* or 'black bile'.

melodrama Derived from the Greek *melos,* 'song' and *drama,* 'a play', the word means no more than a play with songs or music. In actual usage it indicates a type of play with stereotyped characters, simple plot and a crudely flamboyant style of acting. It was the type of play put on in the cheap London theatres known as 'penny gaffs'. The use of a word meaning 'music-drama' in this way dates from the theatrical censorship of the early eighteenth century when only four London theatres were licensed for what became known as 'legitimate' drama. In the cheap, unlicensed houses music and songs were permitted, as were recitations in costume and character. The

150

original acts of what became the music-hall comedian was a song with no more than a few prefatory remarks. Soon the emphasis shifted and the song often survived as a mere vestigial formality. It was against this background that the melodrama as we know it emerged. Officially it was a musical performance.

menial A menial is an inferior servant who engages in menial tasks. It derives from the Old French *mesne*, 'household'. *Demesne* and *domain*, both medieval words for a lord's private estate kept under his own management, have the same ultimate origin.

mentor This word for 'a guide, philosopher and friend' is derived from Mentor, the name of a character who acts in this capacity to Ulysses in Homer's poem.

mercenary The mercenary, the 'soldier for hire', was a phenomenon of the ancient and medieval world who seemed to have become extinct until he made his startling reappearance in our own times. Mercenary derives from the Latin *merces*, which means 'pay'.

mercer This medieval word for what we would now call a draper comes from the Latin *merx*, 'wares, merchandise'. The word merchant has the same origin. This development of the word reminds us of the importance of the medieval cloth trade.

merry Here we have one of the most misleading words in the language. It formerly had no connotations of jollity, but meant to be cheerful and in good spirits. This is the meaning we find in the Christmas carol 'God rest you merry, gentlemen'. It means 'May God keep you in good spirits'. In the famous phrase 'Merry England' we go back even further to the Anglo-Saxon use of the word. In Saxon times *maere* meant 'famous' or 'renowned'.

mesmerism What we now know as hypnotism is developed from the work of Franz Anton Mesmer (1733–1815), who first of all called his technique 'animal magnetism'. This was because his original treatment was to stroke the subject with a magnet. Later he became certain that the effect did not derive from the magnet as he had supposed but from his own will. Mesmerism was, in the opinion of the nineteenth century, on the suspect fringes of quackery. Today hypnotism is an accepted medical technique.

mess A group of soldiers or sailors who commonly dine together form a mess. The name is also given to the place where they dine. It is also the food served to them. It is perhaps not surprising that a word with so variable a usage has more than one root. There is some doubt as to the word's exact derivation but certainly the Latin *mensa*, 'a table', played a part. So did the French *mets*, 'a dish served at table'. It seems to have been the medieval custom to serve four people together and we find traces of this usage in Shakespeare. In *Henry VI* he speaks of the king's 'mess of sons' and in *Love's Labour Lost* there appears: 'You three fools lacked one . . . to make up the mess.' The Biblical 'mess of pottage' is simply a meal of soup.

meum et tuum The only use of these Latin words meaning 'mine and thine' in modern speech is when we say someone lacks the sense 'of meum et tuum' which is a polite way of suggesting he is a thief.

mews Ultimately Latin in origin this word came to us like so many others from the Normans. The Old French *mue* was a place where hawks were kept especially when moulting. Later the word was applied to stables which were commonly placed in courtyards behind blocks of city houses. Mews are now sometimes used as garages but more often have been adapted as small and usually expensive apartments.

mick A generic term, first for an Irishman and then for an Irish (or Irish descended) Roman Catholic. In Britain the Protestant Southern Irishman is scarcely heard of. The Ulster, Liverpool or Glasgow 'mick' will refer to members of the 'heretical' church as 'prods'. In Australia the variant 'protto'

152

is found. Mick derives from the Irish popularity of the name Michael. See also PADDY.

mickey, *taking the* This phrase for teasing or making fun of someone relates to the English stereotyped image of the stupid Irishman. See RILEY, *life of*, for another aspect of this outlook.

Middle America This term was popularised in 1968 by Washington journalist Joseph Kraft for the hitherto neglected 'constituency' on which Richard Nixon hoped to base his continuing power. The concept has some relation to that of 'the silent majority'. In 1969 in an interview published in *Fortune* magazine Nixon and James Mitchell spoke of their wish to appeal to 'the traditional values of middle-class America'.

midwife This Anglo-Saxon word is often the subject of questions as to its origin. In Old English 'wife' was any woman (we find for example ale-wife and fish-wife) while *mid* was 'with', the exact equivalent of modern German *mit*. Thus a midwife is the woman who accompanies or assists another woman in childbirth.

milliner The traditional name for a designer and maker of ladies' hats derives from the Italian city of Milan which at one time was accepted as the home of fashion and elegance. The milliners of Elizabethan times, however, did not confine themselves to hats, since in his *Winter's Tale* Shakespeare has a character who says (of Autolycus the pedlar), 'No milliner can so fit his customer with gloves.'

Mills (*of God*) What we all know about 'the mills of God' is that they grind slowly. The more literate might be able to add 'yet they grind exceeding small'. The sentiment was first publicised in Longfellow's translation of von Logau's *Retribution*.

miniature In modern usage this word is descriptive of art work on a greatly reduced scale, but this was not the original meaning, which relates to the use of 'minimum' or red-lead on the 'rubric' or red introductory words which began the various sections of church service books. The capital letters of these were regularly 'illuminated' with what we would call miniature paintings. Thus the raw material used to write part of the text came to give a name to the style of the illustration.

mini-car The first mini-car was 'unveiled' by its manufacturers, B M C, on 18 August 1959. It had been designed by Alec (now Sir Alec) Issigonis in answer to the pressing demand for a high-standard, high-performance small car. It was an outstanding success and the prefix 'mini' swept through the commercial world as a sales 'gimmick' for anything that was appreciably smaller than the normal article! In 1965 the dress designer Mary Quant produced the 'mini-skirt' (a self-defining term) which was another runaway success, and probably the most radical fashion change of the post-war period, if not of the century. Attempts to exploit similarly the prefixes maxi- and micro- have had nothing like the same success.

Missouri, *he's from* The full phrase says 'I'm from Missouri, you'll have to show me'. It is said to have been popularised by a Missouri Congressman, Colonel Vandiver, and President Truman was fond of it, too. According to context it has two distinct implications. One story derives it from the mines of Leadville, Colorado, where Missouri men were sometimes employed. They were completely ignorant of the nature of the work and everything had to be explained to them, hence the phrase. The other use depicts the man from Missouri as shrewd and hard-headed. He will take nothing on trust nor buy any 'pig in a poke'. All claims must be substantiated before he will go any further. One may guess the interpretation favoured in Missouri.

Mitty (*Walter*) The archetypal fantasist and day-dreamer from the main character of a James Thurber story, translated to the screen as a musical starring Danny Kaye by Goldwyn

154

in 1942. In Britain Keith Waterhouse's 'Billy Liar' (1959 on) is a similar figure.

mob New words are coined to describe new phenomena. 'Mob' was a late seventeenth-century contraction of the Latin *mobile vulgus*, 'the fickle crowd'. The political and social opinions of the common man were beginning to make themselves felt in public affairs and the riotous or revolutionary crowd was a major factor in eighteenth-century politics. Mob normally has sinister or threatening implications, though in Australia it can have a neutral usage as in the phrase 'a mob of cattle'.

mob-cap Oddly enough, this has no connection with the mob above. This type of female headwear, often associated with servants and country girls in bygone days, was a deep cap with a broad frill round it. It derives from the Dutch *mop*, meaning coif, cap or head-dress and is an example of a large class of words in which the second element is a strictly speaking unnecessary variant of the first one.

mods By the early sixties the vague Ted trend had evolved into those polar opposites the mods (modernists) and rockers. Mods spent their money on clothes to an extent hitherto unparalleled among teenagers. They cultivated self-conscious elegance, rejected the motorbike for the scooter and dabbled in soft drugs. We might sum up the mod image as feminised or at least transsexual. The mods were middle class and money conscious, not in any way dropouts. They were the customers of Carnaby Street and fortunes were made out of them. The Press knew them mainly for faction fighting with rockers.

moke This slang word for a donkey was in use among the London costermongers or street traders from the 1840s onward. The natural derivation would seem to be from the Romany (gipsy) *moxio*, 'a donkey'. *Pal* and *shaver* are other Romany words adopted by the same class of people.

mollycoddle In the eighteenth century 'Molly' or 'Miss

Molly' (perhaps with some allusion to the Latin *mollis*, 'soft') was a common expression for the effeminate or physically weak male. To coddle was to pamper or spoil so to 'molly-coddle' is to treat someone in the manner appropriate to weaklings.

monastery The main element in this word is the Greek *monos*, 'alone'. The first monks were hermits who withdrew from the world. They were later gathered into communities by SS Basil and Pachomius in the East and by St Benedict in the West. The primitive name of monk was, however, retained. A monastery is therefore a community of solitaries.

money The origin here is the Roman *moneta*, 'mint', which in turn derived its name from the Temple of Juno Moneta ('the one who warns') to which Rome's first mint was attached.

-monger Now only a part word, for it is always in association with some qualifying element, -monger is simply the Anglo-Saxon *mongere*, 'a trader or dealer'. This derivation explains its double use today, literal in the case of such words as ironmonger but metaphorical in the case of warmonger or scandalmonger. Most famous of all is the London coster-monger, who was originally a seller of costards, a type of apple introduced from Holland in the eighteenth century.

monkey In the Middle Ages all such creatures were indiffrently known as apes, but monkey is derived from the Italian *monicchio*, which itself is a diminutive of *monna*. It means 'little old woman'.

monkey suit A contemptuous term for full evening dress of 'white tie and tails'. The tail-coat is responsible for the name which is most odd when one considers that a sailor's monkey jacket is short and distinctly tailless!

monkey wrench This tool, a type of large adjustable spanner, was first made by a certain Charles Moncke and so named after him. The popular name is an ignorant (or humorous?) variant.

moonshine   When this word is used to mean fiction or fantasy it is no more than a metaphorical transference of a concept to a new situation. Moonshine is without substance or solidity, it is deceptively glamorous and has traditional connotations of mental derangement. To condemn someone's testimony as moonshine is strong condemnation indeed. 'Moonshiners', on the other hand, are illegal distillers of liquor who operate under the cover of darkness. 'Moonlighters' are those hard-pressed citizens who have a second employment after normal working hours in order to keep abreast of the rising cost of living. A 'moonlight flit' is a secret flight under cover of darkness by tenants anxious to avoid paying accumulated rent arrears.

Moot (*a moot point*)   A point well worth serious discussion. A term taken from the London Inns of Court conference-debates for law students and known as moots, an Old English word for a gathering.

moratorium   This is legal permission to delay payment of bills or accounts and comes from the Latin *morari*, 'to delay'.

'More haste, less speed'   The Romans knew the equivalent sentiment, for they had a saying *Festina lente*, 'Hasten slowly', but it was also an authentic English proverb. The Elizabethan scholar Udall, in his translation of Erasmus's *Sayings of the Ancients*, writes: 'Soche persones as do make most hast in the beginning, have commonly (accordyng to our Englysh proverbe) worst spede towards the endyng.'

morgue   This name for the place where unidentified bodies are kept is itself something of a mystery. There is no doubt that the origin must be sought in France, but there is somewhere a missing link in the chain. In one sense *morgue* meant the haughty demeanour of the 'high and mighty', a sort of studied coldness that was believed to be characteristic of the English! In another sense *morgue* was a section of a prison, where new arrivals underwent a long scrutiny so that they would be known on any future occasion. This was, of course, before the

157

days of fingerprinting. Did the manner of the gaolers give the name to the place? And, of course, the dead had to wait until identified.

moron   This is a technical term relating to the classification of mental subnormals. Idiots and imbeciles had already been labelled, but there was a need to distinguish these from a third slightly higher category, physical adults whose mental age had been retarded at the level of an eight to twelve year old. Dr H. Goddard chose the word *moron*, which is Greek for 'dull' or 'stupid'.

morris dancers   This name for one category of England's traditional dancers has been the subject of great controversy. The name 'morris' is undoubtedly meant to be 'Moorish' and an apocryphal story says the dances were brought back by John of Gaunt's soldiers from their expedition to Spain. Folklorists today do not support this view and suggest it was a plausible but false identification. The dancers were no doubt called Moorish because they blackened their faces. They did not blacken their faces to present themselves as Moors.

mosey   To 'mosey around' is to take a slow, exploratory walk. It is an American corruption of the Spanish *Vamose*, 'Let's go'. See VAMOOSE.

mossbros   This term applied to, for example, an evening suit means that it has been hired for the occasion and derives from Moss Brothers (customarily abreviated to Bros) a London firm specialising in this line of business.

Mother Carey's chickens   In the Middle Ages these were 'the birds of Our Lady'. Mother Carey is said to be an ignorant anglicising of *mater cara*, 'dear mother', a variant way of referring to Mary.

mountebank   Another word for a charlatan or trickster. This is of Italian origin being, when first borrowed, *montambanco*, 'one who mounts on a bench'. The *banco* or bench is now more

158

often a box, but the image is still a vivid one of the quack offering his wares to a crowd in the open air.

mouse, *poor as a church*   See CHURCH MOUSE.

muckraker   An expression taken by US President Theodore Roosevelt from Bunyan's *Pilgrim's Progress* (where it avers that 'No man can look upwards with a muckrake in his hand') and applied by him to such 'investigative journalists' as Lincoln Steffens.

mud in your eye, *Here's*   This toast is still informally employed, but few people have thought of its meaning. The speaker is in fact toasting himself, for the saying belongs to the world of horse-racing and the winner will be kicking mud into the eyes of those who follow.

mud, *your name is*   John Wilkes Booth, the assassin of Abraham Lincoln, caught his spurs in the flags decorating the presidential box and fractured a leg in making his escape. He was treated by Dr Samuel Mudd, a country doctor, who did not learn of the assassination until the next day. Although he and his wife then notified the authorities of the suspicious patient, the doctor was arrested a few days later and sentenced to life imprisonment as a conspirator. Because of the hatred and contempt felt for Lincoln's assassin and anything connected with him, 'your name is mud' is said to have originated with this incident. In the 1970s there was a revival in a half-serious way of a campaign to clear the doctor's name.

muff   To be a muff, or to muff something, are both contemptuous expressions used about someone deemed to be less manly and less competent than the speaker. Both are now obsolescent. The suggestion has been made that the original object of ridicule was the man who carried the more normally feminine muff to keep his hands warm.

mufti, *in*   This was an army expression for 'wearing civilian clothes'. A real mufti is a doctor of Muslim law, and on some forgotten occasion an army officer, relaxing in 'undress', perhaps in smoking jacket and slippers, was told he looked like one and the expression caught on.

mug Like jug, this simple word is something of a mystery. It first appeared in the sixteenth century and though it has Scandinavian parallels, for example Swedish *mugge*, 'a drinking vessel', these take us no nearer an origin. As with jug, a personal name has been suggested. Mug is also fairly modern slang for a dupe or simpleton – what the Elizabethans knew as a gull, hence 'mugging' (U S A), robbing passers-by. Mug can also mean face and in theatrical slang 'mugging up' was at first putting on the make-up for a character part. From its character of preparation its meaning was extended to learning the part.

mugwump Originally a term for 'wise chief' among the Massachusetts Indians, it came to be applied to political 'fence-sitters' who would not come down on one side or other of an argument. This led to the humorous definition of a mugwump as an animal that sits on the fence, 'its mug on one side and its wump on the other'.

mulberry Best known because of a children's rhyme 'Here we go round the mulberry bush', the name mulberry has a most odd and paradoxical origin. The scientific name is *morus* from the Greek *moros*, 'a fool'. And why a fool? Because tradition calls it 'the wisest of all flowers that never buds until the cold weather is past and gone'. Perhaps the wisest fool? In the Second World War 'Mulberry' was the code name for a vast prefabricated harbour made of concrete that was towed across for D-Day (6 June 1944) when the invasion of Europe began.

mumbo jumbo Now used for any incomprehensible rigmarole, the name Mumbo Jumbo is first found in the writings of Mungo Park, the explorer of the Niger. He said it was the name of a fictitious god or spirit, actually impersonated by a disguised man, whose terrible visitations and chastisements

160

were used by the men of a village to keep their women in subjection.

mumpsismus Today the word means any mistaken opinion still adhered to after it has been proved to be wrong. It derives from a word in the Latin mass meaning 'we take up'. The story goes that an old priest had it pointed out to him that he had been using the nonsense word 'mumpsismus' instead. He pleaded the habit of years and the familiarity of an old friend and regretfully added, 'I'd sooner have my old mumpsismus than your new sumpsismus any day.'

Murphy's Law In its briefest form this states that 'What can go wrong, will go wrong'. Sometimes known as Sod's Law. Murphy's Law is of American origin. I first heard it in the 1977 television disaster film *Pile up on Highway 14*.

museum Now conceived of as a store-house of objects for display and study, the literal translation of museum should be 'Arts Centre', for it means 'Temple of the Muses' who were the goddesses of the arts. The first place to be called 'museum' was the university founded by Ptolemy at Alexandria, *c*. 300 B.C.

mustard The name of this condiment derives from the 'must' or new wine which was traditionally used for mixing with the mustard seed. Powdered or ground mustard is said to have been introduced by an old lady of Durham in the reign of George I. France has its own story of the origin of the name. Philip, Duke of Burgundy, we are told, gave the town of Dijon, famous for its mustard, the motto *Multum ardeo*, 'I ardently desire', or, in the French of the day, '*Moult me Tarde*'. This was popularly cut down to *Moult-tarde* (to burn much) and again to *moutarde*, which became the French for mustard. A proverb which has both French and English versions says regretfully 'After meat, mustard' when assistance arrives too late to be of any use.

myrmidons (*of the law*) The original Myrmidons (meaning

161

Antmen, from the Greek *murmes*, 'an ant') were the Thessalian tribe who accompanied Achilles to the siege of Troy. After this the word that once implied 'faithful followers' degenerated into 'hired ruffian' or 'brutal police official'.

mythology The Greek *logos* or 'discourse' gives us the final element in the names of many sciences. Mythology from *muthos*, 'the spoken part of a religious ritual', is then the study of those symbolic religious stories which were so significant to the ancients, but are now told as fables for children. A myth is *not* by definition untrue; it is an elaborate metaphor, a symbolic explanation, a parable, a dramatic 'vehicle' to convey a spiritual message. Today without the religious faith that inspired them the classical myths are largely devoid of meaning, though still of enormous literary and artistic significance.

N

N or M This answer to the first question in the Prayer Book Catechism has puzzled many people. The person being catechised should give as answer his name or names, in Latin *nomen vel nomina*, in abbreviated form, 'n' or 'nn', since the double initial was the customary Latin form for plurals. The 'nn' was mistakenly printed as 'm' and this became the standard practice.

nab This word that means to seize suddenly and without warning is of Scandinavian provenance, Swedish having *nappa* and Danish *nappe*. The expression nabman was once used for a police officer.

nabob In the eighteenth century the men who had made a fortune in India and then returned to buy power with their wealth in England were contemptuously referred to as nabobs. It is a corruption of the Hindi title *nawab*, meaning, in general, a 'man of great wealth' and in particular the ruler of a province of the Mughal Empire.

nadsat In January 1972 the Stanley Kubrick film *A Clockwork Orange* from the Anthony Burgess novel of the same name was the focus of much public interest and controversy. Set 'not long from now', much of the story is told in a synthetic jargon compounded of Russian, Romany and Cockney and known as *nadsat*, from the Russian abbreviation of *pyatnadsat*, 'fifteen'.

nagging The continual grumbling of a wife to her husband (or even vice versa) comes from the Anglo-Saxon *gnagan*, 'to gnaw' or 'to bite'. A dull continuous pain is often called a nagging pain.

nail, *hung on the* This now obsolescent expression is a euphemism for pawning, the leaving of a valuable object as a 'pledge' in return for a loan. At one time the 'pawned' object was hung on a nail with a number attached to it, the customer having a duplicate ticket. In later days the nails became purely metaphorical.

nail, *to pay on the* The phrase now means to make prompt and exact payment without making any difficulty over it. It has its origin in market customs of long ago. In the markets of the Middle Ages, and no doubt earlier ones too, bargains were to be made and accounts settled 'in open market' and in the presence of witnesses. Several places are known to have had official 'payment counters' usually in the form of waist-high flat topped pillars known as nails. Examples have been recorded at Limerick and the old Liverpool Exchange, and can indeed still be seen at Bristol. This is how one paid 'on the nail'.

nailing a lie To demonstrably expose a falsehood for what it is is often referred to as 'nailing the lie'. This is said to derive from the storekeeper's practice of nailing counterfeit coins to the counter for all to see. The derivation is not a satisfactory one.

nailing colours to the mast Surrender, especially in a fight at sea, was indicated by hauling down one's colours or flag. Nailing the flag to the mast was a symbol of being ready to fight to the last, eschewing all possibility of compromise.

naked truth, *the* The phrase speaks for itself but has had a fable woven about it. Falsehood and Truth went together to bathe in the river. Falsehood came out first and dressed in the garments of Truth. Truth, unwilling to go dressed as Falsehood, preferred to go naked.

namby-pamby This derisive term is used for the weakly sentimental, the insipidly pretty and the affectedly simple. It is a fanciful play on the name of *Amb*rose Philips, an author of pastorals who died in 1749. His work was ridiculed by better known writers (Carey and Pope, for example) and dismissed as 'Namby-Pamby's little rhymes'.

nap This word for a short sleep not taken in bed is a derivative of the Saxon *hnaeppian*, 'to doze'. The expression cat-nap derives from that animal's ability to be apparently asleep and yet instantly ready to come to the alert. The game Nap is a shortened form of 'Napoleon'.

napalm Napalm is an incendiary material used in jelly form for air-to-ground bombing or for flamethrowers. Its name is often used as symbolic of the horrors of such a war of material against people as has been seen in Vietnam. Napalm is made from a petroleum product, naphthenic acid, and palmetate, an extract of palm oil. The name incorporates elements from both these words.

Naples (*see Naples and die*) A mysterious phrase this, with many suggested origins. It could, for example, be a tribute to the beauty of Naples and its bay. Having seen Naples you have seen the finest sight in the world. Or again does perhaps have a whiff of Vesuvius about it? A third suggestion makes it no more than an Italian pun on the name of a nearby village Muori, which is also Italian for to die. *Vedere Napoli e poi Muori* 'See Naples and then Muori'. Finally Naples was once an English euphemism for syphilis. What happened to many a young man on his Grand Tour? He saw Naples. It was perhaps this English expression that gave a new dimension to the Italian witticism.

napoo   The British Tommy who went to France in 1914 found the language far too much for him and so produced his own version of what he thought he heard. Napoo meant 'nothing' and is a mangled version of '*Il n'y en a plus*', 'There's no more of it'.

narcissism   This technical term for a morbid self-admiration derives from the Greek legend of Narcissus a youth of great beauty who fell in love with his own reflection in a pool believing it to be the nymph of that place. His vain attempts to possess his love caused him to take his own life and the flower that bears his name sprang up where his blood touched the ground.

nark   This word for a police informer, current in criminal circles, is the Romany word *nak*, 'a nose'

natter   This word, though perhaps not Standard English, is not slang but has a respectable Scots origin. It is a close relation of two Old Norse words *knetta*, 'to grumble', and *gnadda*, 'to murmur'.

nature/nurture   This basic antithesis between heredity and environment was first set out by Shakespeare (*Tempest*, IV.i) with regard to Caliban, '...a born devil, on whose nature/ Nurture can never stick...'. The phrase was taken up by Francis Galton, the eugenicist, in 1883 and again popularised by Sir Percy Nunn as a chapter heading in his 1920 classic, *Education: its data and first principles*. The debate continues.

naughty   The word now normally describes the disposition of a badly behaved child. This is a sad weakening of its original meaning. In the Anglo-Saxon tongue it was *na wiht*, 'nothing', implying utter worthlessness. In the Bible we find reference to a basket of 'naughty figs' (Jeremiah xxiv: 2). In Tudor times the word sometimes meant simply evil as when Shakespeare speaks of 'a good deed in a naughty world' (*The Merchant of Venice*, Act v).

navvy The original navvies were the men who dug the first canals in the eighteenth century. The canals were called navigations and the men who dug them navigators; navvy is an abbreviated form. 'To work like a navvy' has become a proverbial phrase and is a living monument to the remarkable and formidable 'army of labour' that gave industrial Britain its network of canals and railways.

'Nearer the bone, the sweeter the meat' This sentiment is first recorded in a ballad of 1559 in the form 'The nigher the bone the flesh is much sweeter'.

'Necessity knows no law' This phrase was made most famous by the German Chancellor Bethmann Hollweg when he used it in August 1915 to justify Germany's violation of Belgian neutrality. It was not, however, coined for the occasion. It had been used by Cromwell in 1655 and also by Milton in *Paradise Lost*.

necessity, *music of* An academic term for 'pop' coined by Professor Wilfrid Mellers of the University of York in his book *Twilight of the Gods: The Beatles in Retrospect* (1973). Professor Mellers stresses the role of the pop musicians as fillers of the aching void in the mind of youth cultists, as dream weavers and occupiers of empty time. The phrase is an analogue of 'money of necessity', the bizarre coinages issued in besieged cities during the English Civil War of the seventeenth century, a parallel that matches well with the basic meaning of the word BEAT.

neck and crop Here neck is the Scandinavian *nakk* meaning

166

a 'knoll' or the 'top of a hill', and *cropp* was an Anglo-Saxon word for the top or head of a plant. The whole phrase then strengthens the idea of 'top' by reduplicating it. To fall 'neck and crop' is to crash completely.

neck-verse The beginning of Psalm 51 used to bear this name from the fact that by reading it a person accused of a capital offence could claim 'Benefit of Clergy', which had in course of time been extended from its legitimate covering of ordained priests to include anyone who could read and indeed who need only be able to read this one verse. Having 'proved his clergy', the offender if guilty was only branded and not hanged. The privileges of these so-called 'clergy' were gradually eroded, but did not disappear entirely until 1827.

needle in a bottle of hay When something is difficult to find we compare the task to that of looking for a needle in a hay stack or in the original version 'in a bottle of hay'. There is no nonsense or paradox here. The key word is from the Old French *botel* which simply meant 'a bundle'. The variant *pottle* exists meaning a measure of four pints.

nem. con. This is simply a contraction of the Latin *nemine contradicente*, 'no one contradicting'. A motion passed *nem. con.* has had no vote passed against it.

nemesis As a proper noun, Nemesis denotes the classical goddess of retributive justice who doled out to men the exact share of good or evil fortune that was their due. The word is now used more loosely in the sense of fate or destiny especially if this can be equated with doom.

nephew Strange though it may seem, this word is a direct derivative from the Latin *nepos*, 'a grandson'. This word also gives us nepotism, a corrupt preference for the members of one's own family.

ne plus ultra This is Latin for 'nothing more further' and is used to imply the ultimate, whether in the sense of the greatest achievement of its kind and therefore impossible to transcend or in a physical sense, the furthest point attainable beyond which one simply cannot go.

nest-egg Commonly used to mean an amount of money put away in reserve, this expression has in fact a slightly more complex idea behind it. The original nest-egg was a pottery egg put into a hen's nest as an inducement for her to add another to it. The monetary nest-egg then gives one a start and is an inducement to add more savings to it. The term goes back to at least 1611.

news We see the true origin of this word in its French parallel form *nouvelles*, 'new things'. The theory that it derived from the four points of the compass, N.E.W.S., is disproved by the fact that this is not the conventional order, and that the old spelling of the word always included a final 'e', 'newes'.

Newtonism Odd confusion of traditional phrases with amusing results said to be characteristic of Sir Gordon Newton, editor of the *Financial Times* 1950–73. For example, he is said to have told an expert in a subject that something was 'right up his pigeon', expressed a desire to aid a friend by saying 'I'd slip over backwards to help him', and admired a picture in an art collection as an 'excellent Rio Tinto'. See the rather similar SPOONERISM.

nice Now, in a mild sort of way, this word means pleasant or agreeable. It started its development as the Latin *nescius*, 'ignorant, unknowing'. It evolved into the French *nice*, which meant 'lazy', and came into English meaning 'over-particular', 'fastidious' and hence 'refined', until it gradually acquired its present sense of inoffensively charming.

niche A niche is a shallow recess or hollow in a wall perhaps for the purpose of containing a statue. It ultimately derives from the Italian *nicchio*, 'a cockle-shell', and the upper part of a niche was often made in the shape of a shell.

nickname This word for a name given in derision or fami-

168

liarity has a Middle English origin in *ekename*, 'an also-name' or 'by-name'. The 'n' of 'an' becoming attached to the word itself.

Nicotine, my Lady This rather coy term for the pleasures of smoking was first used by Sir James Barrie in an essay written for the *St James's Gazette*.

night-cap This word for a last drink before going to bed takes its name from a similarity between it and the actual night-cap our ancestors put on before retiring. They imagined they could not sleep without it.

nightmare See HAG-RIDDEN.

nil desperandum Freely translated as 'Never despair' or 'Don't give up hope', this expression comes from Vergil's *Aeneid*: '*Nil desperandum Teucro duce . . .*' 'With Teucer in command there is nothing to despair of . . .'

niminy-piminy Little heard nowadays, this odd expression was once used to deride an affected mode of pronunciation. It is first recorded in a late eighteenth-century play, *The Heiress*, in which one of the characters is told that the right way to acquire the fashionable manner was to stand in front of a mirror and repeat 'niminy piminy', then 'The lips cannot fail to take the right plie'. Compare the note on namby-pamby.

nincompoop Dr Johnson suggests that this is a corruption of the Latin *non compos mentis*, 'not the possessor of mind', but the earliest forms of the word do not bear the theory out. We cannot assign a certain origin to the word. It may well have been a personal coinage that somehow got info circulation. It is an evocative word that suggests ninny, *non compos* and perhaps even the Dutch *poep*, 'a fool'.

nine days' wonder The Late Latin *novena* is a term used in the Roman Catholic Church for a devotion extending over nine successive days. Once it is completed, some new one with a different intention may well be engaged in and the old, as it were, forgotten. It may be that the phrase 'nine days' wonder' relates to this usage, perhaps from derision among Protestants, but Chaucer in his *Troilus and Criseyde* seems to make an allusion to it. By Shakespeare's time the phrase was proverbial.

ninepins This game, in which pieces of wood (also known as skittles) must be knocked over by a ball bowled at them, goes back to the earliest times and was played throughout Europe. So popular was it, and so cultivated to the neglect of more serious pursuits, that some American communities made it illegal. For this reason the modern commercial development of the game utilised the transparent disguise of 'ten-pin bowling'.

ninny Two origins contend here and perhaps both contributed to the word's peculiar shade of meaning. The Spanish *niño*, 'a child', is a possibility, as is a gently deriding abbreviation of innocent.

nip As a measure of drink the word today is used to imply a very modest amount indeed, but in so far as a nip is an abbreviation of nipperkin it was something more. By some reckonings the nipperkin was a little under half a pint but by others only one eighth. The measure called 'gill' is the subject of similar ambiguities.

nipper This is established London slang for a boy or for children in general. Its original application was rather more specific, being applied to the odd-job boys who helped the costermongers. They were also known as 'cas'alty boys'. They were 'nippers' because they ran about on errands. To 'nip along quickly' means to move fast. The word nipper is used by Mayhew in the 1840s. There is, however, the possibility of even deeper roots. In sailing ships from Tudor times onwards, the anchor cable was too big to go round the capstan so a smaller rope was 'nipped' to it by nippermen. The temporary lashing between the two ropes (the nip) was watched to the cable hatch by nipper boys who then freed it and ran back with the 'capstan rope' to nip it to a new section of cable.

nisi This is simply the Latin 'unless'. The decree nisi of the divorce court is a decree granted *unless* an objection is made and upheld within the prescribed period, usually three months.

nix No problem here. Nix is nothing and is a variant of the German *nichts*, which means the same thing.

nob In the sense of 'one of the upper classes' nob was an abbreviation used at Oxford and Cambridge after a student's name in formal lists to distinguish him as one of the privileged nobility.

nod, *on the* This is another way of saying 'on credit'. At auctions things are bought by a nod, and settling up comes later.

noise The immediate origin of the word is a French equivalent of identical spelling, but to go beyond this is difficult. Latin *nausea*, 'sickness', is one well-supported view and *noxia*, 'hurt, damage, injury', another.

non compos See NINCOMPOOP.

nonce Meaning 'for one particular occasion' this word, like nickname, has been made by a wrong division of a misunderstood phrase which was the Saxon *then anes*, 'the once'. 'The nanes' evolved into 'the nonce'.

'None but the brave . . .' These words were first written by John Dryden in 'Alexander's Feast', an ode composed for St Cecilia's Day, 1694.

nonplussed A man nonplussed has nothing more to say, being so astonished at the turn an argument has taken. The phrase is made from the Latin *non plus*, 'no more'.

no quarter This traditional military phrase meant that no prisoners would be taken. There is no certain origin for this expression and the theories advanced are all unsatisfactory. One suggests that the traditional ransom for a life was one quarter of the man's pay and this understanding is attributed to the Dutch and the Spaniards at war in the Netherlands. Another relates quarter to the providing of quarters, i.e. it interprets this ruthless instruction as a euphemistic 'No lodgings for you'. This is not so much weak as pathetic. The expression exists in French. English borrowed it from there.

No rose without a thorn The poet John Lydgate (c. 1400) spells out this sentiment thus: 'There is no rose springing in gardens but there be some thorn' but whether the common form preceded or followed this we cannot say. Certainly it was proverbial a century later and the motto that accompanies the Tudor rose, 'A rose without a thorn', in Latin *Rosa sine spina*, is an allusion to it.

nose, *pay through the* The meaning is clear enough. It means to pay an exorbitant price because one has no choice. As early as the seventeenth century, 'rhino' was slang for money and *rhinos* is Greek for 'nose'. Noses bleed and the man who is forced to pay is also 'bled'. Some elaborate word-play of this character must lie behind the phrase.

Nosy Parker Traditionally this phrase is associated with Matthew Parker, Queen Elizabeth's Archbishop of Canterbury, but a 'nose' has long been underworld slang for an informer (see the note on 'nark') and 'pauk' is a dialect word meaning to be inquisitive. It could be that the involvement of Parker, though apt, is unnecessary.

nous This word, well established in the popular speech of Liverpool, is pure Greek and means mind or intelligence. It keeps this sense in modern usage.

nouveau *art* This 'style label' for the fashion immediately preceding art deco (q.v.) was first used as the name of his Paris shop by Samuel Bing. Prominent among his wares were Tiffany and Gallé products.

novel We get this word from the Italian *novella*, meaning 'little novelties'. The *Decameron* of Boccaccio (*c.* 1350), a collection of prose tales, was the first to be described thus. The term 'novella' is used today for something shorter than a novel would be but longer than a conventional short story.

numeracy The success of the Soviet 'sputnik' in 1957 seemed to indicate that the time was ripe for a significant restructuring of the Western education system. A report on the education of the fifteen to eighteen age group, popularly known as the Crowther Report, stressed the need for 'numeracy', a term coined for the occasion, to be given equal standing with the schools' traditional aim of literacy. Numeracy means skill with the basic concepts of quantity as a prerequisite of serious attainment in mathematics and physical science. Parallel formations (such as 'oracy') have been attempted without equal success.

nuts in May This phrase from the children's rhyme is not the paradox it seems when we know that it should be 'knots of may', bunches of blossom from the hawthorn or may-tree. Transplanted from country to town many an old rhyme degenerated into a meaningless jingle and a puzzle for the curious.

O

oaf This term for a fool or simpleton has been with us since the Middle Ages when it came into the language (as *ouph*) from Danish, though the idea it expresses was common enough throughout the ancient world. The oaf was in fact 'the elves' child', otherwise known as a changeling, a child deformed or 'wanting', left behind by these creatures of the 'other-world', whilst the real human infant was taken away 'to strengthen the race'.

Oakes's oath This Australian expression for sworn testimony not to be taken too seriously is derived from a story that a certain Oakes when asked if he could positively identify some horns as belonging to a beast stolen from him answered: 'I'll chance it, Yes.'

Oaks, *the*   On the Saturday after the famous Derby a race for three-year-old fillies is held at Epsom. It began in 1779, founded by the Earl of Derby, and takes its name from that nobleman's Epsom house.

oar (*to put an oar in someone else's boat*)   Today this proverbial phrase is usually cut down to 'putting his oar in'. It appeared in elaborated form in English in 1542 in Udall's translation of Erasmus's *Apophthegmata* as follows: 'Whatsoever came in his foolish brain / Out it should were it never so vain / In eche man's bote would he have an oar / But no worde to good purpose, lesse or more.' A later variant (1552) talks of 'An owre in echman's barge'.

oat, oater   Because oats is the regular food for horses the verb 'to oat' became United States usage for feeding both a man and his horse. In the 1760s John Adams was already using it in this way in his diary. When the movies came, 'oater' was the name given to a run of the mill 'horse opera' or Western.

oats, *sowing his wild*   This much-used expression for youthful excesses and follies, often sexual in character, has no clearly indicated origin and finds its only direct parallel in Denmark where the mists of early spring are called *Lokkens havre*, 'Loki's wild oats'. Loki was a spirit of mischief, so there is some association of ideas, but enlightenment is perhaps to be found nearer home. More oats in their diet will increase the friskiness of horses. 'Feeling his oats' describes the horse's 'state of mind' and the term is applied to adolescent boys becoming aware of their masculinity. In their wildness horse and man think of propagating their kind. This is the obvious background of the phrase though the chain of development cannot be seen.

obiter dictum   Once only found in legal contexts, this expression now has a wider use. It is Latin for 'a saying by the way' or 'a remark on the side' and was originally an expression of opinion on some topic by a judge, though not one forming an essential part of his decision.

obliged Now part of the debased 'small change' of everyday speech, such expressions as 'I am obliged to you' formerly had a deeper significance for oblige derives from the Latin *obligare*, 'to bind'. An expansion of the phrase might be 'Your action has created a tie or bond between us. I cannot be morally free until I have repaid you in similar fashion.'

'Odds The word is a 'softened' or disguised form of God and appears in oaths of the Stuart period and later when swearers wished to carry on swearing, but also to evade any charges of profanity, hence 'Odd's bodikins', meaning 'God's little body' and (a favourite oath of Charles II) 'Odd's fish', a corrupted version of 'God's flesh'.

odour of sanctity In the Middle Ages it was generally believed that a sweet odour was given off by the bodies of saintly persons after their death. Conversely, the sweet smell was a proof of the sanctity of the deceased. It is not possible to pronounce on the veracity of this claim, but in cases of exhumed saints the embalming medium may have played a part. In modern usage the phrase is often sarcastic and sometimes suggests a contrast between a doubtful life and an ostentatiously pious deathbed.

odyssey Frequently used today for any long and protracted wanderings, especially those interspersed with hazardous or romantic adventures, this word is a generalised use of the *Odyssey*, one of the two great epic poems of Ancient Greece in which Homer describes the ten years' wandering of Odysseus on his way home to Ithaca after the fall of Troy.

ogre It is often said that this word was invented by Charles Perrault in his *Contes des Fées* of 1697, and this is indeed the source from which it entered the English language, but some

French authorities see it as a formation from *Hongre*, 'Hungarian'. When we relate the Hungarians to the Huns, and recall that in Hungary Attila is still a popular name for a boy, we see the force of the suggestion.

oil on troubled waters It is an undoubted fact that the roughness of the sea can be much reduced by discharging oil on to its surface. Benjamin Franklin experimented with this technique, but it was not until 1855, in Kingsley's *Westward Ho!*, that we find the expression used metaphorically. The example, often quoted from Bede's *Ecclesiastical History* of A.D. 731, in which St Aidan gives a priest a cruse of oil to pour on the sea if it should become threatening, relates more to the saint's faith in the properties of holy oil than it does to the physical phenomenon in which Franklin was interested.

O K Meaning 'all right', this is perhaps the most widely diffused piece of American slang, and has certainly been the subject of more discussion as to its origin than any other. The term was already popular, and debated, in the New England of the 1830s, but has been noted in New Jersey by scholars as early as 1815. Shorter forms, such as 'kay', to indicate assent, were in use among black Americans in the 1770s, and the consensus of most recent opinion is that the Afro-American origin is the correct one. Indeed, it is thought that a large number of other 'Americanisms' will probably be assigned to the same source, namely the regions of West Africa from which most of the slaves came, and in particular to those peoples who spoke Mandingo and Wolof. It does, however, seem strange that the first reported area of currency should be New England, where black Americans were less common, and it is not surprising that there are claims for an Amerindian origin. In this connection Edwin Radford, the original author of this book, had an interesting experience in a visit to the States before the Second World War. Introduced to an American Indian of impressive appearance and with an excellent command of grammatically correct English, he was surprised when the Indian used the term 'O K' and made a jocular reference to it. The reply was: 'My friend before there were any Americans here, we had a word Okeh. It means "May it be so".'

Besides sources as far away as Greece and Finland, there have been curious attempts at what might be called legendary origin from nearer home. Andrew Jackson, 7th President of the U S A, was supposed to have used it as an abbreviation of All Correct, which he spelt 'Orl Korrect' – an undoubtedly ill-founded libel. A similar story makes the hero an illiterate Irish immigrant. Another story tells of an Indian chief, Old Keokuk, who signed all treaties with his initials – which would be more convincing if any treaties survived. And, ruled out by its date, and remarkable only for perverse ingenuity, is the story that it derives from the O K Club (1840), an American Democratic society which supported Van Buren's campaign for re-election. The initials were said to come from Old Kinderhook, New York, where Van Buren was born, but since he was not re-elected, the result was far from O K.

old as Pandon Gates (*or Yatts*) This expression, still used in the north-east of England, was 'a very common saying' as early as 1649. Pandon Gate stood at Newcastle upon Tyne and was of Roman foundation.

Old Bailey London's Central Criminal Court takes its name from a word that was originally Latin *vallum*, 'a rampart', through the French *bailler*, 'to enclose'. The place name then refers to some demolished fortification.

old fogey This disrespectful term for a man advanced in years or simply old-fashioned in outlook is perhaps related to the Danish *fjog*, 'a man in his dotage', but it is quite impossible to note this as more than a probability.

Old Harry One of our many roundabout references to the Devil. It is a variant of Old Hairy, the Devil often being represented as semi-animal in aspect.

Old Nick Perhaps the most common expression for the Devil, it seems to have appeared only in the seventeenth century and attempts have been made to show a connection with the bad reputation of Machiavelli. This is not very likely. Perhaps Nick is quite arbitrary, for from Saxon times the Devil got along quite nicely as *se ealde*, 'the old 'un'. Old Scratt or Scratch, yet another in the series, is quite plainly the Norse *skratte* 'goblin'.

old sweat The name given to an old soldier, especially to a survivor from the First World War, is most probably a borrowing from German where *alter Schwede* was a familiar term for a veteran campaigner and originally referred to the Swedes who ravaged Germany in the Thirty Years' War of the seventeenth century. These borrowings across the lines of battle are not uncommon. The song 'Lili Marlene', taken over by the Western Allies from the Germans in the Second World War, is a similar example.

Old Tom Recorded in 1823 as an affectionate name for gin, it is said to have been popularised when a former employee of Hodge's Distillery in London set up his own 'gin-palace' and perpetuated the name of Old Tom Chamberlain, his former employer, by applying his name to his product.

Olympic Games Originally these were great religious-athletic festivals held every four years in Ancient Greece, and named from Olympia in the Vale of Elis in the Peloponnesus. The festival lapsed in the Roman epoch, but the name was revived in 1896 when the modern series of international athletic competitions began.

omega The word means 'great O' and is the last letter of the Greek alphabet. The phrase 'alpha and omega' means the beginning and the end (alpha being the Greek 'a') and the two letters have become Christian symbols.

omnibus This form of the Latin *omnis*, 'all', means 'for all'. It was first applied to a public vehicle in Paris in 1828. In the next year George Shillibeer, who had been working as a coachbuilder in France, took the idea to London and started a service for passengers along the Paddington Road.

178

one dog, one bull This phrase, which is still sometimes used as an appeal for fair play, originates from the old 'sport' of bullbaiting, in which a specially bred bulldog was set to worry a bull which was restricted by a chain fixed to a ring through its nose. The bull tried to toss and gore the dog, while the dog was expected to show tenacity in gripping the bull by the throat.

one gate for another This proverbial reminder of the obligation to return good offices rendered refers to a story told of one of the Earls of Rutland who, riding alone, overtook a countryman who civilly opened for him the next gate they came to. At the second gate the Earl waited for this to happen again, but the countryman said to him, 'Nay, soft. One gate for another, good fellow.'

one o'clock, *going like* In factories and workshops the dinner break was normally from one to two o'clock and in the larger establishments 'knocking off time' was indicated by a bell, steam whistle or hooter. The speed with which the men left the premises for their 'free' hour provides the explanation of this phrase.

onus Used nowadays for responsibilities or obligations in general, this word is just the ordinary Latin word for a literal 'burden'. Oddly enough, in the legal world where so much Latin survives, the English word is preferred and we talk of 'the burden of proof'.

oof This slang term for money is of Yiddish origin *oof-tish* (German *auf dem Tische*), meaning 'on the table' or in popular English 'cash down', 'on the nail'.

opal The name of this stone is obviously derived from the Latin *opalus*, but this itself is Greek *apallios* which in turn relates to the Sanscrit *upala*, 'precious stone'.

open It is curious to note that in all Germanic languages the idea of 'open' is linked to that of 'up', as though the primitive 'door' of the north was not something to be pushed, or pulled on pivots or hinges, but something (a hanging skin or hide?) to be lifted up.

opera Now a word in its own right this was in origin the plural form of the Latin *opus*, 'a work'. Opera was seen as a succession or an assemblage of musical items.

opportune In the sense of favourable and fortunate we have the core of this word's essential and original meaning. The Romans spoke of a safe arrival in harbour being *ob Portunus*, that is 'by favour of Portunus', the god who protected ports and harbours.

oracle In the ancient world this was a place where the gods might be heard to speak, to declare their will in particular cases and to answer the questions of enquirers. The word relates to the Latin *oro*, 'I speak'. The speaking took many different forms, from the rustling of an oak tree at Dodona to the mumblings of an entranced priestess at Delphi. The oracle at Delphi always used words capable of more than one interpretation, hence the expression 'a Delphic utterance'. A tradition of scepticism about oracles seems to play some part in the phrase 'to work the oracle', meaning to secure the required response usually from some recalcitrant piece of machinery.

Orangemen This name, given to the Protestants of Northern Ireland, and particularly to those organised in the lodges of the Orange Order, derives from William of Orange, the 'King Billy' of Ulster tradition, who defeated King James at the Battle of the Boyne and firmly established the Protestant ascendancy in Ireland.

oratorio This 'sacred musical drama' takes its name from the fact that these words were first performed in the Oratory, or Church of the Oratorians, the religious order founded by St Philip Neri in Rome in 1540.

orchard This is a Saxon word, *orceard*, and meant an 'enclosure', and this, rather than the fruit trees we think of today, is the basic sense of the word. The first element comes from the Latin *hortus*, 'garden'. The late form *ort-yard* shows the roots of the word.

orchestra The word as we use it today is Latin, but the Romans took it from the Greeks, among whom it meant the part of the theatre in front of the stage where the chorus danced. In Greek *orchesis* is 'the art of dance'. As the drama in Roman hands lost its ritual character, while the shape of the theatre remained the same, so the word acquired a new use.

ordeal This word for a severe test, usually involving physical risk, is a relic of old Germanic legal procedure when the judgement of God was invoked by putting an accused person at risk in some way in the belief that God would protect the innocent by a near miracle. Ordeal by fire involved clutching a piece of red-hot iron, or walking blindfold and barefooted among red-hot ploughshares. How much faith was actually put in the ordeal is suggested by the fact that men of importance could submit to the judgement of God by deputy.

Orders, *Holy* The official description of a clergyman of the Church of England is 'A clerk in Holy Orders'. He is a clerk because at one time virtually the only people who could write were clergymen. The Holy Orders were the ranks of the Church hierarchy. In the primitive church the orders were eight in number, namely bishop, priest, deacon, subdeacon, acolyte, exorcist, reader and doorkeeper, In the church today the three effective orders are bishop, priest and deacon. The expression 'to take Orders' is often used to mean becoming a clergyman.

orgies This word derives from the Greek *orgeia* which were the nocturnal festivals for initiates only of the cult of Bacchus and other gods or goddesses. Once used for drunken revelry only, the word in current usage implies uninhibited sexual indulgence.

orrery A clockwork mechanism representing the movements of the planets is so called because an early example was presented to the 4th Earl of Orrery (1676–1731), a patron of the sciences.

oscar Strictly meaning the bronze-gilt statuette annually awarded since 1927 for outstanding performance in the various fields of the film industry by the American Academy of Motion Pictures, the name is often used generally of any striking achievement – 'he ought to get an oscar for it'. The name derived from a secretary's remark that the expression of the statuette reminded her of her Uncle Oscar. The television equivalent, named on similar principles, is the 'emmy'.

ostracise Derived from the Greek *ostrakon*, 'tile, piece of pottery', ostracism was a device used by the Greeks to protect their constitution. Once a year each Athenian could write on a piece of pot the name of a prominent man he would like to see banished. Six thousand such votes would send an unpopular or dangerous politician into exile.

ouija board This, the best-known piece of spiritualistic apparatus, takes its name from the combined French and German words for 'Yes', *oui ja*. The words yes and no are printed on the board, as well as the letters of the alphabet, and the 'spirit' communicators will use any language they fancy.

out-of-sorts Now indicating a vague physical malaise, this was once a term used in the world of printing for a compositor who could not get on with his work because he was short of the necessary letters in his case.

ovation Today this means prolonged applause. In Ancient Rome, where it originated, it was, however, only a 'second-class' triumph such as might be awarded for a victory over slaves. The recipient of an ovation walked or rode into the city on horseback. In a full triumph he would have come by chariot.

oyster part This is theatrical slang for a part in which the

182

player has only one line to say, as, for example, 'Dinner is served'. The oyster, like the clam, is famed for keeping its 'mouth' shut.

P

Ps and Qs, *mind your*   The most likely origin of this traditional warning is the practice of publicans 'chalking up' the pints and quarts consumed by a thirsty customer in the course of an evening. An alternative view relates it to court etiquette. The 'P' here is considered as the French *pied*, 'foot', and the 'Q' as *le queue*, 'tail', i.e. of a wig. This seems improbable, as French *pied* normally became *pie* when adopted into popular English, but it must be admitted that the association of our phrases are with the niceties of behaviour rather than with the dangers of over-indulgence!

Pacific Ocean   *Pacificus* is the Latin for 'peaceful' and this name was given to the great ocean by Magellan in 1520, because he found it relatively free from storms and bad weather, after his tempestuous passage through the strait that now bears his name.

'paddle your own canoe'   See CANOE.

Paddy   The Irishman in England is often the subject of much condescension and under the name of 'Paddy', a diminutive of *Padraig* 'Patrick' (from Ireland's patron saint), features in several popular sayings or allusions. 'Paddy's mare' offered as a means of transport means that you will have to walk for Paddy is too poor to afford a horse. Someone who cannot keep to a schedule might be described as 'All behind, like Paddy with the rent'. The gristle on meat can be called the 'paddywhack' and of course a 'paddy' is a sudden fit of childish rage said to be characteristic of Irishmen. It is interesting to note that in Ulster, when Catholic–Protestant feeling runs high, the contemptuous expression for the Catholic is not Paddy, but Teague or Taig. See also MICK and RILEY.

padre This soldiers' name for an army chaplain or indeed any clergyman has been in use for well over two hundred years and goes back to the contact between the soldiers of the East India Company and the Portuguese in India. *Padre* is Portuguese for 'father', the term commonly used in every language for Roman Catholic priests. The use of padre spread from India to the British Army at home.

paean of praise In Greek *paian* was a hymn of thanksgiving and this is the general sense of our modern usage. Paean is the name given by Homer to the physician of the gods, who seem to have needed the same technicians as human beings do, and at first a *paian* was the form of thanks to this god only. Later, however, the cult of Paean was absorbed into that of Apollo and the ritual shout of praise *Io Paean!* was directed to him. From his widespread cult the word escaped into general usage.

pagan See HEATHEN.

pageant Now used for the dramatic representation of historical episodes often in an outdoor or professional setting, pageant comes from the Late Latin *pagina*, 'a stage'. Pageant was the name used for the wagon-like moving stages of the medieval 'Mystery' plays, in which the guilds of such cities as Coventry and Wakefield, for example, portrayed Biblical episodes appropriate to each trade.

pagoda Contrary to what is usually taken as general knowledge, this word is not Chinese but Portuguese, and is presumably a corruption of some word encountered in a religious connection by the Portuguese in India. Pagoda was also the name given to a now obsolete Indian coin, and 'shaking the pagoda tree' meant 'making a quick fortune in the East'. See MANDARIN for a similar case of a Portuguese word becoming accepted as Chinese.

184

paint, *as fresh as*   This striking simile, still much used to indicate smartness and brightness, was first coined in F. E. Smedley's Victorian novel *Frank Fairleigh.*

painter   The rope by which a smaller boat is attached to its parent vessel, or by which it is made fast to the quay, derives its name from the medieval *panter*, 'a snare'. In French the form *pantière* survives as a net-like device for catching birds. The origin of both is the Latin *panther*, 'a net'. In modern English a snare is a single cord or wire ending in a loop. 'To cut the painter' means to break a long-established connection.

pal   One of our many borrowings from the Romany (gipsy) language, where *pral* is 'brother'.

palace   The adjectival form of this word 'palatial' shows its origin a little more clearly than does the noun itself. The original palace was built by Augustus on the Palatine Hill in Rome, the principal of the seven hills on which Rome was built.

pale, *beyond the*   In medieval times the Pale in Ireland was the area over which the English king actually exercised effective authority. It was often little more than Dublin and the area round it. 'Beyond the pale' savagery (or freedom) flourished unabated. To describe someone's conduct as being 'beyond the pale' implies it to be barbarous and uncivilised.

palladium   How this word came to be applied to a place of entertainment, the famous London Palladium, for example, is an instructive example of the debasement of words. The original palladium was a wooden image of the goddess Pallas kept in the city of Troy as its spiritual guardian. When it was taken away, the city fell. It is said to have gone to Rome to fulfil a similar function there. Later it came to mean anything on which the safety and well-being of a nation might be said to depend; the constitution, the independence of judges, the freedom of the Press. Finally, devoid of any meaning, but still having some vague aura of classical splendour, it joined the

Hippodrome, the Coliseum and the Odeon, and became considered to be a suitable title for a theatre or cinema.

Pall Mall This famous thoroughfare in London takes its name from an originally Italian ball game called *palla*, 'ball', *maglio*, 'mallet'. A boxwood ball had to be driven by the mallet through a ring suspended some distance above the ground at the end of an alley. King Charles II is said to have brought the game back from France and the street took its name from the alley where he played. The adverb 'pell mell' derives from the 'indiscriminate vigour' of the players.

palm, *to take the* The successful Roman athlete was awarded a palm branch, just as the poet was given bay and the hero in battle oak. See LAUREATE.

palmer This poetical/obsolete word for pilgrim derives from the custom of bringing back a palm branch from the Holy Land as visible proof of having been there and then offering it at the altar of the pilgrim's 'home' church. The association with victory would be relevant here too.

palm it off This alludes to the art of the conjuror who causes an article to vanish by concealing it in the palm of his hand and then makes it reappear in some unexpected place. Nowadays to 'palm something off' on to someone usually means persuading them to buy or accept something of inferior value.

pamphlet The origin of this word for a small unbound booklet of a few sheets only, normally on a subject of topical controversy, has been much discussed. A popular poem of the middle ages had the title 'Pamphilet' but this still begs the question of ultimate origins. Johnson's suggestion of *par-un-filet* '(held) by a thread' is not to be despised, nor is the derivation from *paume-feuillet*, 'a leaf of paper for the hand'. In this last connection it is worth noting that English popular usage insists on calling what is properly a leaflet (French *feuille-volante*, American 'flyer') a pamphlet. Finally, although our

186

three most likely origins are all French, the *Petit Larousse* Dictionary insists that the word is of English origin!

panacea This is a direct take-over from the Greek, where the word means 'all healing'. Panacea was personified as the daughter of Aesculapius, god of healing.

panama hat The hat has nothing to do with Panama at all, being made in Ecuador and Peru, but is a corruption of 'palmata hat', since it was first made from the leaves of the plant *Carludovica palmata*, which, although palm-like in appearance, is not even a palm.

pandemonium The word is self-explained when we know it is Greek for 'all the demons', hence its use when we complain that someone is making 'a devil of a noise'.

pander As a verb this means to act as a 'go-between' in some irregular sexual relationship, or even as a professional procurer. It is a proper name devised by Boccaccio and used after him by Chaucer and Shakespeare for a character in their versions of the story of Troilus and Cressida.

panic The Greek god Pan, suddenly manifesting his presence, was believed by the ancients to be the cause of any sudden apparently unmotivated fear. Properly we should use an expanded expression and talk of people being seized by 'panic fear'.

Panjandrum, *the Great* This term is sarcastically used of the 'big fish in a small pond' who monopolises every office open to him. It was a nonsense coinage of the actor Samuel Foote in the eighteenth century. Foote heard another actor claim that he could remember any passage after a single reading. Foote accordingly composed a long string of nonsense of which the Great Panjandrum is just a part. The challenged actor, Macklin, refused to make the attempt with such intractable material.

pan out The hope that things will 'pan out' derives from the gold diggers, and the process by which the prospector swirled water through the gold ore in a shallow pan, trying in this way to 'wash' the heavier particles of gold out of the silt with which they were mixed.

Pantaloon This character in the Italian *commedia dell'arte* (for which see HARLEQUINADE) dressed in loose trousers and slippers, and represented an old dotard. The 'pantaloons' have been part of traditional clowning ever since. San Pantaleone, the patron of Venice, was mildness itself despite his name which means 'all lion'. The contrast between name and character was yet another element in this simple comedy.

pantechnicon The word is now used for the giant vans of the removal firms, but its meaning in the original Greek is 'belonging to all the arts'. In Britain it was first applied to a bazaar for the sale of artistic works in London's Belgrave Square. This failed and the building became a furniture store and the old name became attached to the delivery vehicles of the new concern.

pantomime The name of this originally Graeco-Roman theatrical performance means 'imitation of all things', and the characteristic feature was indeed mime. The first real 'pantomime' in Britain was that of John Rich who opened the Lincoln's Inn Fields Theatre in 1714. This was the start of what was to become a major institution of the British entertainment world at Christmas, though songs and dialogue later made the traditional description something of a misnomer.

paradise The original paradise was the tree-studded pleasure park of an ancient Persian king, and the Greeks took the name into their language as *paradeisos*. The Septuagint translation of the Old Testament into Greek chose this word for the Garden of Eden. Finally the New Testament writers employed the word to indicate the abode of the blessed and it was in this sense that it came into use as an English word.

paraphernalia Now used in a general sense for equipment,

188

apparatus or even luggage, this word was once a technical term of Roman law indicating the personal effects of a bride specifically excluded from the dowry that passed to her husband. The derivation is from *para*, 'beyond', and *pherne*, 'the dowry'.

pariah In current English this indicates an outcast, shunned by all men. It is one of many imports from India, in this case from the southern part of the subcontinent. The word is Tamil and was originally *paraiyar*, 'drummer', from one of the hereditary occupations of the people who are outside the Hindu socio-religious structure. Pariah also applied to the semi-wild dogs that are the scavengers of Indian villages.

parish This word, like so many others with church associations, is of Greek origin and comes from *para*, 'around', and *oikos*, 'house' (the adjective parochial is closer to the Greek). One can see the use of this word as reflecting the 'missionary' situation in which a company of converts gathers 'around the house', though whether this is 'the House of God' or of the priest is not clear.

park, *the wrong side of the* Used to imply a degree of social undesirability, this phrase grew up when Paddington, the London terminus of the Great Western Railway, was built and people began to move, if they could, to the Kensington side of Hyde Park. Compare the US expression 'the wrong side of the tracks'. In the US as in Britain and no doubt elsewhere the railway lines mark a social divide in a city as well as being a physical obstacle to traffic.

Parkinson's Law In 1958 Cyril Northcote Parkinson, until then with a reputation only in the academic world, became famous for his book *Parkinson's Law*, a study of public and business administration. Its basic thesis or law was that 'work expands to fill the time available for its completion' with the corollary 'subordinates multiply at a fixed rate regardless of the amount of work produced'. Parkinson's Law has proved to be but the first of many part-satirical, part-serious analyses

189

of the causes of inefficiency in political, academic and business administration. See also PETER PRINCIPLE.

parlour   Derived from the French *parler*, 'to talk', the word was originally used in monasteries for a room set apart for the reception of visitors. Town Halls often have a Mayor's Parlour for smaller social occasions.

parson   This word for the clergyman of a parish is the same word that has evolved into 'person'. In Latin it was *persona* but indicated a 'personage' of standing. Blackstone, the legal authority, said that in the 'person' of the priest the whole invisible Church was represented.

Parthenon   The great temple of Athens is so called from its dedication to the goddess Athene, also known as *Parthenos*, 'the virgin'.

Partington (Dame) and her mop   This misguided lady is regularly referred to whenever someone's efforts are pitifully inadequate for the situation they have to tackle. She is said to have been a lady of Sidmouth, who in 1824 attempted to stem an unusually high tide by means of a mop and bucket. She found fame when alluded to by Sydney Smith, the wit, speaking on the Lords' rejection of the Reform Bill in October 1831. He compared the Peers to Dame Partington trying to push back the ocean, saying, 'She was excellent at a slop or a puddle, but should never have meddled with a tempest.'

passing the buck   The phrase now means the evasion or denial of responsibility, but it derives from a simple aide-memoire used by players of Straight Poker. According to Hoyle, 'Each person puts into the pool an agreed sum. As a matter of convenience it is frequently arranged that each player, in turn, puts in for all. To avoid dispute as to whose turn it may be, a pocket knife, *known as the buck*, is passed round resting with the player whose turn it is to "chip in" for the remainder. Having done his duty, he then passes the buck to his neighbour on the left.' The expression 'None of your old buck' derives from India, where *bukh* was Hindi for what the soldiers called 'swagger talk'.

patent   The origin of this word for a recognition of the exclusive right to exploit an invention for a stated number of years is to be found in the old term 'letters patent' meaning really 'an open letter', an official statement to the public at large. Patent in this sense is from the Latin *patens*, 'spreading', hence 'opened out'.

patronage   Originally the term related to the custom that whoever built a church had also the right to nominate its officiating priest. Patronage thus came to be the right to nominate clergy to their 'livings' and the British Prime Minister still has a 'Patronage Secretary' who deals with this business. In time the expression acquired a wider usage and came to refer to the power of nominating to any office.

patter   The conjuror uses patter to distract the attention of the audience from his sleight-of-hand; the comedian's flow of joke and comment is called patter as well. The usually suggested origin is from *Paternoster*, the Latin 'Our Father', and the use of the word as largely synonymous with 'gabble' is held to be a popular comment on the perfunctory nature of much Latin prayer, but *patterin* is also a Romany word for 'talking'. The coincidence is suggestive.

Paul Pry   This name, now applied to anyone deemed to be 'nosy', goes back to a role in an 1825 comedy of the same name written by John Poole. Pry always made his entry with the words 'I hope I don't interrupt'.

pay, *the devil to*   See DEVIL.

pay the piper   This phrase is sometimes incorrectly related to the tale of the Pied Piper of Hamelin. Certainly that story stresses the desirability of paying the piper, but the full saying is 'The man who pays the piper calls the tune'. It is a reminder of harsh facts about money talking and the power of the purse.

pea-jacket   This seaman's garment is named from the Dutch *pije* a 'rough coat'. As with CAUSEWAY and SLEDGE HAMMER a second, explanatory element was added when the original meaning of the word had been forgotten.

pearl divers Catering trade slang for dishwashers both in Britain and the United States. He or she plunges into murky depths to earn a living. The same metaphor exists in French.

peats, *turn the* This north country phrase for changing the subject of conversation derives from the use of peat blocks as fuel. When one side became red hot the peat was turned so the warmth would spread into the room and the other side have its chance of becoming heated too.

peccavi, *to cry* *Peccavi* is Latin for 'I have sinned' and the phrase is now a not entirely serious admission of guilt. 'Peccavi' was the subject of one of history's most outrageous puns when General Charles Napier successfully seized the Indian state of Sind in 1843. He reported his victory in the one-word communiqué 'Peccavi', 'I have Sind'.

pecking order It has been observed that any group of people arbitrarily brought together will soon arrange themselves into some sort of order. 'Cock of the walk' gives us one parallel from the farmyard and 'pecking order' another. At the head of the scale will be one hen, able to peck any of the others without fear of retaliation. The next can get away with pecking all but number one. At the other extreme will be a poor wretched bird pecked by all and with no inferior on whom to seek satisfaction. We may make our own parallels with human societies.

pecuniary This adjective, meaning relating to money, is from the Latin *pecunia*, 'money', and this is ultimately derived from *pecus*, 'head of cattle'. Cattle were regularly used as 'money' in primitive society.

pedagogue This word for a teacher is now usually reserved for derogatory application with all the implications of pedantry. It derives from the Greek *pais*, 'a boy', and *ago*, 'I lead', and was originally used for the slave who accompanied a well-born boy to school and carried his books, etc.

pedigree Genealogists imagined that the arrowlike symbol they used in their diagrams had some similarity to a crane's foot which in French is *pied de grue*. A family tree studded with these symbols became known by the corrupted form of pedigree.

pedlar There is no agreed origin for this simple word. It seems to have no analogous forms in French, German or Latin, though some link with *pedes*, 'that goes on foot', which gives Italian *pedone* and English words like pedestrian would seem likely. To follow another line of approach an Old English word *ped*, meaning 'a covered hamper' has been suggested as a possible root.

peeping tom This traditional English legal expression for what is now technically known as a voyeur goes back to the eleventh-century legend of Lady Godiva of Coventry whose cruel husband would only lift an oppressive tax from the people of the town if Godiva would consent to ride naked through the streets. She agreed, but the good citizens foiled the wicked Earl by shuttering their windows and staying at home. Only Tom, a tailor, peeped and he was struck blind by an outraged heaven.

peg away, peg out Both these phrases come from the game of cribbage in which one may steadily build up a score (peg away) or, at last having achieved all that is necessary, 'peg out' or die.

pelf This rather old-fashioned word for stolen goods has the same root as pilfer, that is the Old French *pelfre*, 'plunder'.

penny The first coin to be called a penny was issued in the middle of the eighth century by the Saxon Kings of Kent and Mercia in imitation of the Frankish coin called the *novus denarius*. These pennies were of silver and weighed two hundred and forty to the Saxon pound. The penny soon became the most important coin, but in the course of time was much reduced in size. It was replaced by the first copper penny in 1797, and by bronze in 1860, but the old silver penny continues as part of the annual Maundy issue. The origin of the word penny is disputed. The Latin *pendo*, 'I weigh', has been proposed as has the name of the Saxon king Penda. It is generally agreed that the word is Germanic (a modern German equivalent of *pfennig*) and is perhaps a primitive corruption of the Latin *patine*, 'a round dish'. The former traditional abbreviation to d. in British pre-decimal currency is a memory of the denarius which was the penny's ancestor.

penny dreadful Not much heard nowadays, this expression was used for the cheap 'comics' and thrillers issued for boys before the First World War. They comprised stories of crime and detection as well as of Red Indians and Palefaces. As with the cinema and television, they were blamed for much juvenile crime.

penny gaff This was the name given to the lowest grade of 'theatre' or music hall in Victorian London. The penny was the price of admission. See also GAFF.

peppercorn rent A peppercorn now has no appreciable value and so occupation of the premises or estate for which a peppercorn rent is paid is a virtual gift, but the legal owner retains his ultimate rights and the peppercorn rent is the proof of this. Nominal rents of this kind, e.g. rose rents, were very common in the Middle Ages.

perfume Though few perfumes are smoky, this word originates from the Latin *per fumum*, 'through smoke'. The original perfumes were obtained from aromatic woods and gums which were burnt as joss-sticks are. Hence the name.

persona Modern psychologists have revived an ancient word and idea to express certain mental situations. Considering a man's character as something he chooses to assume. or at least plays a part in choosing, they talk of 'finding a persona', *per-*

194

sona being in the first instance an actor's mask and then, by extension, a role in a play. The word was built from *per*, 'through', and *sono*, 'I sound', since the actor spoke through the mask.

petard, *hoist with his own*   The original petard was a medieval engine of war consisting of a metal bell-shaped container which held a large quantity of gunpowder and was generally hoisted up on a tripod against some obstacle which needed to be demolished. Premature explosion was an ever-present danger and the phrase 'Hoist with his own petard' is still used for the man whose own weapon or device turns against him. On the Continent a petard is still used as the name of a large firework used in New Year celebrations and church festivities.

peter out   Meaning 'to give out', 'to come to an end', this phrase has been traced to the American goldfields where the old black powder used as explosive was known as peter, from the saltpetre it contained. Once a seam had been worked for all it was worth it was described as 'petered out'.

Peter Principle   In 1969 Laurence J. Peter and Raymond Hull published *The Peter Principle: Why Things Always Go Wrong*, which advanced the semi-serious thesis that administrators tend to be promoted until they reach a level at which their incapacity becomes obvious, and then remain at that level because it is next to impossible to demote or dismiss them. Hence most administrators are incompetent. Compare with PARKINSON'S LAW, which began the vogue for such humorous pseudo-scientific analysis.

petrel, *the stormy*   This is the real name of the birds also called Mother Carey's chickens. The Italian name for the bird is *petrello* 'Little Peter' because its low skimming flight, and the way in which it moves its feet as it flies, suggests that it is trying to walk on the water as Peter did. The birds are associated with rough weather, hence 'the stormy' and the description 'stormy petrel' is often given to people who thrust themselves into the forefront of violent controversy.

petticoat   Literally 'a small coat', this garment was first worn by men under a coat of mail or the civilian doublet. There is no reliable evidence as to exactly when it slipped from above the waist of men to below the waist of women, but since the eighteenth century the word has been closely identified with women and their influence, as in the phrase 'petticoat government'.

phaeton   This name for an open, four-wheeled carriage drawn by two horses is obviously named from the Phaeton of ancient legend who longed to drive the chariot of the sun. Since he was a very incompetent driver the name is ill-chosen.

phalanx   This was a fighting formation of Greek spearmen first devised by Epaminondas of Thebes, but brought to perfection among the Macedonians. It is now applied to any body of people solidly standing together in support of or opposition to some cause.

pheasant   The game bird gets its name from the Greek *Phasianos*, 'pertaining to the river Phasis'. The Phasis flows into the Black Sea from Colchis and near it pheasants abound.

Philadelphia lawyer   The use of this expression as a term of praise or testimony of competence seems to go back to 1735 and Andrew Hamilton's defence of J. P. Zenger, when the latter was sued by the Governor of New York for criticisms published in Zenger's *Weekly Journal*. Hamilton, the Philadelphia lawyer, was entirely successful in his classic defence of the freedom of the Press.

Philip Sober   A woman once objected to a legal decision given in her case by King Philip of Macedon. She said, 'Philip, I shall appeal against this judgement.' 'To whom can you appeal?' said the angry king. 'To Philip Sober,' replied the woman. The wisdom and judgement of Philip Drunk and Philip Sober is still often contrasted today.

philtre   This word for a love potion derives from the Greek *philein*, 'to love'.

phlegmatic   This word for the temperament of the stolid slow-moving person derives from the old theory of the four humours according to which a person's character was formed by the predominance of one of four body fluids: phlegm which made a man slow, blood which made a man sanguine or hopeful, bile which made a man peevish and choler which made him angry.

phone phreaks   Since 1967 when a technical journal accidently revealed certain vital information, American and now British 'electronic pranksters' have been exploiting their knowledge of the vulnerable features of the telephone system to make free calls over ever-increasing distances. The 'phreaks' have their honoured pioneers and folk heroes, among them 'Captain Crunch', who used a give away plastic whistle to imitate the vital circuit opening tones, and Blind Joe Engressia who whistled them himself. The word phreak, or freak, is sometimes used for any dedicated enthusiast, the Jesus Freaks for example.

pianoforte   Literally meaning (in Italian) 'soft and strong', the name accurately characterises this keyboard instrument developed in the early eighteenth century, which produced a much bolder sound than that of the harpsichord, though without harshness.

picket   From the French *piquet*, 'a pointed stake', it had the same meaning in English. Such stakes were used for picketing, i.e. tethering horses and fastening down tents, but as pickets with the upper end also sharpened were used in outer defence works, the word came to mean small parties of troops sent to watch out for the enemy. From this use the word came to be applied by 1867 to the men stationed by trade unions to watch for men going to work during a strike. Under the British Trades Disputes Act of 1906, pickets were legalised 'for the purpose of peacefully obtaining or communicating information or peacefully persuading any person to work or abstain from working'.

197

picnic From the French *pique-nique*, this originally meant a meal to which all brought their own contribution. It was in use in England by the end of the eighteenth century, but it is not absolutely certain when it acquired its present meaning of an outdoor meal though the development from one use to another seems a natural one.

pidgin English Often wrongly spelt as 'pigeon' English, pidgin is supposed to be the Chinese speaker's approximation to pronouncing the English 'business', and this 'business English' was a jargon evolved by the early traders on the China coast and in the Pacific who were under the delusion that one had to be infantile to be understood by orientals. Its simplicity of vocabulary and absence of formal grammar proved so useful that local peoples of differing languages began to use it among themselves. Similar developments occurred elsewhere, in India and in Africa, where in the Cameroon it is particularly colourful. In Papua–New Guinea it is the official administrative language, and the pidgin-English spelling of the name – Niu Gini – was recommended for adoption on the attainment of self-government in 1976. The term has come back to Britain in the phrase 'That's my pigeon' meaning 'That's my business' with the unspoken thought '. . . and not yours.'

pie in the sky Cynical phrase for the belief that our earthly sufferings will all be compensated for in the Hereafter which derives from a parody, circulated in a militant Trade Union song book, of a classic Ira Sankey hymn 'The Sweet By and By'. Popular as the original was, the parody seemed even more apt especially in the years of depression: 'You will eat by and by / In that glorious land in the sky; / Work and pray, live on hay, / You'll get pie in the sky when you die.'

Pig and Whistle The origin of this public-house name is often enquired about. It was in Old English *Piggen wassail* from *piggen*, a wooden bucket or milking pail from which drinkers filled their own mugs (from the Gaelic *pigean*), and *Waes hael*,

'Be healthy', the oldest English toast. It recalls the landlord's 'flowing bowl'.

pigeon English See PIDGIN ENGLISH.

pigeon pair The pigeon commonly lays two eggs only which hatch into one hen chick and one cock, hence a family consisting of one boy and one girl is sometimes called 'a pigeon pair'.

pig in a poke The phrase describes one of the oldest of market frauds. A young pig is displayed as a sample. Others are said to be tied up in bags for carrying away. Too often they were not pigs, but cats, and investigation would sometimes 'let the cat out of the bag'. Poke (compare French *poche*) was a medieval word for bag. Pocket was 'a little bag'.

pile, *to make your* Another word from the goldfields, like PAN OUT and PETER. When you had dug out enough, i.e. 'made your pile', you would be rich enough to retire. Older uses of pile and analogues from other languages are not really needed to explain the phrase.

pillar to post, *to go from* The most plausible explanation of the phrase relates it to consecutive punishments in the pillory and then at the whipping post. The phrase is medieval and a version of it is used by the poet Lydgate in 1420. The modern use of the phrase is distinctly suggestive of harassment.

pinchbeck Now used to describe a cheap imitation of the real thing, or even the spurious or counterfeit, pinchbeck derives from Christopher Pinchbeck (*c.* 1670–1732), a Fleet Street watch- and toy-maker, who developed a zinc-copper alloy at the beginning of the eighteenth century. Looking remarkably like gold, and costing a fraction of the price, it was at first a welcome innovation, but by the mid-nineteenth century its deceptive use gave the word an evil connotation. In the modern enthusiasm for victoriana and earlier antique jewellery, pinchbeck settings of paste stones, often of excellent workmanship and attractive design, have become collectors' items.

pineapple   Gangster slang for a Mills bomb from the segmented markings on the bomb casing which assisted its break up on contact.

pin one's heart to one's sleeve   In the days when the tournament flourished a knight would display some token of his lady when he went into combat, hence this phrase.

pink (*in the pink of condition*)   From the Old English *pynca*, 'a point' (compare the tailor's 'pinking' shears) hence peak or apex. Shakespeare (*Romeo and Juliet*, II. iv) speaks of 'the pink of courtesy'. Some commentators have made a confusion with hunting pink and the implication of being sprucely turned out.

pin-up girl   Although she undoubtedly had her predecessors in mid-nineteenth-century Paris and Vienna, and was known in the First World War, the pin-up girl did not find her name until the early days of the Second World War when there was a massive demand for this fantasy material from men in the armed forces of all nations. The original pin-ups were photographs and film stills, but later magazines and newspapers began the practice of printing pictures especially for this purpose. Perhaps the acme of pin-up art was achieved in the Pirelli calendars of 1960–74.

pistol   The 'hand gun' takes its name from *Pistoia* in Tuscany, but paradoxically the original *pistola* was a 'dagger'. The linking concept is that of the small handy weapon.

pit (*of a theatre*)   This term spread from its original use at the old Drury Lane Theatre built by Killigrew on the site of the former Drury Lane cockpit. The name came to be the standard one for the seats immediately behind the stalls in any theatre.

plain as a pikestaff   This favourite simile for characterising the glaringly obvious has been related by some to the staff of the packman or pedlar, but it is more naturally derived from the weapon of the seventeenth-century pikeman. The pike was sixteen feet long and not something easily concealed!

platform (*as political metaphor*)   A speaker often stands on a platform. American usage soon applied 'platform' to the programme for which a man stood as well. Individual items in the programme were 'planks'. The usage, as with so much in America, was originally Puritan and theological. The earliest example I have found is *The Cambridge Platform: A Platform of Church Discipline* from Cambridge (Mass.) 1648. See also BOARDS for a similar development.

plaudits of the crowd   Now a phrase meaning no more than applause – something the performer is given by the audience – the word plaudit once had a slightly different meaning. It derives from the custom of Roman actors coming to the front of the stage and asking for applause. *Plaudite* in Latin is a command, 'Applaud ye!'

play fast and loose   The origin of this was an old fairground swindle called 'Pricking the belt', in which the victim was invited to push a skewer through a folded belt so as to pin it to the table. The 'operator' would then show that the belt was not in fact fast, but still loose, and so win the bet. It was in the same category as the three-card trick.

plebeian   This comes directly from the Latin *plebs*, 'the common people'. In a plebiscite today all electors are asked to return an answer to a question at issue. In Rome the original plebiscite was a law enacted by the assembled plebs.

plod   Gray's line 'The ploughman homeward plods his weary way' is one of the best-known in English poetry, but the derivation of the word 'plod' is sometimes queried. It seems to come from Middle English *plod*, 'a pool', thus originally suggesting a man tramping rather laboriously through mud and water.

plonk   Now popularised as a generic term for cheap wine, this word seems to have had its first wide circulation in Australia. It was originally a First World War soldier's version of the French (*vin*) *blanc*, 'white wine'.

ploughman's lunch Bread, cheese and pickled onions – traditionally the fare of working men at midday, but the phrase itself, usually thought of as being a relic of rural times, was coined in the 1970s by Richard Trehane, chairman of the English Country Cheese Council, as an advertising slogan. It was enthusiastically adopted by the British public house trade.

ploy See GAMESMANSHIP.

poacher This word is a variant of the French *poche*, 'a pocket'. Game, one supposes, was legitimately 'bagged', but surreptitiously pouched or pocketed. A certain type of man's jacket could once be bought fitted with what was openly described as 'a poacher's pocket', which was vastly commodious. Poached eggs are so called because they, too, are kept in a confined space when cooking.

pogrom From the Russian for 'devastation' or 'destruction' as applied to any organised destructive attack on a class or group. The more specialised use for those against the Jews seems to have come from Western writers who employed it in discussing the massacres of the Jews in Russia in 1905–6.

Pollyanna Heroine of children's books by American author Eleanor Hodgman Porter (1868–1920), known as the 'glad child' and characterised by her boundless, cheerful optimism. Hence applied to anyone irritatingly cheerful when everyone else is depressed.

polony The correct name of this red-skinned sausage should be *Bologna*, a town in Italy once associated with this product. (Compare Parma ham and the cakes called Florentines.)

pom, pommie This Australian term for an Englishman, especially one who has come to settle in Australia, has no generally accepted origin. One theory suggests a word play on immigrant/pomegran(a)te. Australian tradition relates the name to the first convict settlers alleging that they had stamped on their clothes POHM (Prisoner of His Majesty) or that they referred to themselves as Prisoners of Mother England.

pommel By a roundabout way the verb 'pommel' or 'pummel', which now means to hit with the fists, derives from French *pomme*, 'an apple'. The knob on the top of a sword hilt was called 'the little apple' or *pommel*. Used as a verb, the word originally meant to hit with the knob of the sword hilt.

popinjay Sometimes still used as a term of contempt for the vain and conceited, the word was at first simply a medieval word for parrot, particularly the artificial parrot used as a target in some archery competitions. It ultimately derives from Greek *papagas*, 'parrot'.

port (*side of a ship*) The port side of a ship is the left and the right-hand side is called starboard, which relates to the primitive steer board or rudder. It is suggested because the steering gear was to the right a ship would normally tie up with its left side to the port. The port-hole of a ship is from the Latin *porta*, 'a gate'.

portmanteau The original use of this article was as a cloak bag from the French *porter*, 'to carry', and *le manteau*, 'cloak'. It came to be applied to any capacious bag.

poser Now used to mean a question that puzzles, the word once referred to the person who sets or poses such question, as for example the university examiners. The two Fellows of New College who examine at Winchester School are called 'Posers'.

posh Now slightly outdated slang for smart, fashionable, superior, 'posh' derives from booking procedure on the old P. & O. shipping line, where the preferred and therefore more expensive cabins were those '*P*ort(side) *O*ut, *S*tarboard *H*ome'. Sir Denys Lowson, a former Lord Mayor of London, was reported as having requested a SOPH booking for a trip to Vancouver by jet in 1971 to avoid the sun's glare on the outward journey. It may well be that SOPH will come to be the preferred seating of the sophisticated passenger flying west as POSH formerly was of the experienced traveller sailing east.

post-haste Posting was travelling along a route where relays of fresh horses stood ready at intervals. To go 'post-haste' was to go as quickly as possible, far more so than if one took one's own horses all the way.

posy This was not, as it is today, a small bunch of flowers but is to be identified with *poesy* and refers to the verse motto that was once commonly sent with a gift of flowers. A posy ring has a motto or verse inscribed round it. We might also note that anthology meaning a collection of poems is based on the Greek for 'a collection of flowers', *anthos* 'flower', *lego* 'gather'.

pot, *gone to* Now used to suggest a state of ruination, the older usage implied gone beyond all hope of recovery, for the underlying metaphor relates to stolen gold and silver gone to the melting pot never to exist in their original form again.

pot luck A reminiscence of the days when a pot always stood boiling on the fire. To invite a visitor to take pot luck means he must not expect special preparation, but must share whatever is in the pot that day.

Power corrupts The dictum that 'Power tends to corrupt and absolute power corrupts absolutely' was made famous by Lord Acton (1834–1902) but in 1794 William P. Carey had already written. 'It is the dangerous quality of power ... to corrupt those who possess it' and even he seems to be suggesting that it was already something of a cliché. Perhaps the fame of Acton's version is related to the fact that it was *his* comment, albeit an oblique one on the question of Papal infallibility.

praise from Sir Hubert This old phrase gratefully acknowledging some commendation was originally 'Approbation from Sir Hubert Stanley is praise indeed' and comes from the play *A Cure for the Heartache*, written by Thomas Morton and first seen at Covent Garden in 1797.

'Praise the Lord and pass the ammunition' This title and chorus line of a song that became popular in 1942 is said to have been a phrase used by a United States naval chaplain at Pearl Harbor, Captain W. H. Maguire. At first Captain Maguire had no recollection of having used these words, but a year later conceded he might have done so.

prang Wartime slang in the Royal Air Force for an attack from the air, this has a suspicious resemblance to Malay *perang*, 'war', and *perangi*, 'to attack'. A Zulu word *prang*, meaning spear, has also been alleged as a root.

precarious Today normally used to describe something only maintained with difficulty, e.g. a precarious foothold, the word formally related to land tenures. It derives from Latin *precor*, 'a prayer', and means 'obtained by prayer'. Anything precarious has been granted in response to entreaty and is only held at the pleasure of another. It is this implied lack of security which has given the modern sense to the world.

prestige Now meaning high reputation, even fame, the French word of the same form indicated illusion, deception and impressive outward appearance. This last sense has shaped the English usage.

printer's devil See DEVIL.

profane *Fanum* is the Latin for 'temple' or 'shrine' and *pro* (also Latin) meant here 'before' or 'outside'. Profane therefore means 'outside the shrine' in contrast to the sacred which is found within.

proletariat Popularised by Karl Marx as a name for the working masses, this derives from the Latin *proletarii* which in turn derives from *proles*, 'offspring', for the common people were considered as contributing nothing to the state except numbers.

pronto Another United States borrowing directly from Spanish. It is related to the English 'prompt'.

propaganda Current usage of this word associates it with tendentious political 'news' and campaigns of indoctrination.

Propaganda might be cynically defined as 'lies for a purpose'. Its first use was perfectly objective. It comes from the title of a committee set up in Rome in 1620 by Pope Gregory XV to regulate missionary activities. The body had as official title 'Congregatio de propaganda fide'. The name was abbreviated to the Propaganda.

psychedelic This is simply Greek for 'making the soul clear', but is usually rendered 'mind expanding', 'extending the consciousness', and is a term much favoured by those who believe the distorted perceptions of those who use such hallucigenic drugs as cannabis or L S D have some contribution to make to the creative processes of thought and art.

psychenauts Dr Jean Masters and her husband R. E. L. Masters of the New York Foundation for Mind Research coined this word in 1973 to describe those who see themselves as probing 'inner space', in this case the as yet inadequately charted depths of human personality and consciousness as observed in trance states, etc.

punch Once a favourite drink introduced from India, punch takes its name from the Hindi word for 'five', *panch*, from its five ingredients, wine or spirits, hot water or milk, sugar, spices, and lemon juice.

pundit This word now commonly used – perhaps a little sarcastically – for a learned expert is from Hindi *pandit* and means a Sanskrit scholar skilled in the lore of the Brahmins, the Hindu priestly caste.

purchase Now no more than a synonym for 'buy', the word once had more active implications coming from the French *chasser*, 'to hunt', and *pour*, 'for'. The shop window is a fairly modern development and the medieval 'shopper' would have to seek out the seller he wanted.

purple, *born in the* It was the custom of the Byzantine emperors that their children should be born in a certain room decorated with the royal purple. Once quite literally meaning 'born in the purple room', it is now a metaphor meaning born into one of the families of the ruling class.

purse strings, *to hold the* A purse was once a little leather bag closed with a draw string. Whoever 'held the purse strings' controlled the opening of the purse. The metaphor is a very exact parallel to the original fact.

Q

Q E D These three letters are an abbreviation of a Latin phrase *quod erat demonstrandum*, 'which was to be proved'. Their first use was at the end of theorems in Euclid's *Geometry*. To use these letters is a claim to have made your point, to have shown that something is indeed the case. Q E F, from *quod erat faciendem*, 'which was to be done', has a similar usage.

quack Sometimes used as a familiar, even disrespectful, term for any doctor, the word quack should be confined to the medical charlatan, the market-place dispenser of alleged 'cure all' drugs. The Dutch *kwakzalver*, 'one who boasts of his cures', seems to be the origin, with the intermediate English form of 'quacksalver'. The 'quack' suggests the noise of a quacking duck and 'salve' is ointment. Quack has also been related to *quakes*, the shivering fits associated with malaria. But popular speech says quack, and the Dutch parallel is too close for mere coincidence.

quad, *to be in* Meaning 'to be in prison', this derives from the quadrangle or yard for exercise which was a common feature of prison layout. It is sometimes incorrectly spelled quod.

quadrille The name of this square dance is adopted from the French, which in turn derives from the Spanish *cuadrillo*, 'a small square'. The dance itself originated in the eighteenth-century innovation of *quadrilles des contredanses* in French ballet, consisting of a dance in five sections or 'figures', performed frequently by four pairs of dancers. From the stage it passed to the ballroom in the shortened form of 'quadrilles' and importation to England had been effected by the last quarter of the eighteenth century.

Quakers The religious body that calls itself the Society of Friends was given its strange nickname by a Derby justice in the days of George Fox, its founder. Fox urged the justice to 'Quake and tremble at the word of the Lord' and was promptly dubbed 'a Quaker'. There is, however, a record of the word being used some years earlier in 1647 with reference to 'a sect of women come from beyond the sea, called Quakers, and these swell and shiver and shake . . .' Other sectarian groups were later nicknamed Rollers and Jumpers.

quandary This word for a state of difficulty or perplexity exactly describes the position of those who discuss its origin. Some suggest *condarye*, a Middle English version of *hypocondarye*, or hypochondria, 'a morbid state of mind'. Johnson condemned it as 'a low word' without any more explanation. There seems much to be said for the idea of a garbling of the French *'Qu'en dirai-je?'*, 'What shall I say of it?'

quangos These much debated political creations originated in the USA as an abbreviation of 'quasi autonomous non governmental organisations' non-profit-making corporations, nominally independent but in fact relying on contracts and other business from government agencies. The British quango (for example a regional water authority) is much more directly dependent upon the government. Quangos are much execrated as 'jobs for the boys' from one side and as extensions of bureaucracy from the other.

quarantine The isolation of those suspected of contact with infectious diseases took its name from the Italian *quarantina*, 'forty (days)'. When ships came to Venice from the plague-stricken East they went into a special dock and stayed there

208

forty days. If by then no signs of plague were visible they were then allowed to come out and unload in the normal way.

quarry As the object of a hunt the word derives from the Old French *cuirée*, 'hide'. The skin of the creature with what meat still adhered to it was, along with certain offal, always given to the hounds or hawks. To call the animal 'the quarry' while it still lived was to anticipate events. 'Quarry', as applied to a pane of glass or a floor tile, merely means square and comes from the French *le carré*, 'square'.

quarter backs, *Monday morning* If not actually coined, this evocative phrase was certainly given a wider currency by President Gerald Ford at a White House press conference in June 1975 in connection with his expressed preference for not discussing issues raised in the controversial Rockefeller Commission Report on CIA activities. He had no wish to join the ranks of the Monday morning quarterbacks who sagely criticise decisions taken in a game in which they did not play.

quarter-deck The quarter here is from French *écarter*, 'to set apart'. The quarter-deck is set apart for officers. 'Quarters' are also derived from this 'set apart' idea, e.g. married quarters in barracks. The quartermaster once allocated accommodation as well as issuing supplies.

quassia This is perhaps the only botanical name which honours a Negro. The medical properties of this American plant were first noted by Quassi, a Surinam Negro, in 1730 (modern African usage would favour the spelling Kwasi). Quassi told a man called Dahlberg, who informed Linnaeus. The latter coined the name quassia.

queen In Old English this was *cwen*, 'woman', no more. The other derivative, *quean,* is obsolescent for 'worthless woman', 'hussy', 'slut'. From its decent middle ground the word has both risen and fallen.

'Queen Anne's dead' This caustic rejoinder to the retailer of old news is first mentioned in a ballad of 1722, eight years

209

after her death. The death of Anne was of great political significance and led to the coming of the Hanoverians. It could scarcely have gone unmarked by any.

queen's tobacco pipe This was the popular name for a furnace in the London Docks where smuggled tobacco was burnt. This burning ended towards the end of the nineteenth century.

queen's weather It was generally believed that whenever Queen Victoria appeared for a public occasion the weather would be fine and warm, so a fine warm day was often called 'Queen's weather'. This is perhaps the last example of belief in the 'magic of monarchy'. Beginning with a notably wet coronation day, the reign of Elizabeth II seemed at first likely to reverse the traditional meaning.

Queer Street, *to be in* Meaning to be in financial difficulties, the term has been derived from an alleged tradesman's practice of putting a query (?) beside the name of customers whose financial soundness was questioned. A queer is slang for a homosexual.

queue A straight borrowing from the French, this is literally 'a tail'. The German word for a queue is *Schlange*, 'snake'. It is odd that the disciplined English had no word of their own.

quibble This seems to derive from the Latin *quibus*, 'to whom', so common in legal documents that it came to symbolise the hair-splitting and subtleties believed characteristic of the legal profession.

quick In the expression 'a quick-set hedge' or the Biblical expression 'the quick and the dead' we see the original Saxon *cwic*, 'living'. When 'cut to the quick' our semi-dead skin has been penetrated and our living flesh hurt.

quintessence The Greek meaning of this is 'fifth essence'. To the standard Greek ideas of the four elements or forms of matter the Pythagoreans added a fifth, ether, conceived of as more subtle, more pure, indeed more itself than the others.

quisling This generic word for a traitor is formed from the name of Vidkun Quisling, a Norwegian officer and diplomat who prepared the way for the German invasion of his country. He was executed after the liberation in 1945, leaving his name as an unenviable legacy.

qui vive, *to be on the* *Qui vive* (literally 'Who lives?') is the French equivalent of our sentry's 'Who goes there'. To be 'on the *qui vive*' is to remain alert and watchful.

quiz A synthetic word invented in 1780 by Daly, a Dublin theatre manager, for a wager that he would introduce a new word into the language in twenty-four hours. The mystery word was secretly chalked up on every wall and bare space in the city and in a few hours everyone was discussing it. It came to be used for 'enquiry' and a root in inquisition has been suggested as likely. Since the Second World War it has been widely used for competitive tests usually of general knowledge.

R

Rs, *the three* This famous phrase still bandied about in any discussion on education is attributed to Sir William Curtis MP and sometime Lord Mayor of London who, having made a fortune by selling ships' biscuits during the Napoleonic War, took to pronouncing on the schools curriculum question. The three Rs are reading, 'riting and 'rithmetic – the original core curriculum.

rabbi Although the word is loosely used to describe a Jewish minister of religion, it was at first a title of respect awarded from the first century to doctors of the law. It means 'My master'.

rabbit This essentially London slang term for 'talk' especially excessive and unnecessary talk derives from rhyming slang 'rabbit and pork' but it does seem to owe something to the animal itself with its perpetually moving jaws.

Rachmanism Under the Rent Act of 1957 rents in Britain were controlled at an artificially low level in comparison with the market value of the property, but only so long as the original tenant remained in possession. This led unscrupulous landlords, especially in certain areas of London, to harass tenants to obtain vacant possession. The property was then sold or re-let at high rents, sometimes to prostitutes, etc. Such tactics became known as Rachmanism, after Peter Rachman (1920–62), a Polish immigrant, who indulged in the practice.

rack and ruin The English language has a fondness for these alliterative phrases. In this one rack is a variant of wreck, which was formerly written wrack.

racket According to John Kobler's *Capone*, 'racket' in the sense of swindle or criminal activity derives from the rowdy benefit galas held by the old New York social clubs. Gangsters would organise fictitious 'benevolent clubs' and collect money for 'rackets' that were never held nor ever intended to be.

radicals As a term describing a political tendency this derives from the Late Latin *radicalis*, 'pertaining to the roots', for the radicals favoured thorough-going political reform.

radar This word belongs to the class of acronyms, words made up from the initials of a longer phrase, in this case Radio Ascertainment of Direction And Range.

rag The first use of this word was in the sense of ragged, and rag was a piece of that which is ragged, hence a worthless scrap, etc. It derives from a Scandinavian word *rogg* in Icelandic, *ragg* in Norse, *rugg* in Swedish, all meaning 'rough matted hair'. Incidentally, the word rug has the same ultimate origin and it is curious to note that Rugg was once a common name for a dog.

rag on every bush, *to have a*   This old phrase refers to a man who pays attentions to more than one lady at a time. Although only noted in print form *c.* 1866 it obviously has a history behind it, since it would seem to relate to the practice of tying a rag to a nearby bush after having visited a wishing well to make a wish. This may still be seen at the famous Cloutie Well near Culloden in Scotland.

ragout   This name for a seasoned meat stew comes from the French *ragoûter*, from the Latin *regustare*, 'to restore the taste', a reference to the spicy seasoning.

ragtime   Perhaps best defined as the phase of pop music that preceded jazz, the word ragtime is first noted in 1901 in America. Its vogue came to a climax on the eve of the First World War. In 1912 a show at the London Hippodrome was entitled *Hello Ragtime.* Presumably derived from the ragged or irregular beat, the term soon gained a wider usage in the sense of haphazard, careless, happy-go-lucky. In the work of the American Negro ragtime king Scott Joplin (1868–1917), ragtime attained the level of a serious art, although his work was not fully recognised until the 1970s.

rain cats and dogs   This idiomatic description of heavy rainfall cannot easily have an origin ascribed to it. One suggestion relates it to old Norse weather-lore, the cat being related to rain and the dog to wind. Another more plausibly suggests the Greek *catadupa*, 'cataract' or 'waterfall'. The phrase was first used in print in 1653, which favours the Greek as against the Norse theory.

raincheck, *to take a*   In the United States, for a small extra charge, a raincheck is issued with the ticket bought for outdoor sporting events. In the event of rain, this entitles the purchaser to a free ticket on a later occasion. Hence, in refusing a drink or an invitation to dinner, Americans will often say 'I'll take a raincheck on it', meaning they would be glad to accept another time. The system, for obvious reasons, has never taken root in the British climate, but the phrase is

213

often used without knowledge of its origin, simply by adoption of American usage, from films and novels.

raise the roof See HOUSE, *to bring down the*. The same general observations apply.

ranch The original Spanish American *rancho* referred to the hut or 'bunkhouse' in which herdsmen or cowboys lived. Gradually the word was applied to the whole estate.

ransack Now used in the sense of 'pillage' and requiring an object after it, this verb once made complete sense itself. It comes from Icelandic *rann*, 'house', and *saka*, 'to seek'.

rap, *not worth a* Ireland in the 1720s was suffering a great shortage of small change and the vacuum was filled by certain counterfeit copper halfpence known as *raps*. They soon fell to something like a quarter of their face value. Today the word *Rappen* is the Swiss-German equivalent of centime, the smallest unit of Swiss currency.

razzle, *on the* The phrase came like so many to Britain from the United States. Now to 'go on the razzle' is a somewhat outdated term for a spectacular celebratory jaunt. (Compare 'whooping it up' and 'painting the town red'.) Its first appearance is in 1890 in *Miss Nobody*: 'I'm going to razzle-dazzle the boys with my great lightning change act.'

read oneself in This term refers to the first duty of a new parish priest. He must read the Thirty-nine Articles, the fundamental beliefs of the Anglican Church, from the pulpit of his new church and make a Declaration of Assent to them. The expression is sometimes used metaphorically of other inaugurations.

recluse The origin here is Latin *recludere*, 'to shut away', and a recluse is one who shuts himself away.

recreant A survival from the age of chivalry, this word for a coward or craven is of Old French origin. It is now only used in deliberately archaic styles.

214

rector   From the Latin *rego*, 'I rule', the title rector distinguishes the Church of England clergyman, whose predecessors received the tithes themselves, from the vicars who were the clerical deputies of some other person or corporation who received the tithe income. See VICAR.

red herring, *to draw across the path*   A red herring was a dried and smoked one, an early relation of the kipper, which was notorious for its strong flavour. To draw a red herring across anywhere a fox had been would, it was believed, effectively destroy his scent and prevent the hounds from pursuing him. Anyone who seeks to divert the course of an argument or investigation is said to be the user of a red herring.

red-letter day   In olden days the Saints' Days that were the subject of special festivities were indicated in the Church Calendar in red letters. The expression came in time to mean a special occasion, a day to be remembered.

red light district   This now internationally understood expression for an official or unofficial brothel quarter seems to have been first employed in the famous Dodge City. See also TENDERLOIN.

red rag to a bull   The phrase, used to indicate a high degree of provocation, derives from the belief that the colour red had an enraging effect upon bulls, a belief perhaps derived from the capes of the Spanish bullring. It is in fact the movement and not the colour that arouses the bull.

red tape   Charles Dickens is believed to have been the first to use this expression to characterise officialdom's rigid sticking to obstructive and timewasting rules of procedure. The tape used in government offices to tie up bundles of papers is in fact pink.

reduce   Although this word is commonly used in the sense of 'to make less' it is still sometimes found in a slightly different sense which is in fact its original one. It comes from the Latin *re*, 'back', and *duco*, 'I lead'. When one talks of 'reducing a

215

dislocated joint' or 'reducing an officer to the ranks', it is easy to see how the current meaning grew.

reffo In the years immediately after the Second World War this was a common term in Australia for a newly arrived European immigrant, particularly one from Eastern Europe. It was a contraction of refugee.

regatta The first regattas were held in Venice and were contests between gondoliers. In Italian *regatta* was 'a struggle' or 'contention'. Now it applies to any organised competitions for watercraft.

rendezvous Literally translated from French this would be 'Betake ourself . . .' or more simply 'Go to . . .' It came into English as a military term for a prearranged meeting place and its context is still normally a military one. It is normally used as a noun but sometimes as a verb: 'Units will rendezvous at 0700 hours.'

restaurant The first restaurant, as such, opened in Paris and is said to have displayed the legend *Venite ad me . . . et ego restaurabo . . .*, 'Come unto me . . . and I will restore you . . . It is unlikely that such a blasphemous parody would have been displayed under the old régime and certainly, after the revolution, many former chefs to the nobility gave their talents to a wider public and the word hôtel (formerly the nobleman's town house) began to change its meaning.

revue As a theatrical term this word first appeared in English in 1912. *The Tatler* in October referred to '*Kill that Fly*, the new revue which is crowding the New Alhambra'. The word is French and basically means a detailed inspection. It came into theatre language to describe a satirical look at the events of the past year.

rhapsody Used today to mean fulsome praise, it also has the more technical meaning of a composition of loosely connected episodes. It comes from Greek *rapto*, 'to sew', and *ode*, 'song'. The first rhapsodists were Greek troubadours or their equivalent who devised 'selections from Homer'.

riddle The riddle was a favourite entertainment of the Saxons and developed elaborate forms. It derives from *raedan,* 'to read, to guess'.

riddle of the sphinx This classic puzzle of the ancient world was asked by the sphinx (a monster whose name means 'strangler'); those who could not answer were killed. It goes 'What animal has four feet, then two feet, then three feet and only one voice. Its feet vary and when it has most it is weakest?' Oedipus gave the right answer, at which the sphinx killed herself in despair. 'MAN who crawls on all fours as an infant, walks on two feet when grown, but in old age moves upon his feet and a staff.'

ride, *take someone for a* The first use of this phrase and of the method of killing it implies is authoritatively ascribed to one Hymie Weiss of the Chicago O'Bannion gang in 1921. The victim was forced into the front seat of a car, driven away to a suitable spot, shot through the back of the head and dumped by the wayside.

riff-raff A contemptuous expression for the socially despised, this expression came from France, where *rif et raf* meant 'every last bit', in other words the rubbish, the leftovers, the sweepings.

rift in the lute The lute in this expression is not the musical instrument, but a Latin-based word for the clay or cement-like substance used to seal a crack or render a joint secure. A rift in the lute then presages a break up of some sort.

right as a trivet Trivet was a three-legged stand from Latin *tri,* 'three', *pes,* 'foot'. The three-legged tripet or trivet, if standing at all, must be upright. Nothing could be more (up)right than a trivet.

right foot foremost This means 'with every intention of doing the job well'. To set off with the left foot first would augur bad luck, so one should start in the most auspicious way, 'right foot foremost'.

right-hand man   In our right-hand orientated society the right has always been the place of honour. A chief assistant is a trusted companion. He is moreover as indispensable as a right hand. A superior would be more easily defended by a swordsman standing to the right. All these ideas merge in the expression.

rigmarole   This word for a long and confused narrative has been in known use since the early eighteenth century, but is said to be a corruption of the Ragman Roll, a document with many pendant seals recording the titles of the Scots noblemen who paid homage to Edward I in 1291. The explanation is well attested but does not convince.

rile   Meaning to annoy or make angry, this is a variant of an old verb *roil*, meaning 'to stir up', as for example the sediment in a pool or stream thus clouding the water.

Riley, *live the life of*   No origin can be pinpointed for this phrase indicative of irresponsible ease and pleasure, but it plainly relates to the stereotyped figure of the feckless Irishman, for which see PADDY.

ring leader   Always used in the sense of one who has led others into some mischief this has been derived from the ring dances which were associated with medieval witches' sabbaths, etc.

R I P   This is an abbreviation of the Latin *Requiescat in pace*, 'May he [or she] rest in peace'.

Ritz, ritzy   Still widely used as suggestive of the world of high fashion and high society after popularisation in the thirties by Scott Fitzgerald and Cole Porter, and defined in a famous dictionary as meaning 'ostentatiously rich' these words derived César Ritz's famous London hotel 'The Ritz' opened in 1906. It was intended to be the most luxurious hotel in the world and the English language has accepted it as such.

rival The word has descended from Latin *rivalis*, 'one living on the opposite river bank'. The original rivals then lived on the opposite banks of a river.

roam The original 'roamer', from the Old French *romier*, was 'one who had made the pilgrimage to Rome'.

roast, *rule the* A variant spelling is 'roost' and there are accordingly two theories as to its origin. Roost suggests the barnyard and the dominance of one cock. Roast suggests the master of the house carving at table. The phrase goes back to the fifteenth century, but diversities of spelling confuse the issue. By the seventeenth century the 'kitchen' association seems to be dominant.

robbing Peter to pay Paul This phrase has been ingeniously associated with the varying fortunes of St Peter's Abbey of Westminster and St Paul's Cathedral. In 1550 Westminster was given cathedral status, only to be demoted ten years later and its revenues diverted to St Paul's. Unfortunately for the supporters of this theory, the words were used by Wycliff in the fourteenth century. In fact Peter and Paul have been taken as contrasting figures from very early times.

robin redbreast According to legend the robin tried to pull the cruel thorns from the head of the crucified Jesus and to staunch the flow of blood with the feathers of its breast, thus staining it red for all time.

rod in pickle, *I have a* Birch rods used for corporal punishment were kept in brine (or pickle) to keep the twigs pliable. To have a rod in pickle is to have an unpleasant surprise in store for someone.

rogue See VAGABOND. The general opinion seems to be that rogue is a variant of Roger, but the French *rogue*, which is of

Celtic origin and means 'arrogant', reflects one aspect of the 'sturdy beggars' who terrorised Tudor society.

rogue's yarn   This was the old name for the strands of coloured thread woven into ropes used by the Royal Navy so they could be easily identified if stolen.

romany rye   *Rye* is *raja*, 'gentleman', and the whole expression (made well known by George Borrow in his book of the same title) is a gipsy term for the outsider who learns their language and comes to live among them.

Rome plough   One of the technological innovations of the Vietnam war was the use of huge fifty-ton bulldozers to flatten and sweep away whole tracts of jungle, in order to deny any shelter there to the Viet Cong forces. They were given the evocative name of Rome ploughs in reference to the utter destruction wreaked upon Carthage, the ruins of which were swept away and the site ploughed up that its very memory might perish.

rostrum   Now a place from which a speaker addresses his audience, the name once meant (in Latin) the beak or prow of a ship. The orator's platform in the Roman Forum was decorated with the prows of captured ships.

rota   Latin for wheel and applied by extension to any scheme for rotation of duties. Roster, similarly used, has its origin in the Dutch *rooster*, 'a grid', and is used for a diagrammatic arrangement of those who are to perform duties.

Rotten Row   The name of the famous horse-riding track in London's Hyde Park is a corruption of *Route du roi*, 'the king's way', 'the royal road', from the Palace of Westminster to the forest.

roué   This word for a debauchee goes back to Regent Orleans of France, who declared that his companions were all profligates who deserved the punishment of 'breaking on the wheel' (*la roue*).

round robin There is no real robin involved here but a *ruban*, which is French for 'ribbon'. The signatures to such a document, which is normally a protest or statement of grievances, are arranged in a circle so that no one name heads the list and appears as that of the originator of the protest.

Rubicon, *to cross the* See DIE (*the die is cast*).

rum Used in some such phrase as 'a rum cove [chap]' or 'a rum business' to indicate a suspect person, a suspicious affair, rum has had a derivation from *romany*, 'pertaining to gipsies', claimed for it.

run amok See AMOK.

rush, *not worth a* The phrase has been given a medieval origin and explained as, relating to visitors or guests, 'not important enough to have fresh rushes strewn on the floor for them', but in this case one might expect 'not worth rushes'. The rush light, on the other hand, was a sort of rudimentary torch and one may more plausibly interpret the phrase as 'not worth the waste of a single rush light'. Compare the proverbial phrase, 'The game is not worth the candle'.

S

sabotage The word derives from the French *sabot*, meaning 'wooden shoe' or 'clog', but *sabot* is also the 'shoe' that holds the iron rail on to the wooden sleeper beneath it, and it is from the loosening or removal of these *sabots* by striking French railwaymen that the word sabotage as we use it takes its meaning.

saccharin This synthetic sweetener, which is a by-product of coal tar, derives its name from the Latin *saccharum*, 'sugar'. The adjective saccharine is sometimes used metaphorically for artificial 'sweetness' of voice or manner. Saccharin was discovered by accident in 1879 when C. H. Fahlberg, who was carrying out experiments at Johns Hopkins University, went home to supper and found the bread tasted sweet. Realising suddenly that the sweetness came from his hands, not the bread, he rushed back to recheck his laboratory equipment and find the source of the new compound.

sack, *to get the* The origin of this most widespread euphemism for being dismissed from one's job is said to have been the custom of workmen leaving the bag or sack in which they first brought their tools with their employer. If they lost the job they 'got the sack' and took their tools away with them. Frankly it does not convince but a better suggestion has yet to be made. Since the introduction in Britain of National Insurance on the eve of the First World War, the expression 'to get your cards', i.e. be given your insurance cards to take away, has become quite as common.

sacrament The use of this word for the most solemn rites of the Church derives from the Latin *sacramentum*, 'military oath of loyalty'. The parallel between the spiritual 'warfare' of the Christian and the life of the soldier goes back to the writings of Paul in the first century.

sad Derived from the Anglo-Saxon *saed*, which meant 'sated' or 'tired', this word took on the meaning of heavy, firm or even the quality of being resolute. In Wycliff's Bible, the 'house built on a rock' is 'on a sad stoon'. Even today bread may be sad if it is too heavy and there is such a thing as sadcake. Our modern usage of sad keeps the idea of mental heaviness.

safe This comes first from the French *sauf*, but ultimately from the Latin *salvus*, 'unhurt', 'well', 'preserved', in short 'safe'.

safety matches Disposable matches were first developed by John Walker of Stockton-on-Tees *c*. 1826 and later marketed by Samuel Jones under the name of Lucifers, a term still in use as late as the First World War. The safety match, which would only strike when rubbed on a specially prepared surface, was developed in the 1850s by the Swedish chemist

Bottger. Present-day matches use a more sophisticated chemical 'mix', but the principle remains the same.

sail close to the wind This is an allusion to the keeping of a vessel's head so close to the quarter from which the wind is coming that she is in danger of being caught by a gust and keeling over. So, metaphorically, engaging in practices just short of the illegal means a real danger of discovery and exposure.

St Leger Run annually in September at Doncaster in Yorkshire, this race takes its name from its first organiser, Colonel St Leger of Park Hill, Doncaster. For three-year-olds, it was first run in 1776 but not given its present name until 1778.

St Luke's summer A mid-October period of fine weather is traditionally associated with St Luke's Day on the 18th. The American term for the same phenomenon is 'Indian summer'.

St Vitus' Dance This folkname for the nervous affliction called chorea, in Greek 'the dance', because of the convulsive twitchings that characterise it, arose from an inexplicable medieval superstition. St Vitus was a Christian martyr with no association with dancing, but the belief grew that anyone who danced before his statute on his feast day (15 June) would enjoy good health for the year. It is this association that led to the saint's name being given to 'the dancing sickness'.

salary From the Latin *salarium*, 'salt money', a soldier's allowance for the purchase of salt, come a pair of metaphorical phrases, i.e. 'not worth his salt' and 'true to his salt'.

Sally Lunn The tea-cake of this name was first cooked by a Bath pastry cook of the eighteenth century. She hawked her wares through the streets until a baker named Dalmer began large-scale commercial production and the cakes became famous.

salt a mine This expression for scattering gold-dust in order to mislead likely purchasers of a mining claim first appears in print in 1864 with reference to the diggings in Australia. 'Miners sometimes salt an unproductive mine by sprinkling a few grains of gold dust over it.' The key idea could be the sprinkling, or it could be the adding of 'flavour'.

salute The Latin *salus*, 'health, safety', is the origin of this word, the basic good wish.

salvo Closely related to the previous entry, this is an artillery discharge in honour or welcome and its name is derived from the Latin *salve*, 'Hail'.

Sam Browne belt This article of army officer's equipment was named after its first deviser, a general who played a distinguished role in the Indian Mutiny of 1857.

Sambo This largely obsolete, patronising name for the North American Negro derives from the Spanish *zambo*, 'bow-legged'. In Spanish its use was confined to coloured people of racially mixed origin.

san fairy ann This, like PLONK and NAPOO, is another piece of 'bastard French' brought home by soldiers in the First World War. It was an attempt at *Ça ne fait rien*, 'It does not matter'.

sandwich The name, though not the actual invention of the article, goes back to John Montagu, 4th Earl of Sandwich (1718–92), who was so addicted to gambling that he could spare no time for meals, preferring to take his food in the form that came to be known as a sandwich.

sang froid From the French *sang*, 'blood', and *froid*, 'cold', and meaning in English an admirable calm when others are in panic, it is the quality envisaged by Kipling in the poem 'If': 'If you can keep your head when all about you / are losing theirs and blaming it on you . . .' In French, however, the implication is rather of indifference and lack of capacity to feel.

sansculottes   Literally French for 'without breeches', i.e. the wearers of trousers instead. This term was used for the anti-noble faction in the French Revolution of 1789. It may be compared with the *descamisados*, Spanish for 'shirtless ones', who were the working-class supporters of Juan Perón in the Argentine.

sarcophagus   This is the name given to a stone coffin, usually one embellished with sculpture and inscriptions. The name is Greek and embodies a curious belief coming from *sarx*, 'flesh', and *phagein*, 'to eat'. This was originally the name of a stone believed by the Greeks to consume flesh. They therefore used it for coffins.

sardonic laughter   Homer was the first to use the expression. It derives from the *herba sardonia*, 'herb of Sardis in Asia Minor', so bitter to the taste that it causes the facial nerves to contort into the semblance of a smile. Sardonic laughter is not voluntary.

sassenach   This is Scots Gaelic for Englishman, and is a Celtic version of Saxon. It was also applied by the Highlanders to the Lowlanders.

satire   The hairy-legged satyr of the Greek gods, disrespectful though he may have been, has no connection with this Latin word, which was originally *satura*, 'full', as used in the term *lanx satura*, literally 'full dish', but used in the sense of a mixed dish. It is from this concept of a 'mixed dish' that our literary use of satire comes.

sauce   We took this directly from the French but its ultimate origin was the Roman world and the Latin *salsa*, 'salt', 'salted'. The first sauces were dishes of boiled, salted vegetables as a side dish.

Savile Row   Generic term for the high-class West End of London 'bespoke' tailoring trade, still accepted as the best in the world. The first firm to set up business in Savile Row was

Henry Poole & Co. in 1846. Cork Street and Conduit Street also have their famous tailors but it was Savile Row that won a place in the dictionaries.

scamp Now often used of a mischievous child, and always in an affectionate way, the word was once found in a very different context, for it comes from the French *escamper*, from Latin *ex campo*, 'away from the battlefield', and was used of a deserter who fled from the battle.

scapegoat In the ritual for the Day of Atonement, described in the Biblical Book of Leviticus, one of two goats was chosen by lot to be sent into the wilderness, symbolically bearing away the sins of the people. From this, anyone who is made to suffer or answer for somebody's else's crimes is called a scapegoat. Scape is a shortened form of 'escape'. Similar symbolic 'unloadings' of sin are found among primitive peoples, for example in Borneo.

Scarborough warning This traditional phrase means in fact with no warning at all. One view relates this to a sudden seizure of the castle in 1554 by Thomas Stafford, while another relates it to an alleged local practice of hanging robbers first and investigating their case afterwards. The phrase HALIFAX GIBBET LAW tells the same tale of Halifax.

scenery The oddity of this word is that while today its associations are essentially natural, its origin is totally artificial. It comes from the Greek *skene*, 'a covered place', and relates to the stage of a theatre. Thus, if it does not actually imitate, as Oscar Wilde suggested, nature has here certainly been given a name from Art.

school An astonishing origin this! The Greek *schole*, from which our word is derived, meant 'leisure'. To the Greeks this was logical enough, for the cultivation of the mind was to them an obvious use for leisure. The Romans also had what seems to us an oddly derived 'school', which was in Latin *ludus*, which also meant 'game, pastime'. Their connecting thought was the idea of training for the games, e.g. a training place for gladiators.

scissors This is derived from the French *ciseaux*, the plural of *ciseau*, which in Old French was *cisel* and in popular Latin *cisellum*, the same word being also the root of our 'chisel'. The spelling has been influenced by the Latin *scissus*, 'cut apart', 'split', 'divide'. In some regional forms of English, scissors can be a singular noun.

score In primitive times any reckoning would be done by means of notches on a stick. See TALLY. In Old Norse *skor* was a 'cut'. In Saxon the primary meaning of *score* was 'twenty', but behind this lies the idea of a series of cuts.

scot free Scot was a medieval word for tax, e.g. church-scot. Scot and lot was Saxon law jargon for payment according to assessment. To escape 'scot free' means without loss or penalty.

scoundrel The word means 'one who should be shunned', from the Saxon *scunean*, 'to loathe or shun'. English dialects still have the word 'scunner', meaning 'to be repelled by', for example, a loathsome smell.

scrambled egg A soldier's contemptuous expression for the masses of gilt emblems on officers' caps. BRASS-HATS makes a different comparison, but in the same spirit.

scratch, *to come up to* The scratch is the line at the start of a race. The first meaning of 'He will never come up to scratch' was 'He will never actually appear at the starting line', metaphorically, 'will not meet our expectations'. See also COME.

scrounge This word only came into wide use during the First World War and was a euphemism for stealing or, at best, for acquiring without undue formality. Later 'a scrounger' came to mean a man who always borrowed off pals, and never had food or cigarettes of his own. A writer in 1909 had noted 'scrounging' as a country boy's word for apple-stealing, and this is near enough in time and sense to suggest the origin of the soldier's term.

227

scruple The original Latin *scrupulus* was 'a small stone', and later the smallest weight. By extension it came to mean 'small and delicate considerations', and then the anxiety of mind these might occasion among the conscientious.

scuttle In the sense of 'scuttling off', this has a Scandinavian background and must be related to *scut*, 'a tail', though the history of the transformation is obscure.

seamy side (*of life*) Meaning the wrong side, the worst side and that better left unseen, this metaphor derives from the fact that carpets, tapestry, embroidery, etc., if turned over, show rough seams and loose ends, a result of the manufacturing process but not to be seen by the public.

search This word is a version of the French *chercher*, which is based in turn on the Latin *circare*, 'to go round in a circle'. Very often this is what we instinctively do when searching for something.

secular Meaning that which belongs to this life and time, as opposed to eternity, the word derives from Latin *saeculum*, 'the age', 'period of time', which by extension came to mean 'the world in which we live'. Thus secular clergy are the ordinary parish priests, as opposed to 'regulars' who are 'dead to the world', living under a monastic rule and spending much of their time in the contemplation of eternity.

serene, *all* See ALL SERENE.

sergeant-major's tea Old soldiers sometimes used this term for tea in which there was milk, sugar and possibly a dash of rum. The implication was that, however short the men might be, the sergeant-major would look after himself.

setting the Thames on fire The key to this paradoxical phrase is the fact that Thames should be spelt temse, and was an old word for 'sieve'. It was said that an over-vigorous sifter might even set his temse on fire! The phrase is now confined to references to people who never will.

settle a bargain, settle terms These phrases are metaphorical now, but find their origin in the name of a material object, the long wooden seat we still call 'a settle'. This social seat was the scene of much activity. People settled down for a quiet evening, settled their quarrels, settled their bargains. The word is a Saxon one, *setl*, 'a seat'.

sexton Although his office is a minor one today, the name of the sexton has an exalted ancestry, for it is a corruption of *sacristan*, the monastic officer who had charge of the sacred vessels and vestments used at the altar.

shadow, *may it never grow less* This good wish, sometimes used facetiously today, came from the East and relates to the traditions of magic. Students in the art would be chased by the Devil at a certain stage in their progress, and if he caught them he would seize all or part of their shadow. (See DEVIL.) The traditional wish then was that the recipient might be 'delivered from evil'.

S H A E F These initials found in narratives or news stories of the Second World War stand for 'Supreme Headquarters Allied Expeditionary Force' and refer to General Eisenhower's planning H Q for the Allied invasion of Europe. It was first established 15 February 1944 at Norfolk House, St James's Square, London, and moved in March 1944 to Bushy Park, near Kingston upon Thames. (See D-DAY.) Information given to the world's journalists at the thrice-daily press conferences there was usually passed on to the public with some such introduction as 'It was learnt at Shaef today . . .'

Shakers The American religious sect of this name developed in New York State in the 1770s and was founded by 'Mother Ann' Lee, a former Quaker of Manchester, England. The Shakers derived their name from the ecstatic dancing which was a feature of their worship.

shakes, *no great* As a phrase meaning 'not up to much' this must be based on a provincial word 'shake', meaning 'to brag', and hence means 'nothing to brag or boast about'. Attempts to suggest it relates to a poor throw at dice do not convince. It is not the shaking of the dice, but the rolling or throwing that scores and would thus be referred to. The word *schakare*, 'maker of boasts', is found in 1440.

shambles A number of towns in Britain (Nottingham is one) not only retain the name of Shambles as a street name, but also the original purpose. In Saxon *scamel* was a bench or stall on which meat was displayed for sale. The shambles then was 'the street of the butchers', and 'a shambles' as descriptive of a scene of slaughter was a natural extension of this idea. The modern use of shambles for mere disorder is a weakening and debasement.

Shangri-la The name of a (fictitious) ideal community of ageless beings located in the Himalayas described in James Hilton's novel *Lost Horizon*. A filmed version starring Ronald Colman was a great success and served to popularise this new name for Utopia. A remake in 1973 was less successful. In the time of F. D. Roosevelt, the presidential retreat in Maryland was called Shangri-la but Dwight Eisenhower thought this too fanciful, and renamed it after one of his grandsons 'Camp David'. Today a reference to Shangri-la usually means a golf-course de luxe property development in Menorca.

Shanks's mare, pony This humorous phrase for walking is based on 'shank', the leg bone between knee and ankle. Properly called the tibia, it was in Saxon *sceanca*. The notably tall Edward I was popularly surnamed 'Longshanks'.

shanty As a sailor's worksong this derives from the French *chanter*, 'to sing'. As a North American log cabin it is from *chantier*, also French, and meaning among other things 'scaffolding' or 'staging'.

shaver This slang term for a boy is the Romany *chavvie*, *chavo*, 'boy'.

sheet-anchor This nautical term for the largest anchor of a ship is widely used in a symbolic sense for anything on which safety ultimately depends.

sheets (*three in the wind*) The sheet is a rope attached to the lower end of a sail and used to regulate it. Totally slackened, the sheet was said to be 'in the wind'. 'Three sheets in the wind' describes a man badly out of control due to drunkenness.

shekel The principal coin-weight of the ancient Hebrews, the shekel is still sometimes used in references, especially facetious or envious references, to money. Such a phrase as 'raking in the shekels' is perhaps rather more opprobious than objective, and may once have reflected the Jewish usurer archetype.

shillibeer George Shillibeer, who attempted to develop London's first bus service, did not find the venture profitable, and so moved on into undertaking. The vehicle that bore his name was another unsuccessful venture. It was a combined hearse and mourners' carriage. See also OMNIBUS.

shilling The 's' of the formula £-s-d, referring to pre-decimal British currency, stood for *solidus*, a Roman silver coin, but the actual word shilling is pure Saxon, *scilling*, 'cutting'. The Saxon shilling was at first a money of account only, that is a unit of reckoning without any actual coin corresponding to it. Golden rings or armbands were the first Saxon currency and 'cuttings' from these were roughly adjusted to the Roman solidus unit.

shindy This slang word for a noise or altercation has no firm origin assigned to it although it has been linked to the Irish *shinty*, a game of the hockey type, but the variant 'shindig' also exists. Speculation continues.

shire This English word for county is the Saxon *scir*, which meant 'cut off' in the sense of 'allocated'. The shire was the administrative division allotted to an Earl. His continental equivalent was the *Count*. Though English took over *county* and *viscount*, the native Earl was never displaced.

short counsel is good counsel This proverb is generally associated with the death of Bishop Walcher of Durham in 1080. When he was mobbed by a hostile crowd at Gateshead the cry was 'Short rede, good rede: slay the bishop.' (*Rede* is Saxon for 'counsel' or 'advice'.) The bishop retreated into a church but was burnt to death in it.

short shrift Now used to mean speedy punishment, this was not quite the original sense. Shrift is the act of hearing a man's confession and granting him absolution for his sins. A man due to be executed was allowed but 'short shrift'. The simple injunction to 'Say your prayers' was a post-Reformation equivalent.

shovel offertories It was once the custom at a funeral for the sexton (who dug the grave) to stand by the church gate holding out his shovel for contributions from the mourners.

show a leg there This traditional naval 'invitation' to be up and about is not quite complete in the form shown here and most commonly used. It should continue: '. . . or a purser's stocking'. In the old days women were tolerated below decks and when the bo'sun's mate called out the hands in the morning a leg in a stocking put over the side of a hammock indicated that the occupant was a woman, and so allowed to remain until the men had cleared out.

shrapnel In 1784 a Lieutenant (later General) Henry Shrapnel (1761–1842) devised a shell which when opened in flight by a bursting charge scattered a large number of smaller bullets. The shell was soon named after its inventor. Nowadays shrapnel is used to refer to fragments of burst shell casing or to bomb splinters.

shrew It seems an odd thing that while you insult a woman by calling her a shrew, you compliment a man by calling him shrewd. The words have different origins. The shrew takes her

232

name from the medieval *schrewen*, 'to curse', but shrewd comes from the Saxon *screawa*, 'one who bites' or as we should say 'makes his mark'.

sidesman   This name for the man who collects the offerings of the congregation in church derives from 'synod's man', a synod being a district assembly of clergy, and a synod's man one sent to attend such a meeting. In practice the modern sidesman is assistant to the churchwarden.

side track, *to*   This vivid and very useful phrase grew up on the early American railways and is a good example of 'technological metaphor'. It is interesting to note that, whereas in Britain the railways took over much of the vocabulary of the coaching world (the very words coach, carriage, booking office and the cry of 'Right away' are examples), American railmen borrowed from the steamboats, hence berths and 'All aboard'.

silent majority, *the*   This expression gained wide political currency after its use by President Nixon on 3 November 1969 in a speech on the Vietnam War. It was not, however, an original coinage, having appeared in a similar sense in the pages of *Lectures in Foreign History* (1925) by the Oxford historian J. M. Thompson.

silhouette   This type of picture took its name from Etienne de Silhouette, Controller-General (Finance Minister) to Louis XV of France. He was associated with policies of retrenchment, and these cheap cut-out portraits gained their name by association with ideas of cheapness and economy.

silly   The Saxon *soelig* (Modern German *selig*), meaning 'happy, blessed', is the root of this word which, via 'innocent' and then 'guileless' or 'simple', has reached its present meaning.

silver hook, *to angle with a*   Now it means to offer a bribe. If you cannot catch your fish yourself you can always buy some. This is to 'angle with a silver hook'.

silver spoon in one's mouth A silver spoon was a common christening present, but the child of rich parents had no need to wait until the christening for such a gift. He would have the use of silver spoons from birth.

sinecure This is Latin for 'without care' and is used for a situation in which the work is nominal only, though the salary is very real. The word was originally used in church circles, where the priest's work is sometimes referred to as the 'cure' of souls.

sine die Latin for 'without a day', the implication being 'for the further discussion of this question'. A case adjourned *sine die* is in fact closed.

sing small Meaning to accept a more humble position, this is a rather pointless variant of 'sink' small.

sinister See ADROIT.

siren From the Greek *sirenes*, 'entangler', the siren of mythology was a creature half woman, half bird whose sweet voice lured sailors to their doom. By extension the name was given to alluring women (compare VAMP), but the basic association was with sound. For this reason only the air-raid warnings of the Second World War became known as sirens, the name being most inappropriate from any other point of view. The word siren is now used for the sound signals used by police cars and ambulances and the mythological usage is quite obsolete.

sirloin of beef A traditional misspelling of the name of this joint of meat has led to a group of stories which describe an English king (variously Henry VIII, James I or Charles II) being so pleased with a joint served to him that he 'knighted' it for all time. The truth is that the joint is really *sur* loin, *sur* being French 'on' or 'above', and this joint coming next above the loin. The 'baron' of beef (two unseparated sirloins) takes its name by analogy.

234

sixes and sevens, *all at* This expression used to indicate a state of confusion has been (not very plausibly) related to dice players' jargon. The tradition of the City of London is that it relates to the dispute between the Merchant Taylors' and the Skinners' Companies as to which was sixth, and which seventh, in order of precedence. The dispute was resolved by the Billesden Award of 1494, when Sir Robert Billesden the Lord Mayor ordered that the Companies should take it in turns to be ranked as sixth and seventh respectively.

skedaddle Meaning 'to leave hurriedly', this term seems to have, as yet, no proven ancestry. There are allegations of Scandinavian roots and suggestions of dialectal forms in both England and Scotland before the word came into prominence in the United States. At the moment the matter must rest there.

skeleton at the feast This vivid phrase for that which acts as a grim reminder of the fact that 'in the midst of life we are in death' really needs no historic origin, but it is a fact that the Egyptians used a skeleton at their banquets to remind revellers of their mortal state. In a Roman triumph a slave stood in the chariot with the victorious general to whisper in his ear, 'Remember you are mortal'.

skin of my teeth, *to escape by the* It will probably surprise users of this cliché to know they are quoting the Bible. The phrase was first used in Job xix: 20.

skinheads By 1970 a new youth cult was in existence drawing its strength from an even younger, poorer and less sophisticated group. These were the skinheads, so called from their near shaven heads. Large boots (of specified brands) and braces were the cult badges. Weekly violence in loose association with football matches was the main activity, together with assaults on Pakistani immigrants, but oddly enough skinheads have shown some sympathy to the West Indians and have adopted reggae music as their own. Too poor even to think about a motorbike, puritanically opposing mod permissiveness, the skinhead might (if articulate) justify himself as the polar opposite of the HIPPY (q.v.).

slate, *put it on the*   See CHALK IT UP.

slave   The original slaves were the Slav peoples of Eastern Europe. The Norsemen sold them into Central and Western Europe in the Middle Ages, and this racial name became a common noun. The Roman word for slave, *servus*, survives as serf.

slave, *white*   This term for a woman compelled by terror into a life of prostitution finds its traditional origin in an incident in the career of Mary Hastings, a Chicago 'madame' of the 1890s. She is said to have lured girls into her house and having 'broken them in' sold them to other brothel keepers. One victim managed to throw out from a window a note with the message 'I am held as a slave'. She was rescued and a newspaper featured the story and coined the term 'white slavery'. Similar stories of women being kidnapped for enforced prostitution continue to crop up, a recent example being in Amiens, France, in 1969. They are often without foundation.

sledgehammer   The Anglo-Saxon word for a hammer was *slecg*. When English was under Scandinavian influence the word was 'clarified' by the addition of the Norse 'hammer' – which meant exactly the same thing! These 'doublets' are not uncommon. CAUSEWAY and PEA-JACKET are other examples.

sleep like a top   A spinning top is said to sleep when its movement is so rapid as to be imperceptible. Even granting this usage of sleep, the phrase is a very odd one.

sleep on a clothes line, *so tired I could*   In the nineteenth century in London and other cities down-and-outs who could not afford the cheapest bed sometimes slept on 'the twopenny rope'. The men sat on a bench and leaned on a line stretched tightly in front of them. Early in the morning the landlord would cut the rope and the sleepers would be promptly awakened.

sleeve, *to have something up your* The phrase here is from the practice of the conjuror, who often secreted objects in his sleeve and then suddenly produced them again to the surprise of his audience. The expression now always means 'to have a surprise in store'.

sleuth Now often used as a somewhat facetious word for a detective (Sherlock Holmes, the intrepid sleuth) the word once belonged to the sleuth-hound or bloodhound who followed a trail. The derivation is from *sloth*, Old Norse for 'trail'. The word also survives in the hunter's vocabulary as 'slot'. Detectives were first called 'sleuths' by Angus Reach in *Clement Lorimer or the Book with the Iron Clasp*, a serial which began publication in 1849.

slogan This was once a Gaelic word and originally *sluagh-ghairn*, 'shout of the army'. Current usage restricts it to a mere catchphrase or advertising jingle.

slope off The Saxons had a word *hleapan*, 'to jump'. From it we derive leap, but also 'lope', meaning to run with long easy strides. There is also the Saxon *slupan*, 'to slip', and 'slope' in the sense of hurried departure seems to combine both roots.

slops, slopchest This old word for sailors' working clothes or the chest in which they were kept derives from the coarse cloth of Salop, the standard abbreviation of Shropshire.

Smith, *Harvey* In Britain in August 1971, the show jumper Harvey Smith was accused of improper conduct at the Hickstead show-jumping ground. He was alleged to have raised two fingers at Mr Douglas Bunn, one of the judges, a gesture widely used to indicate utter contempt, the modern version of the 'fig' of Elizabethan days. Smith was threatened with the loss of his prize money but was later exonerated. As a result the phrase '. . . so I gave him the old Harvey Smith' gained some currency.

SNAFU A cynical phrase from Service life, of American origin in the Second World War. Spelled out, the message, intended to be encouraging though realistic, is Situation Normal All F(ouled) Up.

snag This Scandinavian word at first referred to any jagged projecting point, whether a broken tree branch or a sharp, malformed tooth. Its use is now largely metaphorical for any difficulty or obstruction.

snide Originally describing counterfeit coin or trashy 'jewellery' this word came to mean base, contemptible and has now in the phrase 'snide comment' assumed the sense of 'derogatory insinuation.'

snob The word is said to have been invented by Thackeray to describe George IV. The root of the word is the entry s. nob. (short for *sine nobilitate*, 'without nobility') which stood against the names of commoners in the college lists. Those without nobility, but with pretensions to it, were accordingly called snobs. In Cambridge the word snob was long used for the townsman as distinct from the 'gownsman' or member of the University

snooker This game, embodying features of billiards, pyramids and pool, appeared in the 1870s among army officers at Ootacumund in India. Its actual inventor is said to have risen to the rank of Field Marshall! Players who managed to leave the cue ball in virtually unplayable positions were called 'snookers', the slang term for first-year cadets at the Royal Military Academy, Woolwich and hence, to their seniors, 'the lowest form of life'. 'Snooker' tactics became characteristic of the game and gave it the name we know today.

social security As a phrase this goes back to the days of Franklin D. Roosevelt's New Deal policy of the 1930s. There was, for example, the Social Security Act of 1935. In 1943 *England's Road to Social Security* by Karl de Schweinitz was published, and the term gained much currency during the Labour Government of 1945–51.

soldier Since it derived from Latin *solidus*, 'a piece of money', the word soldier at first implied a mercenary or 'soldier for hire'.

song, *all this for a* This is said to have been Burleigh's angry retort when Queen Elizabeth ordered him to give one hundred pounds to Edmund Spenser the poet in return for his presentation to her of *The Faerie Queen*. The phrase 'going for a song' arises from this episode.

sop, *to be given a* The origin of this reference is the phrase 'a sop to Cerberus'. In Greek mythology Cerberus was the three-headed dog that guarded the gates of the underworld. Those who wished to enter the forbidden realms must give a sop, or wine-soaked cake, to Cerberus so that he would let them pass. One thinks of modern burglars giving liver to guard dogs. The phrase is now used for any pacifying bribe.

SOS It is quite untrue that this maritime distress signal in the Morse code really stands for 'Save our souls'. The three dots, three dashes and three dots were chosen for ease of transmission and recognition. See MAYDAY.

sound As a name for a narrow body of water, this is the Saxon *sund*, 'swimming'. A piece of water narrow enough to swim was a sound.

spade As a contemporary slang term for a coloured person, this derives from the old simile 'black as the Ace of Spades'. Has this been reinforced by the traditional advice that one should not shrink from 'calling a spade a spade'?

spade guinea The guinea was a British gold coin minted in the late eighteenth century and valued at twenty-one shillings. This coin acquired its nickname because the shield on the reverse resembled a spade. Brass near-facsimiles were made for use as counters or gambling chips, so that the poor could enjoy the brief illusion of playing for gold.

speculation We derive this word from the Latin *speculator*, 'spy', 'scout', 'observer'. By transference, it acquired the meaning of investigator, researcher, enquirer, hence its use to mean thought and imagination, but its modern commercial usage takes us back to the origin, for the speculator in business thinks he has spotted a good thing.

Speewah, *the* A legendary estate in the Australian outback where everything is bigger and better than anywhere else, a kind of mini-Texas of the Antipodes.

spell of duty, of work The Old English *gespelia*, 'substitute', is the root of this word and, strictly, one does a spell as a member of a shift, or of a gang taking over from a previous group of workers.

spencer Originally, this was a short overcoat, double-breasted and without tails, which was devised in the late eighteenth century by, and named after, the 2nd Earl Spencer (1758–1834). He wagered he could set a new fashion, simply by wearing it in the streets, and he won. In the early nineteenth century the same name was being given to a short, bodice-type jacket worn by women and children. In the later nineteenth century and early twentieth it was more frequently a knitted under-garment of fine wool or cotton, sometimes with short sleeves, worn for additional warmth.

sphinx See note on RIDDLE OF THE SPHINX.

spick and span Now meaning neat and well turned out, the phrase was at first descriptive of newness, 'spick and span new'. Spick was a 'spike' or 'nail', and span a 'wood chip', and the expression was first used of ships fresh from the ship-wrights and carpenters.

spike his guns Now it means to foil someone's plans, but it was at first quite literal. The old muzzle-loading cannon could be rendered quite useless by having a spike driven into the touch hole through which the charge was ignited.

spinster Now little used (substitutes such as 'bachelor girl'

240

have been experimented with), this word for an unmarried woman once described her main occupation. In pre-industrial days, the textile trade was conducted at cottage level. Weaving was a man's trade, women span. The wife would manage the household, while the unmarried girls were left with the spinning.

spiv Although a good authority says the word was used in the late-nineteenth-century racing circles for a sharper, or one who generally 'lived on his wits', spiv did not emerge into wider usage until the Second World War. In that context it was used for sellers of 'black market' goods or procurers of scarce 'off ration' commodites. The connection with its old sense is obvious. 'Spivs and drones' became a Press and even administrative synonym for 'shirkers and idlers'. A half-hearted campaign was even launched against them. The style of dress alleged to be favoured by spivs (and exemplified by that of comedian Arthur English) had strong similarities to that of the post-war 'Teds'. Folk etymology saw spiv as a reversal of V I Ps, officialese for distinguished visitors or very important persons.

splice In view of the fact that this is a slang term for 'marry', it is curious that its real meaning is 'split' or 'divide' (Dutch *splitsen*, German *spleiszen*). The word was at first nautical. A seaman would strengthen or mend a weak or damaged rope by cutting it at the weak point, and then, interweaving the strands of the two ends, reuniting it. Hence the 'marrying'.

sponge, *throw up the* A term from the boxing ring. For a second to throw up the sponge was a signal that he wanted to concede a win to prevent grave injury to the fighter he was backing. 'Throw in the towel' is used in the same way.

spoonerism The slips of the tongue that lead to the utterance of such things as 'You have hissed all my mystery lectures' instead of the intended 'You have missed all my history lectures' are called spoonerisms from the Rev. W. A. Spooner (1844–1930), Warden of New College, Oxford, who had this unfortunate habit. In a sermon he once said, 'The Lord is a shoving leopard'. See NEWTONISM.

spooning   An all but obsolescent expression now, this was once a specific reference to a Welsh courting custom in which the lover declared his intentions by carving a wooden spoon with appropriately symbolic ornament and presenting it to his sweetheart.

spouse   As a word meaning husband or wife, this is not quite true to its origins. It comes from Latin *sponsus*, 'fiancé', and *sponsa*, the feminine equivalent. The Italian expression *due sposi*, 'a newly married couple', shows the same development as has obviously taken place in English.

spruce up   *Pruce* was the old form of Prussia and is still preserved in the French *Prusse*. To 'spruce up' was to go out for a Prussian standard of smartness!

square the circle, *to*   This means to attempt the impossible and derives from a classic puzzle in mathematics: how to draw a square exactly equal in area to any given circle.

staid (strait-laced)   These two words, both indicating restricted sympathies, excessive seriousness of mind and a high degree of prudery, derive from the literal tight lacing of stays or corsets, once a common practice among women who aspired to be fashionably dressed.

stalemate   Whereas checkmate in chess wins the game, stalemate brings it to a stop with neither side an effective winner. When one player has his king only and must move, yet there is no square to which he may legally go, this is stalemate. The *stale* is a French form of 'stall', here meaning 'to be fixed', as in mire.

stalking horse   This specially trained animal allowed a hunter to conceal himself behind it in order to creep up on game undetected. The phrase is now used for any ostensible purpose that is not the real one. From the Saxon *stealcian*, 'to stalk'.

stand sam, *to*   This meant 'to be the victim of a highwayman'.

Sampsman was an old slang word for a highway robber and is perhaps linked to the German *sammeln*, 'to gather, to collect', via an Old English equivalent.

starboard and larboard   The two sides of a ship took their old names from the Saxon *steor*, 'steering or rudder' side, and the *leere*, 'empty' side. See PORT.

steep, *that's a bit*   The traditional origin of this expression of incredulity is said by the poet Samuel Rogers to have been as follows. George IV (better known to posterity by his previous title of Prince Regent) made the completely false claim that he had ordered a troop of cavalry to charge down the side of the impossibly precipitous Devil's Dyke near Brighton. Upon which the Duke of Wellington merely observed to him 'Very steep, sir, very steep.'

steeplechase   Cross-country horse races derive their name, it is said, from a chance occasion when a number of foxhunters agreed to race in a direct line and over any intervening obstacles to a distant church steeple, the winner to be the first who touched it with his whip. Racing 'over the sticks' (brushwood fences) is carried out under 'National Hunt Rules' in Britain, whilst ordinary racing is 'flat racing'. The steeple in question was that of Doneraile Church, in County Cork, Ireland, and the first steeplechase riders were named O'Callaghan and Edmund Blake.

stem the tide, the flow   There is really no story of origin here, for the Old Norse *stemma* means 'to stop the flow of' something and we are simply using the same word.

stepfather, -mother   This word for a nominal relationship arising from a second marriage is Saxon and derives from a word meaning 'by bereavement'.

sterling   This traditional qualification of the English monetary unit, 'the pound sterling', derives from the medieval merchants of the Hanse (a Baltic-based trading association), who were known in England as the 'Easterlings', 'Easterners'. Their weights and coinage were of well-known integrity.

243

steward The first holder of this village office was a *stigweard*, or Saxon 'sty ward', who looked after the village pigs. Only later did he evolve into estate manager.

stick, *to cut one's* Meaning 'to up and away' this phrase is usually explained with reference to the idea of cutting a staff for a journey. Suggestions of pilgrims cutting palm staves to prove that they had been in the Holy Land are no more than flights of fancy. A better explanation is found in the English rural custom by which a farmhand hired for a year could indicate that he did not wish to renew the contract by cutting a stick from the hedge and placing it in the chimney corner of the farmhouse. This convention obviated what might have been an embarrassing encounter.

stickler Used now for anyone who is particular about details, it originally meant an umpire in traditional wrestling. The word long survived in this sense in Cornwall, though it is oddly enough not Celtic but Saxon *stightlen*, 'settle a dispute'.

stir This slang term for prison is from the Romany *stiriben*, *stiripen*, 'prison'. 'In stir' became a standard expression in the underworld. Did stir suggest the term porridge, also slang for a prison sentence? Or does this simply derive from that most common breakfast food?

stock In all its senses one may trace this back to the Saxon *stocc*, 'a log', 'a stick'. A man's woodpile was his wealth and guarantee of winter comfort. It came to mean any accumulation and was the old economists' word for capital.

stoker This has the same origin as stock. The original stoker fed wood fires only.

story In many contexts the word 'story' is identified with positive falsehood, yet it is actually Greek in origin and means 'history'.

streaking The craze for seeking to make the front page by running naked through a public place hit the headlines in March 1974. The distinction of inaugurating the new 'sport' is disputed between the University of Texas at Austin and Memphis State University. The name derives from the quick dash – like a streak of lightning.

strike   The word for strike is a local coinage in each country, and we see little sign of international borrowing. Our English word relates to the 'striking', i.e. taking down of sails and yards on a ship to ensure it could not sail.

stump up, *to*   This is (somewhat doubtfully) derived from the practice of American 'stump orators' taking collections after their addresses to a crowd. The stump is the tree-stump favoured by impromptu speakers as a platform. In England the 'soap box' was preferred. 'Stumping the country' is systematic political campaigning.

sundae   The law of Virginia forbade the selling of soda-fountain drinks on a Sunday, so a drugstore proprietor of Norfolk, Virginia, 'thickened' a drink with fruit and ice cream until it became, in the eyes of the law, a meal. It was a Sunday drink. Hence the name.

swallow (*one swallow does not make a summer*)   It is interesting to note that over two thousand years ago Aristotle knew a version of this saying. In his more southerly clime, one swallow did not make a spring.

swan-song   Meaning a last, truly memorable, splendid performance, this term derives from an ancient, but quite unfounded belief, that the swan sings but once in its life, superbly, just before it dies. 'Swans sing before they die, 'twere no bad thing/If some folks were to die before they sing.'

swindle   Of German origin, the word, though certainly not the practice, was introduced by Jewish immigrants to Britain in the mid-eighteenth century.

sycophant   In ancient Athens a law was once passed forbidding the export of figs. In time this became generally ignored, but remained 'a dead letter' on the statute book. To inform against a man who broke this long-lapsed prohibition was a form of vexatious conduct sometimes indulged in out of malice or a desire to attract the attention of the authorities to oneself as a conscientious citizen. The verb *sycophantein* originally meant 'to lay information against another for exporting figs', and in effect a cross between a toady and an informer, something for which our language still uses the word 'sycophant'.

T

T, *it fits to a* The T is the draughtsman's T-square, a rule with a crosspiece at one end exactly at right angles and enabling exactly parallel lines to be drawn.

tabby Why a tabby cat? Because it displays the wavy markings of watered silk once associated with Atabi, the silk-weavers' quarter of old Baghdad.

table d'hôte The literal meaning of this French phrase is 'the table of the host'. Travellers who agreed to eat at the host's table might well expect to pay less than those who wished to order something special. Compare the more plebeian POT LUCK.

taboo In its original sense this Polynesian word meant 'sacred', and therefore not to be touched by the unauthorised. It does not directly mean 'forbidden'.

tailor This was in the first instance a borrowing from the French *tailleur*, 'cutter', and that had a Latin original, *talea*, 'something cut'. So much has the origin of the word been forgotten that tailors employ assistant 'cutters'.

take a rise out of him A metaphor from fishing, this refers to the casting of a fly on to the surface of the water to make it rise. To trick someone into doing something foolish is to 'take a rise out of them'.

taken aback See ABACK.

take the cake See CAKE-WALK.

talent The first use of this word was as the name of a Greek weight of precious metal usable as a coin. Its transformation into the sense of natural ability or skill begins with the symbolic application of the Parable of the Talents in Matthew xxv: 14–30.

talisman Properly a talisman is a ring or other object engraved with characters and capable of producing magical effects by means of its inherent power. The exact origin is uncertain, but it seems to be a corruption of something from the Islamic world, possibly Persian.

talk turkey This means to talk profitable business, to talk to some purpose. It is derived from an apocryphal story about a white man and an Indian who hunted together and agreed to share the game piece by piece. They killed two turkeys and three crows. The white man gave a crow to the Indian, a turkey to himself, another crow to the Indian, another turkey to himself. When the Indian objected he was told, 'You have three birds, I have only two.' He replied, 'Stop talking birds. Talk turkey.'

tally The original tally was a wooden rod on which notches were cut to mark numbers or amounts according to a conventional system. The tally was then cut down the middle and one half given as a receipt. In case of dispute the two parts could be brought together to see if they tallied. The word has the same origin as tailor, the French *tailler*, 'to cut'. The English Exchequer used tallies until the end of the eighteenth century, and when the vast accumulation was disposed of in 1834 the Houses of Parliament were accidentally burnt down. See also SCORE.

tally ho   This traditional cry of hunters to incite the dogs to the chase when the quarry is seen is Norman French, virtually unchanged from the original *ta-i-aut*.

tandem   This name for two horses driven one behind the other, or for a bicycle for two people, must have been a university joke, for *tandem* is a Latin adverb meaning 'at length'.

tank   At first an Indian word for an irrigation reservoir, tank was adopted for any large water container. When in the First World War a new type of armoured vehicle was devised they were, for security purposes, described as 'bulk water carriers'. Sir Ernest Swinton, their chief inventor, suggested they should be called tanks, and the name stuck.

tanner   This slang for the old sixpenny piece in pre-decimal British currency has been derived from the Romany *tano*, 'small', but it was not the smallest silver coin, nor through much of the last century was sixpence an insignificant sum!

tantalise   This word for the raising and then disappointment of hopes derives from the mythological character Tantalus, punished in this way for giving to mortals the food of the gods. He stood in water up to his chin. When he bent to drink it receded. Fruit hung within his reach. When he stretched out his hand it withered. A 'tantalus' is a lock-up stand for spirit bottles. They may be seen, but cannot be taken out and opened without the key.

tapis, *sur le*   This French phrase means literally 'on the carpet' but does not have the same meaning as that phrase in English. It means 'up for discussion or consideration' no more.

tar   As name for a sailor see JACK.

tar brush, *a touch of*   This phrase of former days was once a 'polite' way of conveying that someone had a coloured ancestor. Racial prejudice is rarely expressed directly.

tarred with the same brush The reference here may well be to the practice of marking one's flock of sheep in some distinctive way, though the tone of the phrase implies the bad character of those so marked. The origin cannot be clearly established.

tattoo Now used for a military display or pageant, especially one held after dark, tattoo (formerly *tap-to*) was a Dutch word for the drum signal ordering the publicans to 'shut up shop' and recalling the troops to barracks. Tattoo as incised or punctured body decoration derives from the Tahitian *tatau*. Although the practice was known in Europe, it was most characteristic of the Pacific cultures.

tawdry This word, meaning 'cheap and gaudy', is a corruption of St Audrey's lace, as sold at St Audrey's Fair, at Ely in Cambridgeshire. The original lace was by no means tawdry, but the cheap imitations were. Audrey is a popular form of Etheldreda in whose honour the fair was established.

teach your grandmother to suck eggs This classic allusion to the tendency of the young to instruct those much more experienced than themselves exists in several variants. In 1542 it was '. . . to teach our dame to spin'. In 1611 we get '. . . teach his grandame to grope ducks'. The egg-sucking theme first appears in the writings of Jonathan Swift (1667–1745).

teddy bear This popular toy is of comparatively recent origin, having been named after Theodore 'Teddy' Roosevelt (1858–1919), twenty-sixth President of the United States 1901–9, who was a keen hunter.

Teddy boys, Teds By the mid-fifties in Britain wartime austerity was at last gone and the first rumblings of 'the youth revolution' could be heard. Gangs of working-class boys began to affect a style of dress with long jackets, narrow trousers and thick-soled shoes. Though known as 'Edwardian', this costume owed something to the 'spiv' of the wartime years. Their favouring of rock 'n' roll music was the bridge that linked this group with the later rockers/greasers.

teeth are drawn, *his* In an old fable a lion agreed to have his teeth drawn and his claws cut so he might marry the beautiful maid he covets. When the deed was done, the maid and her father killed the lion. Conversely, the enactment of a law 'with teeth' is sometimes called for, meaning something capable of really tackling the problem in question.

teetotal The word is always said to be derived from the stuttering utterance of one Joseph Turner of Preston, Lancs, who, at a meeting in favour of total abstinence from alcohol in 1833, said, 'Nothing but t-t-t-t-total abstinence will do . . .' The expression was seized upon in derision, but taken up by the movement of abstainers to describe their position.

'Tell it to the marines' See MARINES.

tenant A tenant is a person who holds property and the word is ultimately from the Latin *tenere*, 'to hold'. The French form is *tenir* and *tenant* is the present participle. In England, in strict legal theory, all land is 'held' from the Crown. The principle was established at the Norman Conquest.

Tender-loin district New San Francisco euphemism for 'red light district'. The term first surfaced in 1974 when the first National Hookers' Convention was held in that city.

tenterhooks A tenter ground was a place where freshly prepared cloth was dried and stretched between 'tenterhooks'. The word is from the Latin *tendere*, 'to stretch'. To be on tenterhooks is figurative language for being in a state of suspense and anxiety.

tenth nation *the* Term coined by Dr Patrick Hillery for the twelve-million strong community of 'guest workers' on whom the EEC depends. The 'tenth nation' is mostly drawn from Yugoslavia, Turkey, Portugal and Spain.

Test 'Ashes' See ASHES.

tête-à-tête This expression for an intimate or private conversation is French and means literally 'head to head'. In English there is a similar phrase in 'Let us put our heads together', with the unspoken continuation 'and devise a solution between us'.

tether, *at the end of his*   A tether ('tedder' is a dialect variant) is a rope or chain which restricts the grazing of the tethered animal to a circle around the point to which the tether is fixed. In metaphor the expression implies being frustrated to the point of distraction.

'There but for the grace of God . . .'   This famous phrase was first uttered by John Bradford (1510–55) and, when first uttered, was completed 'goes John Bradford'. He said it on seeing criminals on their way to execution.

thespians   As a name for actors this derives from Thespia, Greek poet of the sixth century B.C., accepted as the 'father of Greek tragedy'.

thieves, *as thick as*   Now used to mean that two people are in very close collusion. Theodore Hook in *The Parson's Daughter* (1833) first used our form of it, adapting from the French *comme larrons en foire* 'like thieves at a fair'.

thimble   The Old Norse *thumall* meant the thumb of a glove and a leather 'thumb-stall' was the first effective thimble. Metal thimbles did not come into England until the seventeenth century.

third degree   This was an originally American term for the harsh interrogation of a reluctant prisoner. It derives from Freemasonry, or rather from the popular opinions of it, specifically that the initiation into the Third Degree was a particularly frightening experience.

third sector   Term coined by American writer Theodore Levitt, in a book of that title, to denote the large-scale charity/campaign/pressure groups which vie with government and big business in the making of public policy.

third world This term for the ex-colonial 'emerging' nations who are not committed to either the United States or communist power blocs has been ascribed to Professor Peter Worsley the Manchester University sociologist.

thistle Tradition says that the thistle was adopted as the emblem of Scotland after an unsuccessful attack by the Danes on Stirling Castle, which was foiled when one of the would-be attackers cried out after treading on a thistle, thus revealing the danger.

three-legged mare Highwayman's slang for the gallows, either because of its three parts or because of its tripodal base. Although current in the seventeenth and eighteenth centuries this type of expression has a Norse or Saxon ring about it.

three sheets in the wind See SHEETS.

threshold The word is Saxon and links with the idea of threshing or beating. It is the step that is trodden by all who enter conjecturally *thersewald*, 'beaten wood'.

thug In current English, a ruffian, but originally an Indian devotee of the goddess Kali, who in return for the honours they gave her, permitted her worshippers to prey upon all travellers provided they were killed in a prescribed manner and in secret. The sect was extirpated in the nineteenth century by British officials.

thunder, *to steal someone's* This is sometimes believed to derive from classical mythology but in fact the phrase was coined to fit his own case by John Dennis (1657–1734), major critic, very minor playwright and inventor of the theatrical thunder sheet. He is said to have complained that while the theatres thought little of his plays, 'They steal my thunder.'

tiara The Papal mitre with the triple crown is the original European tiara, but the word itself comes from Persia via Ancient Greece. In Persia and the land of the Medes it also signified a head-dress denoting high office.

tick, *have it on*   This means to buy on credit and is an abbreviated form of 'on the ticket', i.e. a note would be made of the debt. Compare ON THE SLATE, CHALK IT UP.

ticket, *that's the*   This phrase reminds us that ticket is a variant of *etiquette*, which has the meaning of 'appropriate conduct'. 'That's the ticket' means 'Just the right thing'.

tiger, *paper*   When in August 1946 Mao Tse-tung was interviewed by an American journalist Anna Louise Strong, he several times used the expression 'paper tiger': 'The atomic bomb . . . is a paper tiger'; 'All reactionaries are paper tigers'. A firmer mastery of English must have produced the less colourful 'empty threat' or even 'pantomime dragon'. The interpreter suggested 'scarecrow' but Chairman Mao insisted on his own choice and a memorable phrase was born.

tinker's damn, tinker's cuss   See DAM.

toast   It was an old custom to put toast into tankards of beer to improve the flavour and, according to a surely apocryphal story recounted in *The Tatler*, this practice led to a bizarre incident at Bath and the giving of a new expression to the language. The story is as follows. A celebrated beauty (of the time of Charles II) was in the Cross Bath when one of her admirers took a glass of the water, in which the fair one stood, and drank her health to the company. A bystander, half drunk, said he would jump in the water, for, 'though he liked not the liquor, he would have the toast', meaning the lady herself. Hence, it is said, 'The present honour which is done to the lady we mention in our liquor who has ever since been called a toast.'

tobacco   According to the Spanish writer Oviedo, *tobaco* was the Y-shaped tube through which the Caribs of Haiti inhaled smoke. This is confirmed by the fact that the island of Tobago gets its name from the resemblance of its shape to that of the Carib pipe. Another Spanish writer, Las Casas, uses tobacco for the primitive 'cigar' smoked by some Indians. It was the

Spaniards who really fixed the name to the herb rather than to the instrument.

tobyman A slang term for highwayman, *toby* being the 'high road'.

toff The gentlemen commoners of Oxford, the noble students at the University, were permitted golden tassels or tufts on their academic caps or 'mortar boards'. Toff is a corruption of tuft.

togs This has been a slang word for clothes for some three hundred years and seems to derive from the Roman toga.

Tommy Atkins As representative of the typical British soldier this name goes back to 1815, when a specimen form in the 'Soldier's Account Book' of that year showed the name Thomas Atkins. Every soldier had a copy of the 'Account Book' and so 'Tommy' came to stand for the average soldier as G I Joe has done in the United States. The story that Tommy Atkins was a soldier mortally wounded under Wellington in the Netherlands in 1794, and that the Duke of Wellington personally chose the name for inclusion in the army document seems to be a legend of modern origin.

tommy gun About 1919 the American general John Taliaferro Thompson (1860–1940) was the joint inventor of the light form of machine gun, fired from the hip or shoulder, which was called the Thompson machine gun, and was adopted by the United States Marine in 1928 and then by the Coast Guard. When the detachable stock was removed, for firing from the hip, it was small enough to be carried easily and unobtrusively, and derived forms of it, known as tommy guns, were the favourite weapon of American gangsters in the 1930s, hence the nickname 'the Chicago piano'. It is also a traditional weapon of the Irish Republican Army terrorists. The shortened form of the name is now applied to all weapons of this general type.

tommy rot Tommy shops were the company-owned food

254

stores where the worker paid under the now forbidden 'truck' system was compelled to receive part of his wages in over-valued goods. 'Tommy rot' was what they gave you at the tommy shop. Tommy is still used by some industrial workers for the food they take to eat at work.

ton up (boy, girl) The 'ton' is motorcyclists' slang for the speed of 100 m.p.h. 'Doing a ton' is achieving this speed, illegally, on the public highway and to have done this is 'having the ton up'. The expression 'ton up boy' is sometimes loosely used for any young motorcycling enthusiast.

tooth and nail, *to go for something* This proverbial phrase indicating 'with the utmost vigour' is at least as old as 1533 being used then by the writer Nicholas Udall (1504–56).

toothpick, *Arkansas* This very old American expression for a dagger is a sophisticated (Eastern Seaboard) comment on the crudities of frontier life.

topsy-turvy This expression has been in print since 1528 but as yet no authenticated origin can be ascribed to it. A probable origin is the obsolete *terve*, meaning 'to topple'.

torch This originates from the Latin *torca*, from *torquere*, 'to twist', for Roman torches were lengths of twisted rope.

Tory As a political designation in Britain this goes back to the time of Charles II. The word 'tory' had been an Irish word for brigand, and was first applied to Irish guerrillas who warred on British settlers, the guerrillas naturally being Roman Catholics. Hence the word was applied to English supporters of the claims of the Roman Catholic James to succeed his brother on the throne. In the eighteenth century it was the name of the country party still suspected of lingering Jacobite sympathies. It yielded place to 'Conservative' from 1830 onwards, as the official name of the party, but is still very much alive as a term of quasi-abuse by political opponents. In the American War of Independence 'Tory' was a term often used for the 'loyalists'.

towel, *throw in the* See SPONGE.

trade winds These have nothing to do with trade in the modern sense though this is the popular (and false) explanation of the word. The true derivation is from the Anglo-Saxon *tredan*, 'to tread' (in a regular track being understood), as in the fuller expression 'to tread out a path'. *Tredan* is also the origin of our modern word 'trade'.

tram, tramway This derives from the Old German *traam*, 'a beam', or Swedish *tram*, 'log'. The first tramways were in and around coalmines and they ran on wooden rails.

traps As a slang term for luggage this is a shortened form of 'trappings', the elaborate 'horse furnishings' that once symbolised a man's status in society.

trick, *worth two of that* This phrase, still in current usage, is in fact pure Shakespeare coming from *I Hentry IV*, II. i.

triffid Species of imaginary plant created by John Wyndham in his novel *The Day of the Triffids* (1951). Seven feet high and cultivated for the valuable oil obtainable from their thick bulbous stems, they were equipped with a fatal poisonous sting, were able to move about on three stick-like legs, and were possessed of a collective intelligence and ability to communicate with one another. Following a successful radio serialisation the name was popularly given to any large rampant weed.

trooper, *to swear like a* Of all military men it is the trooper who has been saddled, in popular speech with all the worst features of military swagger. In former times one could eat and lie like a trooper as well but today anything but 'swear' is obsolete.

trounce Meaning to beat severely, this is related to the Old French *troncer*, 'to cut off', as one does a piece of wood. In fact it means to cudgel someone, or even, using a related word, to 'truncheon' them.

256

trousers The French verb *trousser*, 'to bundle up', is the odd origin of the name of the garment. Our word truss is a close relation.

trousseau Derived from the French *trousse*, 'a bundle', this is, of course, the 'bundle' a bride gets together in preparation for her marriage. See entry on TROUSERS for some associated words.

troy weight This weight system, now reserved for precious metals, was that used at the great fair of Troyes in France.

truck (*to have no truck with*) To have no dealings with. From the French *troquer*, 'to barter'. One abuse in the early days of the Industrial Revolution was the truck system by which wages were paid in goods, not cash.

trump, trumps See CARDS.

tryst This word for an appointed meeting (compare RENDEZVOUS) is, in fact, a variant of trust.

tuft hunter One who seeks to mingle with the mighty. See TOFF.

tumbler Certain early drinking glasses had a rounded base or even a pointed one and so would stand only when empty and inverted. Any other way and they would tumble.

tweed This word for a soft woollen twilled (two-threaded) fabric is the result of bad handwriting. A consignment of such cloth was sent to a James Lock in London in 1829 and labelled *tweal*. Since it came from the vicinity of the River Tweed the name was misread, but has since remained the standard description.

tweezers The origin here is the French *étui*, a small case of instruments for personal use. It is nearly enough the contemporary 'manicure set'. The plural 'tweeses' was derived to mean 'small instruments' and evolved into 'tweezers'.

twig it Twig, meaning 'to see the point' or 'understand', derives from the Irish *tuigim*, 'I understand'.

tycoon This US term for a big-business man is of direct Japanese origin, being *T'ai Kun*, dominant figure'.

U

U *and* non-U In *Noblesse Oblige* (1956), both edited and contributed to by Nancy Mitford, she popularised an analysis of English vocabulary and usage, devised by Professor Alan Ross, in which pairs of words of apparently identical meaning are distinguished as U (preferred by the upper class) or non-U. Lavatory and toilet; looking-class and mirror; napkin and serviette, are all listed as blatant betrayers of social standing. The thesis is perhaps more interesting as a documentation of the English obsession with social class than as a guide to practical usage, for few things are as ephemeral as the 'established'. Professor Ross applied a similar classification to English pronunciation in *How to pronounce it* (1970).

uckeye This soldiers' slang of the First World War for 'All right' is a corruption of the Hindustani *uchcha*.

ugly as sin This phrase first appeared in print in Sir Walter Scott's *Kenilworth* in 1821.

ulster (*coat*) A type of overcoat, frequently mentioned in the Sherlock Holmes stories. Long, full-fitting and often with a waistbelt, it was made in the rough woollen cloth known as frieze, and was first marketed as the 'Ulster overcoat' by a Belfast firm in 1867. It became popular for its warmth and weatherproof qualities.

umbrage, *to take* *Umbra* is Latin for 'shadow' or 'shade' and umbrage is the resentment we feel when overshadowed or neglected. The word 'umbrella', meaning 'little shade', has the same origin.

umpire As in the cases of 'apron' and 'adder', this is a word which has lost a significant first letter. 'Umpire' should be 'numpire', from Old French *nompair*, derived in turn from Latin *non*, 'not', and *par*, 'equal'. The umpire is the 'odd' man with the casting vote to settle points of dispute.

umpteen This handy term for some indefinite though decidedly large number (only the synthetic language Esperanto has a direct equivalent in *umdek*) originated in Army signallers' slang during the First World War. Ack-emma and pip-emma, from a.m. and p.m., are other well-known examples.

uncle As a euphemism for a pawnbroker this word has no clearly established origin. It was in use in the 1750s. A suggested derivation from Latin *uncus*, 'hook', is implausible.

Uncle Sam Despite many picturesque legends, such as those about Sam Wilson an army supplier of Troy, N Y, there is little serious doubt that this expression is no more than a facetious interpretation of the initials U S which were first widely 'advertised' on the side of government wagons. Uncle Sam is first recorded in print in 1813 (*Troy Post* of 7 September) and in a book (*The Adventures of Uncle Sam*) in 1816. The cartoonist's picture of Uncle Sam owes much to the earlier symbolic figure of Jack Downing (q.v.).

under the rose, *told* Meaning in strict confidence, the phrase derives from the ancient use of the rose as a symbol of silence and discretion, the flower of Venus, consecrated by her son Cupid to the God of Silence. Discretion must preserve silence about the affairs of Venus. The plaster ornament in the centre of a ceiling is sometimes called the rose, as it was a standard motif for that position, all conversation in the room then being 'under the rose'.

under the weather The first record of this phrase in print is in Robert Louis Stevenson's novel *The Wrecker* (1892), 'You must not fancy I am sick, only . . . under the weather.'

underwriter This term from the world of insurance is in fact quite literal. This person alone, or with others, writes his name under the written text of the policy to announce that he (and the others if any) accepts the risk. Underwrite can thus be used in the wider sense of guarantee.

university From the Latin *universitas*, 'the whole', because at the universities the whole range of learning, *universitas litera-rum*, was available to students. By extension *universitas* came to mean a guild or corporation, in England of masters who accepted students, but in many Continental cities of students who chose or hired teachers.

unlucky in love, lucky at play We find an indirect reference to this proverbial saying in Swift's *Polite Conversations* of 1738 as follows: 'Well, miss, you'll have a sad husband, you have such good luck at cards.' This is, however, most unlikely to be its first actual use.

Unready, *Ethelred the* In Saxon this king was nicknamed *unrede*, sometimes half-translated as redeless. *Rede* means 'good counsel', *unrede* is the opposite. A poetic rendering would be 'Ethelred of Evil Counsel' or, mundanely, 'Ethelred the ill-advised'.

unturned, *leave no stone* This faithful old cliche, still in popular use, first appeared in the fifth century B.C. After the defeat of the Persians at Plataea the Greek Polycrates sought in vain for the treasure they were believed to have abandoned. Going at last to the Oracle at Delphi, he was told to leave no stone unturned. He went to the tent of the defeated Persian general and found the treasure under the floor.

unwashed, *the great* This contemptuous term for the common people was coined by Edmund Burke in the age of the French Revolution. He also coined the phrase 'the swinish multitude'. The choice of words indicates Burke's political tendency with admirable clarity.

'Up Guards and at 'em' These words of incitement to one last, magnificent effort are always attributed to Wellington at Waterloo. The Guards did not in fact make the final charge (this was made by the 52nd Light Infantry) and Wellington did not say these words.

upper ten This term for the aristocratic 'upper crust' of society was first coined by an American author, N. P. Willis (1806–67). It was originally 'the upper ten thousand' and denoted the estimated number of 'High Society' people in New York.

up the spout This is an allusion to the pawnbrokers who sent the pledged articles up to the storeroom via a 'service hoist' device. Once redeemed, the goods would be sent back 'down the spout' again.

usher In the eighteenth century this was the common word for an assistant teacher. Today it denotes a minor court official or, usually in the feminine form of 'usherette', a cinema or theatre attendant. It is the French *huissier* (from *huis*, which derives from the Latin *ostium*, 'a door') and loosely means 'door-keeper'.

usquebaugh This Irish word, properly *uisge-beatha*, 'water of life', is the original name of whisky.

utopia An ideal, but impracticable, state of human society. Sir Thomas More coined the word, from the Greek *ou*, 'not', and *topos*, 'place', hence meaning 'nowhere', for the imaginary island of socially advanced ideas he described in his book of the same title, *Utopia*, in 1516. Plato had had the similar idea of describing an ideal republic, and utopian literature has become a recognised genre, although the states described in later books tend to be satirised and not ideal.

V

vade-mecum This rather old-fashioned phrase for a small book or manual of essential information is simply the Latin for 'Go with me', indicating the book's function as a friend in need. We have mentioned above the similarly used word 'manual' from the Latin *manus*, 'a hand', and implying, as with the vade-mecum, portability and usefulness. The old

261

manual fell out of use in the Renaissance period when scholars wishing to display their new Greek learning used the word *encheiridion*, which is no more than the Greek for manual, and comes from *kheir*, 'hand'. In the nineteenth century 'handbook', from the German *Handbuch*, was put into circulation. It had in fact been known to and used by the Saxons, but had been despised by the learned until its resurrection in modern times.

vagabond The origin of this is Latin *vagari*, 'to wander', but in the course of time it has picked up certain romantic associations (as in the operetta *The Vagabond King*) which are quite lacking in the word 'vagrant' which has exactly the same origin. This romantic aura was perhaps picked up by association with actors who, because they were 'strolling players', were condemned by the law as 'masterless men' and 'rogues and vagabonds'. It is curious to note that the law's term 'rogue' is of unknown origin, but was picked up from the semi-criminal subculture it was seeking to suppress.

valance Not often seen nowadays, a valance was formerly a kind of short curtain round the framework of a bed or, if the bed was a four-poster, round the canopy of that. The usual origin suggested is from Old French *avaler*, 'to descend'. Other possibilities are from Valencia in Spain, formerly a great centre for textiles much used for bed linen, or even from Valenciennes, the famous lace-making town of north-east France. The bed valance frequently had lace on it.

valentine In the twentieth century a valentine is a specially styled greetings card sent to someone of the opposite sex on St Valentine's Day (14 February) as a token of romantic attachment. The card may also be satirical, though rarely nowadays openly cruel, which was often the case in the nineteenth century. These usually anonymous greetings derived from the custom, which continued into the nineteenth century, of choosing a sweetheart on St Valentine's Day, which was by tradition the day on which the birds chose their mates. It is

262

said that there was a similar custom in ancient Roman times on 13 February and that the Christian clergy vainly tried to substitute the choosing of patron saints for the choosing of sweethearts. Today what is left of the valentine custom is due more to the greeting-card industry than to popular interest, as today's social system has little place for such indirect courtship.

valet This name for a gentleman's personal servant comes from the Old French *vaselet*, which in turn is a shortening of the still older *vassalet*, meaning 'vassal'. In feudal days a 'vassal' was someone bound by oath to an overlord and 'vassalet' was a diminutive of this. Today, a shop offering 'valet service' presses and repairs clothes, one of the main duties of the traditional valet. The obsolete word 'varlet', moulded by a variant pronunciation, has the same ultimate origin, but as with so many words concerning the socially despised (blackguard and villain are other examples) took a downward path and gained associations of obsequiousness and treachery.

vamoose This is another derivative of the Spanish *vamos*, 'Let's go'. (The other is 'MOSEY'.) The word came into use in the American South-West as a result of contact with the Spanish-speaking settlers there, but, as is often the case, somewhat changed its meaning. In American English 'vamoose' is more often an instruction to a third party than a suggestion to one's companions.

vamp The oldest meaning of this word is 'the upper front part of a boot or shoe' and comes from the Old French *vampe*, a form of *avantpied*, 'before or in front of the foot' (*avant* + *pied*). Since one could 'revamp' a shoe the word took on the extra meaning of patching up, repairing or improvising especially of improvising musical accompaniments by means of the slightly varied repetition of a few musical phrases. The term was also used in a similar literary sense. In the United States a 'vamp' was a slang term for a fireman, and this most

263

probably takes us back to the 'boot' associations. There is also another vamp of quite different character and origins, the unscrupulous woman who uses her charm to enthrall, exploit and finally ruin the men who fall under her spell. The type was not unknown to the nineteenth-century theatre, but it was the cinema that publicised the type and name of vamp, which in this usage is generally agreed to be a derivation from 'vampire'.

vampire The word itself is common to several Balkan languages, for example Serbian and Turkish, but is also found by adoption in Hungarian (properly Magyar) and it is from this source that it came into the English language. In Balkan folklore a vampire was one of the 'undead', an apparently deceased person who maintained a nocturnal life by coming out of the tomb to feed upon the blood of the living. The vampire tradition owes its widest circulation to Bram Stoker's famous novel *Dracula* (1897). The fifteenth-century prince of Rumania Vlad V, known as 'the impaler', seems to have been the original of 'Count Dracula', but he was never a vampire in any sense of the word. It is, however, far too late to break the association between the name and the activity!

van The vehicle into which we load goods for transport gets its name from an abbreviation of caravan which is the Arabic *qairawan*, the train of laden camels carrying merchandise. The application of caravan to the gipsy vehicle is a comparatively late one. The proper Romany word here is *vardo*, best translated as 'living wagon'. The van of vanguard, the leading units of an army on the march, derives from the French *avant*, 'in front'.

vandals Today a vandal is anyone guilty of wanton destruction. The original Vandals were a Germanic tribe who, under their king Genseric, sacked Rome in A.D. 435. The Vandals eventually settled in Spain and Northern Africa, but their name has been unpleasantly immortalised by their destructive foray into Italy.

Vatican The palace of the Pope (and the surrounding Vatican City) takes its name from the Mons Vaticanus or Vatican Hill of Ancient Rome, and the word Vaticanus derived from the Latin *vates*, 'prophet' or 'soothsayer'. Our modern word vaticinate, 'to act as a prophet', has the same origin.

vaudeville This American word for light theatrical entertainment (British usage would prefer the word 'variety') comes from the French phrase *chanson du Vau de Vire*, 'song of the Vire valley'. The Vire is a river in Normandy and its valley was the home ground of Olivier Basselin, a poet and song writer of the fifteenth century, whose topical and satirical songs created a style that was to flourish in later centuries.

vegetate This verb is often used as descriptive of a dull life in the country and is a typically urban sneer. To the student of origins it might seem more than a little unfair, since the word's root is the Latin *vegetatio*, 'growth', and *vegetare*, 'to enliven'. However, whatever the origin of the word's form may be, modern usage contrasts the lively movements and responses of the animal world with the passive and fixed life of the plant. Today people suffering such severe brain damage as to make normal action and reaction impossible are often described as being 'reduced to vegetable existence'.

vendetta This Corsican word for the blood feud, a virtual state of private war between two families in which the duty of killing one of the enemy clan is passed on from one generation to another, takes its name from the Latin *vindicta*, 'vengeance'. Our word vindictive, which means 'seeking vengeance', has the same root.

venial sins Venial is from the Latin *venia*, 'pardon, forgiveness', and the expression is used in the teaching of the Roman Church to distinguish lesser offences, which may be forgiven, from those mortal sins which result in spiritual death.

ventriloquism The art of the ventriloquist, now used exclusively for entertainment, was almost certainly not unknown to some of the ancient priests of the oracles. Our word is from the Latin but the Greeks had an exactly parallel form because both peoples subscribed to the same theory of this undetectable speech, namely that it somehow came from the stomach. The word derives from a form of *venter*, 'the belly', and *loqui*, 'to speak'.

verb. sap. This veiled warning is an abbreviated Latin phrase, *verbum sapienti*, which means 'A word to the wise man . . .', the implication being that what has been said is but a hint of a fuller story that could if necessary be fully told.

verdict Like so many legal expressions in English, this term comes to us from Norman French in the first instance, but ultimately from the Latin. Its French form was *verdit*, from the Latin *vere dictum*, 'a true saying', which explains exactly what a jury is supposed to give to the court.

verger The name of this church official derives from the Latin *virgarius*, 'the carrier of a rod or wand'. The verger now often does little more than show people to their places and act as a kind of janitor, though in a cathedral church he is something more dignified and a member of the bishop's entourage. The same word for rod (Old French *verge* or Latin *virga*) was also used to indicate the physical extent of an official's power or jurisdiction in the sense of 'the area within which the sign of office may be displayed'. The verge or limit of jurisdiction of the king's court (an important matter because offences committed on this territory were treated with more seriousness) was a constantly shifting one, moving with the king as he travelled round the country.

vermouth This characteristically bitter drink now has Italian associations (see IT), but is in fact of pure German origin deriving from the Old English *wermod* and German *wermut* which are also the root of the bitter herb *wormwood*. The name means 'brain protector' from imagined medicinal effects.

Vesta This name for the Roman goddess of the hearth, the focus of Roman religion in its family aspect, had a strange revival in the nineteenth century when it was used as a brand

266

name for a certain type of match. Incidentally the word 'focus', used above, is simply the Latin word for 'hearth'. The 'vestal virgins' were the priestesses of the national hearth, and the fate of the nation was felt to be dependent upon their chastity. Their name has come to symbolise an absolute devotion to virginity.

vestry We get this word from the Latin *vestiarium*, 'a robing room', where church vestments were kept when not in use. The modern French *vestiare*, 'a cloakroom', preserves this literal sense. However, as local government developed in England, the vestry was commonly used as a meeting place for the representatives of parish ratepayers and the word vestry came to be used interchangeably with 'parish council'.

veto This word for a ban is a direct borrowing from Latin, in which it means 'I forbid'.

via Another simple Latin borrowing in which the word for road is used in the sense of 'by way of' or even 'through'. The *via media* is 'a middle way' in the sense of a compromise which avoids extremes on either side. It is a traditional description of the religious outlook of the Anglican Church.

vicar The use of this word, derived from the Latin *vicarius*, 'a deputy', for the priest in charge of an English parish can only be explained historically. This English use of 'vicar' arose at the time of the abolition of the monasteries by Henry VIII. Monastic wealth, which often included the local churches, was put into the hands of lay nobles who became the recipients of the income from the property and therefore responsible for carrying out the services. They put in clergymen as 'deputies', hence the name 'vicar'. If the priest himself received the income directly he was a *rector*. Nowadays the distinction has no practical significance. The 'Vicar of Bray' is an expression used to describe a systematic turncoat who changes his faith and political loyalties with overmuch alacrity. Simon Symonds, the seventeenth-century Vicar of Bray in Berkshire, is said to be the original personage celebrated in the song on this theme.

villain Originally 'villein', the word once implied no more than 'peasant inhabiting a medieval vill or manor'. But, as we have noted elsewhere (in the entry on VALET), the upper classes attributed every vice and 'villainy' to the humble.

vino veritas, in This is Latin for 'There is truth in wine'. When a man is drunk he often leaves discretion behind and blurts out things he has been keeping to himself. An English variant of this is 'When the wine is in, the wits are out'.

violet In the traditional language of flowers the violet symbolises shyness and modesty. It is curious to recall that in Greek legend the flower sprang from the blood of Ajax, the notorious braggart and boaster, who killed himself at the siege of Troy.

viz. There is a double source of mystification here, not only the use of a contracted Latin expression in English, but also the fact that it is customary to read it aloud as something else, usually the word 'namely' or the Old English phrase 'to wit'. The term 'viz.' is used when one goes on to give details of something that has been generally indicated. It is a short form of the Latin *videre licet*, 'one is permitted to see'. In the days when parchment was valuable and everything written by hand many regularly used expressions had an arbitrarily contracted form.

volume Today this word means a book or more exactly one of a set of books. It is the Roman *volumen*, 'a roll or scroll', which was the normal form of an ancient book.

voodoo The island of Haiti evolved this strange cult which combine elements of West African paganism with perverted fragments of the Roman Catholicism which the slaves either picked up or had superficially imposed upon them. The name derives from *vodun*, a variant of an Ashanti word for 'spirit'. The voodoo cult in which participants invite possession, or

268

'riding' by the gods, spread through the Caribbean and into the slave areas of the United States. Religious bigotry among speakers of French led to an attempt to associate the word with *Vaudois*, the name given to a group of Protestant 'heretics' in the Alpine district of Savoie. There is no justification for this association.

Vox populi, vox Dei   'The voice of the people is the voice of God'. The first record of this sentiment is when Alcuin of York (735–804 A.D.) warned the Emperor Charlemagne to take no notice of it!

W

wager   This word for a bet or a stake comes (via French) from the popular Latin *vadium*, 'a pledge'. The same primitive root grew in another direction into the German *Wette*, 'a bet'.

wager of law   This little-known and now obsolete legal procedure available in actions for debt permitted a defendant to take an oath that he owed nothing, supported by eleven neighbours who would also swear, this time that they believed him to be telling the truth.

waits   Now a traditional name for Christmas carol singers, the word is the Old French *waite*, 'a watchman' (compare the traditional phrase 'watching and waiting'). The waits were formerly retainers of noble households, or even of a municipality, whose function it was to keep watch and cry out the hours of the night – sometimes adding information on the state of the weather. The use of certain stereotyped greetings by carol singers is really all that justifies the localised use of the name 'waits'.

wake   The root idea of this word, which has more than one use, is that of the vigil, the night of prayer preceding the day of some religious festival. When northern towns in England celebrate 'Wakes Week', this is a community holiday which was formerly associated with the feast day of the patron saint of the parish. The holiday would begin with the wake and continue with the feast. The wake in which Irish mourners sit up through the night in the presence of the corpse also exemplifies the vigil idea. This kind of wake has also been known to assume a celebratory character.

walk This simple word for what would seem a simple concept did not assume its present sense until the Middle Ages. Its origin is the Saxon *wealcan*, 'to roll'. One thinks of the showman's traditional cry 'Roll up, roll up', perhaps a vestige of the old association of ideas.

wall, *to give or take the* In the medieval street the cleanest and safest path was that on the wall side. In England it is the custom for a lady to be given 'the wall side' as a matter of courtesy. In earlier times 'the wall' was also given to persons of higher social standing – or stronger character. When Samuel Johnson visited his aged mother she asked him, 'Do you give or take the wall?'

wall, *to go to the* This old phrase means to be pushed aside, to be supplanted. As a medieval writer, Sir John Cheke in *The Hurt of Sedicion*, says 'When brethren agree not in a house, goeth not the weakest to the wall?'

wallop As a slang term for a beating this is not found before the nineteenth century. Old French and Middle English knew the word *walop*, 'to boil' and, with the regularly occurring substitution of 'g' for 'w', as *gallop*. If one rider out-galloped another he had 'walloped' him, and this may well be the origin of the later usage. Students of history may recall the 'pot walloper' franchise at Preston, Lancs. There, before 1832, any man who could boil a pot on his own hearth had the right to vote.

walnut This nut was known to the Saxons as being *wealh* or 'foreign'. It ultimately came from Persia.

270

wangle The earliest reference to this word in print is in 1888 in Jacobi's *Printer's Vocabulary* where it is defined as a slang term for faking, or arranging matters to one's own satisfaction. Wangle first gained general currency in the First World War.

war-paint The first use of these words in English was with literal reference to the Red Indians preparing themselves for battle by painting their faces to make themselves terrifying. It is more often used today as a facetious reference to the use of cosmetics by women.

washout Now a failure, or disappointment, a washout was originally a cancellation – the slang instruction to navy signallers who formerly recorded the message received on a slate.

WASP This acronym derives from the initial letters of *W*hite *A*nglo-*S*axon *P*rotestant and sums up the concept of 'the all American blue-eyed boy' as distinguished from those denominated wops, micks, spades, kikes, etc. Only a WASP would be eligible for membership of the Ku Klux Klan for example and the term gained currency in those hard times when the Klan had to advertise for members.

wassail This ancient word for a festive occasion, health-drinking, or even a drinking bout, is pure Saxon and is in fact a toast *wes*, 'be', *hal*, 'hale, healthy'. A medieval story tries to link it with an incident in the tale of Hengist and Horsa, traditionally first of the English to come to Britain. Although the phrase may well be very primitive it is not known in our earliest literature. The wassail-bowl, however, was a feature of traditional Christmas festivities until very recent times.

wavy navy This was the British naval slang term for men of the Royal Naval Volunteer Reserve. The gold lace rings on R N V R officers' sleeves were wavy instead of straight, hence the nickname.

wayzgoose This curious word was once used for a printers' annual outing. It means stubble goose (*wayz* being an obsolete word for stubble), for a goose is still the traditional meal on these occasions.

weathercock   Why is it so often a cock on a windvane? The answer to this frequently asked question seems to be a Papal injunction of the ninth century that churches should set up the emblem of the cock, in allusion to St Peter's denial of Christ. As a writer of 1619 puts it, we '. . . should thereby remember our sinnes and with Peter seeke and obtaine mercy . . .' So well established was the practice that often any windvane is called a weathercock.

wedlock   Now it means simply the state of being married, but its Saxon form *wed*, 'pledge', *lac*, 'gift, offering', refers to the gifts made at betrothal. There never was any reference to 'lock' in the sense of something secured, symbolically shut, etc., as has often been imagined.

welsher   Originally applied only to racecourse bookmakers who disappeared instead of paying out, this word has been the subject of much debate. In England there is much support for the view that it merely continues the tradition begun in the nursery rhyme, 'Taffy was a Welshman, Taffy was a thief'. Welsh writers are inclined to invoke an original welsher, Bob Welch of Epsom. The term has been in use for well over a century and research may prove it to be very ancient indeed. Welsh is, of course, a Teutonic word for foreign and variants of it crop up all over Europe, and 'foreigner' is one form of personal abuse that springs readily to every human tongue.

west, *gone*   The fact that the sun apparently sinks in the west has no doubt been the reason for the location of so many 'otherworlds' from those of Ancient Egypt to those of the Red Indians in the west, and in many tongues and cultures 'gone west' or some equivalent means to have died. Sheer chance made the words part of the criminal slang of old London for the Tyburn gibbet was on the west side of the city, near the modern Marble Arch. Nevertheless, the phrase does not seem to have had a popular circulation until the First World War.

272

wetback Mexicans entering the United States in defiance of the immigration laws often do so by swimming the Rio Grande which forms the Texas–Mexico border for some 1500 miles, frequently still being wet when caught, hence 'wetbacks'.

wham bam, thank you ma'am This evocative phrase, used in criticism of the coital techniques favoured by the typical 'male chauvinist pig', crossed from the United States to Britain in mid-1973. It would seem to stem from Women's Lib circles.

Whig As a political term, Whig is the mirror image of Tory, noted elsewhere. Whig or whiggamore was the term for a Scottish bandit or plunderer, as tory was for an Irish one. From this it came to be applied in the seventeenth century to the rebel Covenanters of the Presbyterian Church in Scotland (hence strongly Protestant), and then in 1679 to the supporters of the Parliamentary bill excluding James, Duke of York, from the succession to the English throne because he was a Roman Catholic. Afterwards Whig was the name of the 'reforming', as opposed to the 'conserving' Tory party until 1832 when, following the passing of the great parliamentary reform bill, it became known as the Liberal Party. In the United States the name Whig Party was used 1836–54 by one of the two major parties which opposed the radical policy of Andrew Jackson and defended commercial interests.

whist According to Cotton's *Complete Gamester* of 1680 the game takes its name from 'the silence that is to be observed in the play'.

whistle for it, *you'll have to* On land, the phrase is a sarcastic one, but at sea in sailing-ship days the superstition was that a wind could be raised in a calm by the sympathetic magic of whistling. As you blew, so it would.

white elephant See ELEPHANT.

white feather See FEATHER.

Whitsun This is a corruption of White Sunday in allusion to the custom of the early Church for new converts to wear white from Easter to Pentecost. The converts were called *albati*, 'the white-robed'. Pentecost Day was called *Dominica in albis*, 'White Sunday'.

wild as an undipped devil This ancient simile is still sometimes heard and relates to the belief that the devil was in man until his baptism or dipping. If a child cried at baptism this was the devil quitting him, and the north (devil's) door of the church stood open for the devil to leave by.

wild oats See OATS.

wind, *raising the* A euphemism for obtaining credit or funds, this originates in a simple analogy. Without wind the ship cannot sail. Without credit the business cannot function. And no doubt the man who sought to raise the wind was often told to whistle for it.

Wind, *of change* 'A wind of change is sweeping through Africa'. A historic phrase used by Conservative Prime Minister Harold Macmillan during a 1960 tour of Africa. At Accra it excited little notice but caused a sensation when used in the Republic of South Africa. The authorship of the words is much disputed. John Wyndham (Lord Egremont), Sir Arthur Clark and Sir David Hunt are among those suggested but none have claimed the distinction.

window The origin of this word is the Old Norse *vindr*, 'wind', *auga*, 'eye'. The window provided for both seeing and ventilation.

wipe the clock An American term for stopping unexpectedly and quickly. It was first used on the railroad where a full application of the air brakes so reduces the pressure that the hand on the gauge or clock races round to zero.

winkling out In the autumn of 1972 this expression, presumably derived from the art of taking the boiled winkle out of its shell with a pin, though already extended in military usage to the systematic clearing of, for example, a newly entered sector of lurking partisans, gained wider currency as applied to the 'easing out' of sitting tenants who were obstructing speculators who preferred to deal with the more attractive 'vacant possession' properties only. Tenants who declined offers to leave were put under heavy pressure reminiscent of the worst days of Rachmanism.

wiseacre This rather disparaging term for anyone who claims more knowledge than his fellows has, of course, a story attached to it. A landed gentleman is said to have boasted of his property in front of Ben Jonson at the Devil Tavern in Fleet Street. 'What care we for your dirt and clods?' said Jonson. 'Where you have an acre of land, I have ten acres of wit.' 'Good, Mr Wiseacre,' said the gentleman. A similar story is told of Beethoven who, on receiving a visiting card from someone who proclaimed himself 'landowner', sent his own back with the added word 'brainowner'. However, wiseacre is really no more than an anglicised form of the Dutch *wijsseggher* or German *Weissager*, 'wise speaker', 'soothsayer', 'prophet'.

with it One of the features of the 'affluent society' that grew up in post-war Europe has been a phenomenal development of cults, fashions and 'in groups' and with them corresponding linguistic phenomena. To be 'with it' implied being up to date, aware of the latest vogue, etc. It has interesting analogues in French, *dans le vent*, 'in the wind', and Italian, *d'entro*, 'inside'. Not to be 'with it' clearly implied you were 'past it'. In the United States 'hip' and 'hep' once had something of the same meaning.

worsted The yarn was thus named because it was originally spun at Worsted in Norfolk. The name of the village is now spelled Worstead.

X

X This mark on barrels of beer once indicated that excise duty had been paid and that the beer was therefore of a certain recognised strength. The marking of two or three X's on a barrel by the brewer came to be a conventional indication of quality. The X was also used in a similarly unregulated way as a suggestion of superior quality by the makers of pewter measures and drinking vessels.

Xanthippe In literature this term sometimes occurs as a nagging and bad-tempered wife. It was the name of the wife of the Greek philosopher Socrates. Whether she made him a philosopher or he made her a shrew is an interesting subject for speculation.

Xeres Xeres de la Frontera, near Cadiz in Spain, is the original home of the wine we now know as sherry. Xeres was its first name which written roughly as pronounced became *sheres*, then *sherris* and finally sherry.

xerography Photocopying machines are now a standard part of modern office equipment. The name xerography, by which this copying process is often called, is a modern coinage from two classical Greek elements *xeros*, 'dry', and *grapho*, 'I write'. This dry copying is effected by the use of a negatively charged powder on a positively charged surface, thus dispensing with the cumbersome wet developing process of earlier copying machines.

X-rays Formerly known as Röntgen rays after their discoverer, X-rays are so called because they were such a striking example of an utterly unknown force or factor in action. Their property of being able to penetrate normally opaque substances was discovered by accident at Würzburg in 1895 and inaugurated a new era in medical science.

XXX This, the Roman numeral thirty, gave the old 30th Regiment of Foot its nickname 'The Three Exes'. The 40th (in Roman numerals XL) were called 'The Excels'.

xylophone   The earliest mention of this musical instrument in Britain is in the *Athenaeum* magazine in 1868. The xylophone consists of a graduated series of flat bars of wood which are struck with a small wooden hammer. *Xylon* is Greek for 'wood' and *phone* is 'a voice'.

Y

yacht   This, like many other nautical words (skipper and deck, for example), came into our language from Dutch, where it was originally *jacht*, from *jagen*, 'to chase', an allusion to the fast-sailing qualities of this type of vessel.

Yankee   Two origins are proposed for this word and it is possible that both played their part in its evolution. One suggests a derivation from *Yengees*, an Indian pronunciation of 'English'. On the other hand *Janke*, as a diminutive of the Dutch *Jan*, 'John', was in use as a derisive nickname as early as 1683. It has also been linked with *Jan Kaas*, 'Johnny Cheese', another nickname for Dutchmen that became attached to the English who took over New Amsterdam and made it New York.

yankee dime   The Yankees were often accused of being over careful with money and ready to pay with anything but cash. A yankee dime is a kiss. A similar view was taken of Quakers, and people spoke of a Quaker 'fip', a fip being a five-cent coin.

yarborough   This card player's term for a hand containing no trumps was originally used for a hand containing no card over the value of nine and takes its name from an Earl of Yarborough, who enlivened his games by regularly betting against the appearance of such a hand in any game in which he took part.

ye   In Saxon and Middle English there was a single letter called *thorn* which was used for 'th'. *Ye* then is simply an archaic way of writing 'the' and it should not be read as 'yee', despite the custom of so many educated people.

yellow press This expression for newspapers specialising in scare articles and alarmist campaigns is American in origin and first appeared in the 1890s when the Press, or some of it, fomented fears of 'the Yellow Peril', the presumed threat to the rest of the world of the rising populations of China and Japan.

yeoman Controversy still rages round the origins of this term. In the middle ages in England it was used to indicate a class of independent small landowners below the rank of gentleman, but qualified to vote in Parliamentary elections and to serve on juries. The term dates back to the thirteenth century. In the Middle English sense it meant a trusted attendant and fighting man of lower rank than the 'squire'. The order of precedence was: knight, squire, yeoman, knave. That order survived in 'yeoman service' in *Hamlet*. Suggested origins are from a conjectured Saxon form *ga-man*, 'man of the district', or from a form *yoman*, 'young man'. One can compare the German *Junker*, 'youngster', which rose in the social scale until it came to be the term for a substantial and indeed noble landowner. In modern English the word yeoman has implications of solid worth.

yoga This Indian religious philosophy seeks, by the cultivation of interacting physical and mental techniques, to attain union with the infinite. Yoga is a parallel formation to our own word yoke.

yokel This disparaging word for a countryman is of obscure origin but seems to derive from the Saxon *geac*, 'a cuckoo'.

yorker This is a cricket ball delivered by the bowler so as to pitch immediately under the bat. It is called a yorker because it is said to have been developed in Yorkshire where cricket is treated with deadly seriousness. The word is sometimes used as a metaphor for something very awkward to deal with.

Yorkshire toast, *the*   Yorkshiremen have a peculiar character attributed to them by other Englishmen, and indeed they attribute similar characteristics to themselves, as expressed in this toast. 'Here's to us, all on us. May we never want for ought, none on us.' The so-called Yorkshire motto is in the same style. 'Hear all, see all, say nowt. Eat all, sup all, pay nowt and if ever tha does owt for nowt, do it for thi'sen.'

Yule, Yuletide   This is an old Norse and Germanic word for the midwinter feast now identified with Christmas. It is possible that our word 'jolly' has the same ultimate root.

Z

Zantippe   This is a variant spelling of Xanthippe, on which there is an entry above.

zany   Now used as a synonym for clown or fool, 'zany' derives from the old Italian entertainment, the *commedia dell'arte*, from which we also derive such characters as Harlequin and Pantaloon. Zany, a corruption of *Giovanni*, 'John', was the comic servant.

Zap   In the sense of failing ('I zapped again') this word derives from the jargon of competitive parachute jumpers and represents 'zero all points'.

zenana   This is the Hindu or Persian equivalent of the Muslim harem, that part of the home reserved for the women only. It derives from the Persian *zan*, 'woman'.

zenith   The Arabs made great contributions to the development of astronomy and mathematics, and much of their terminology remains in use. The zenith is the point in the heavens directly above the observer's head and comes to us via French and Spanish, for it was in Spain that Muslim and Christian culture had their closest contact. The opposite of zenith is nadir, a point considered to be directly below the observer, as it were 'under the world'. Both words have a wide metaphorical use.

zephyr breezes   We sometimes call any soft, warm breeze a zephyr, but properly it should be restricted to those from the west. The name derives from the Greek *zophos*, 'west'. The spirit or deity of the west wind, Zephyrus, was said to produce flowers and fruits by the sweetness of his breath.

zero   Another scientific term from Arabic, 'zero' derives from Arabic *sifr*, 'the nil point'. We also derive 'cipher' from the same source. The zero had not been needed when calculation was done on an abacus board, since an empty space simply made calculation easier. However, its presence in the Hindu-Arabic system of figure notation, which was gradually adopted in Europe from *c.* A.D. 1000, made it easier to deal with the larger numbers, etc., of modern arithmetic when calculations were made with pen and paper.

zero hour   The officially appointed time for the commencement of a military operation. The plan is explained in terms of 'zero plus 3', etc. Only at the last moment need zero hour be actually specified. (Compare D-DAY.)

zest   This word is found in cookery books in its original sense, which is as meaning the peel of an orange or lemon. In the sense of 'something that gives a relish or added flavour' it attained a wider use and has come to mean something akin to enthusiasm. Beyond its immediate French origin *zest* goes back to the Greek *schizein*, 'to divide', and refers to the pith that divides the sections of a fruit.

Zinoviev letter   Just before polling in the 1924 election the *Daily Mail* published a letter, purporting to be from Grigori Zinoviev a Soviet leader, to the new British Communist Party, inciting them to renewed revolutionary efforts. The intention was, one presumes, to damage the Labour Party, by association. It was the original 'Reds under the beds' scare. In 1966 *Sunday Times* writers established that it was a forgery emanating from a Russian emigré group.

zodiac The signs of the zodiac, well known to all readers of newspaper astrology columns, derive their name from the Greek *zodiakos*, 'of animals'. The zodiac is a belt of visible sky which seemed to mark the path of the sun and planets as they (apparently) moved round the earth. This track was divided into twelve equal parts each identified with a prominent constellation. Many of these had animal names, the Ram, the Bull, the Crab, etc., hence the description *zodiakos*, 'of the animals'.

zoo Originally an abbreviation of 'zoological garden', a place where animals could be watched and studied, this has now become a word in its own right. Like the parent word *zoology* it comes from the Greek *zoon* 'a living creature'. A London music hall song of the 1860s, 'Walking in the Zoo is the O K thing to do' popularised the contraction.

zoom Now a technical term used by air pilots for a steep-angled climb and by cameramen (in zoom lens) for the rapid change from long shot to a close-up, the word was once no more than a sound imitative of machinery in speeded-up motion.

zounds Our ancestors were much addicted to picturesque oaths, yet unwilling to break the commandment about 'taking the name of God in vain'. Their compromise we call the 'minced oath'. This one is a corruption of 'God's wounds'.

Supplement to the 1989 Edition

Since its first appearance in 1973 *To Coin a Phrase* has attracted much comment – largely enthusiastic – from its readers, many with their own localised stories of a phrase and its origins; but every so often came the cry 'Why haven't you mentioned . . .?' It is in answer to some of these enquiries and to catch up on new coinages that look like establishing a place in the language that this supplement has been compiled.   A.W.S.

A, *Type A behaviour*   In 1974, American doctors Friedman and Rosenman published *Type A Behaviour and Your Heart* and in it tried to identify and characterise 'the inevitable victims of heart disease'. These they saw as being hyper-aggressive and hypercompetitive, the recognisable features of many hard driving (and hard driven) business executives. 'Type A behaviour' is now almost a condition of employment in some sectors of the economy and the resultant 'burn out' an accepted risk.

Acid House   The media-featured pop/youth cult of late 1988 and early 1989. It involves an alleged revival of psychedelic drug use and 'House' style music – very loud with much electronic synthesis and stroboscopic light effects designed to parallel, or at least suggest, the experiences of the LSD (Acid) user.

arty-crafty   This disparaging term, now perhaps subsumed into the wider concept 'ethnic', is used to characterise individuals professing aesthetic ideals superior to those of our consumer society and reflecting their 'hand woven' creed in their dress and general lifestyle. The term derived initially from the Arts and Crafts movement of the 1880s, which sought to promote 'the beautiful adornment of common objects', and ultimately from the propaganda of John Ruskin and William Morris. Note also the variant 'arty-farty' which stresses the pretentious triviality of much such effort.

ballpark, *a ballpark figure*   US 'computerese' for a realistic estimate or forecast of some quantity – a hit that stays within the ballpark – of reasonable expectation. The ballpark is, of course, where baseball is played.

'because it is there'   These famous and oft quoted words are said to have been the response of 1920s climber George Mallory when asked why he wanted to climb Everest. The actual words were first seen in a *New York Times* story of March 18 1923. Modern commentators are inclined to the view that a reporter first coined this 'heroic epigram'.

Bermuda Triangle   A name sometimes applied to the sea area delimited by Bermuda–Florida–Puerto Rico in which mysterious incidents with occult implications are said to occur. If an interesting case is not near enough to the area as conventionally defined then a wider one 'the Limbo of the Lost', a substantial sector of the Atlantic between Venezuela, Virginia and the Azores, is invoked instead. The whole Triangle legend, one of the great growth industries of our time, seems to be rooted in an Associated Press release of September 1950 about a number of ships that had vanished near Bermuda and were still apparently unaccounted for. The phrase 'Bermuda Triangle' was first used in *Argosy* magazine (February 1964) by V. H. Gaddis. 'Deadly triangle' and 'devil's triangle' are variants of the original. There has been some attempt to postulate a similar death-trap area 'The Devil's Sea' off Japan.

best seller   This term emerged in the USA in the 1890s and had made its way to Britain by 1912. It entered popular usage in the 1920s in connection with A. S. M. Hutchinson's successful novel *If Winter Comes* . . . . Nowadays a book is sometimes billed as a 'best seller' even before publication. In these cases the implication is one of a book, usually written to a proven formula, aimed at and indeed pushed towards an essentially 'non-bookish' market and sold by news-stands and supermarkets rather than by bookshops.

Big Bang   In astronomy this was the popular name coined for the theory that our universe began at a specific moment in time with the explosion of some small dense body. By a presumptuous analogy, the term is also used to describe the radical reorganisation of the London Stock Exchange which, as from 27 October 1986, saw the inauguration of a new age in finance and speculation.

bimbo   This currently popular US label for a young woman of perhaps limited intelligence but undoubtedly powerful sexual magnetism first made the headlines in connection with the Gary Hart–Donna Rice story during the Presidential campaign of 1988, but the word has a long history. Ultimately from Italian *bambino* (baby) it has since the 1920s meant both any young woman and a prostitute (compare English 'tart') but it has been shrewdly suggested that *bimbo*, the stereotyped name of the Italian organ grinder's monkey, must have played a part in shaping current usage. Bimbo = monkey business?

Blitzkrieg   This is German for 'lightning war' and was popularised by constant usage during World War II. Blitzkrieg is properly used for a sudden, decisive strike by combined air and land forces, classically the dive bomber and the tank. The coinage of the word has been ascribed to Hitler himself, but some authorities credit its first use to *Time* magazine of 25 September 1939. British military commentator Basil Liddell Hart has claimed the coinage as his, and German General Walter Nehring has contributed to the discussion by denying the word to be of actual German origin. The abbreviation 'blitz' became the normal British term for the German air raids.

'Blood is thicker than water' Far from being some ancient Saxon adage, this is a coinage of the mid nineteenth century. During the bellicose Lord Palmerston's Second Chinese War (1856–9), British ships were suffering heavy casualties while attacking the Pei Ho Forts. US Commodore Josiah Tatnall, who was in the vicinity, used his ship *Toeywan* to help retrieve the damaged British vessels and rescue the survivors. The next day, in conversation with the British commander, he explained his decision to intervene in the words that have become famous.

blue chip A term of US origin for a highly favoured, solid performance equity or share, usually in a well-known, well-established company. However a 'when the chips are down' investment is still a form of gambling and, at the gaming tables, the blue 'chips' (tokens used instead of actual cash) were those of the highest value.

brig This word, originally US naval for a ship's cell and later more widely applied to military prisons, probably has its roots in gold-rush San Francisco when John Geary, alcalde and later first Mayor under US rule, purchased the brig *Euphemia*, abandoned in the Bay when all her crew deserted, as the city's first temporary prison.

bodger, to bodge a job 'Bodger' today is a loaded word with clear implications of ham-fisted incompetence or at best an accepted inadequacy of materials and workmanship in order to save on costs. But the original bodgers were the peasant chairmakers of the High Wycombe (Buckinghamshire) area. (The German *Böttcher* – a cooper – shows the same word in another woodworking association.) The bodgers produced, by traditional handicraft methods, simple and serviceable objects. When chairmaking was transformed into high art by the Chippendales, Sheratons and Hepplewhites, the bodger was correspondingly downgraded and 'bodge' was assimilated in popular usage to 'botch', a medieval word of unknown origin meaning 'to repair badly'.

bottle, *He's got no —. He's lost his —.*   Bottle as a synonym for courage is a now well-established London usage and seems also to have become part of the football fans' sparse vocabulary, usually in the negative forms cited above. It has been uncertainly derived from London rhyming slang, for example, from 'bottle and glass' meaning 'class' or alternatively 'arse', with the implication of losing control of the bowels while in a state of terror, but these cannot both be valid explanations. The expression was not known to Grose, the pioneer recorder of slang, so its currency in the late eighteenth and early nineteenth century must be doubted. Partridge notes (*c.* 1870) 'to turn out no bottle', meaning to be a failure, but this is not quite the same. Possibly an origin may be found in the well-attested 'bottle holder', a second in the old bare-knuckle boxing ring, who 'made a knee' for his principal, held his bottle and generally got him into condition to go back for the next round. (A *Punch* cartoon once showed Lord Palmerston as 'bottle holder' to the emerging Liberal regimes of Europe.) As this usage was winning a place in the vocabularies of the politically conscious, the older native word for courage, 'bottom', was falling into disfavour. There is an anecdote in which Dr Johnson is laughed at for using it. Can 'bottle' be 'bottom' euphemised? Are there echoes of 'bottle' as the source of Dutch courage?

brace of shakes   An expression indicating a mere moment of time and usually conjectured to be of maritime origin deriving from the shaking of the sails as the ship comes round into the wind. However, the jocular and rural 'two shakes of a lamb's tail' seems just as likely an origin.

broaching a subject This phrase is straight metaphor. One originally broached casks or bales by sticking something sharp into them so the contents could run out or be got at. The broach was a spike. The French form *broche* now means a roasting spit. It is the fastening pin behind that gives the name 'brooch' to the hinged dress ornament.

bucket shop Used in the 1930s for often fraudulent and always shady broking firms which were not members of the Stock Exchange, the term in the 1980s is often applied to travel firms who undercut officially fixed air flight prices by 'special offers' to would-be passengers. The implication of the name is the same in both cases: *Caveat emptor* (Let the buyer beware). It is said that 'bucket' was an early 19th-century US term for a swindle, but the word also has associations with backroom brewing and illicit drinking dens.

bulimia, *(bulimia nervosa)* This distressing condition, involving voracious eating followed by self-induced vomiting or violent purging because of a morbid fear of becoming fat, was identified as a significant contemporary syndrome by Gerald Russell in 1979. The word itself is the Classical Greek 'ox hunger' – the monstrous, insatiable craving for food that could dominate the thinking of a community prone to famine. In the general sense of an inordinate appetite – or simply greed – the word has a long history in English. As 'bulimy' it is recorded as early as 1389.

busking This name for the activity of musicians who play on the street or in subway tunnels perhaps goes back to Spanish *buscar* (to seek). The French *busquer fortune* (to seek one's fortune) is even more explicit. The busker is 'trying his luck'. In a parallel but now obsolete development 'busking' could once mean 'to cruise as a pirate'.

camera, *in camera* A Latin expression used of law cases heard in private and originally in the judge's own room, though nowadays the public are simply excluded from the normal court. 'Camera' is simply 'room'. Before the handy 'box camera' was invented, 'camera' normally referred to the *camera obscura* (dark room), a small building with an aperture in the roof through which an image was projected on to a screen or table. It ended as a sea-side or fairground attraction. 'Camera' was adopted into Latin from Greek where it meant 'vaulted over'.

cereals   This name, which in farming can still mean all cornlike crops, derives from Ceres, the classical corn goddess. Modern cereals in the sense of corn-based breakfast foods began in the 1890s at Battle Creek Sanitarium (Michigan), a formerly Adventist institution with a health food tradition. There John Kellogg first 'flaked' wheat and maize (corn). In 1898 Charles Post, a former Battle Creek patient, decided to emulate Kellogg by inventing Grape Nuts (toasted wheat and barley) and then went on to create 'Post Toasties'. W. K. Kellogg, brother of John, then joined the fray with his Corn Flakes and Rice Krispies. The Great American Cereal was born. See also SUNNY JIM for another cereal story.

chauffeur   It seems odd that this French word, apparently meaning 'warmer' or 'heater-up' should have its current signification. In French, however, there was a logical progression from *chauffeur* as the man who 'blew the fire' in a forge, to the stokers who fuelled the new steam engines and then on to the individual 'engine man' of a private car. The case for this development is, I think, far stronger than that which relates it to the 'hot tube' ignition system of such cars as the Daimler Riemenwagen which had to be well warmed up before the car would start. With 'chauffeur' came in 'garage', another interesting French development.

chips, *You've had your*   This threat, widely used in World War II, indicates that a time of favoured indulgence has definitely come to an end. The phrase had its origin in the old naval dockyards where sawn off ends and other small bits of surplus timber were dismissed as mere 'chips' and considered the legitimate perquisites ('perks') of shipwright or carpenter. They could be taken out of the yard without question. In cases of abuse – and a reliable authority asserts that pieces of furniture and even the woodwork of entire houses were frequently made from 'chips' – the privilege could be, and often was, withdrawn. Hence the phrase, 'You've had all the chips you are ever going to get here!'

Cinderella complex, *the* This phrase was coined by Colette Dowling as the title for her 1982 book in which she sought to identify and analyse the real dilemma of women in society: dependence at the domestic hearth as 'Daddy's little girl' versus the prospect of a new life with the handsome prince postulated by the fairy tale. 'Some day my prince will come' as Disney put it. This desired move from one unequal rights situation to what can only be another leaves little scope for the options of militant feminism.

cleaners, *taken to the* Still heard in racing circles and probably of 1930s American gangster (or at least movie gangster) origins, this evocative phrase implies that the victim has been deprived of all he had – his pockets totally, indeed carefully, emptied as one does when sending a suit to be cleaned. In a similar vein 'laundered' money has been the subject of various fictitious transactions so that it might acquire a 'clean' origin when in fact it has been derived from some criminal or otherwise inadmissible source.

cock up This widely used British expression for a badly bungled job cheerfully accepted for the most part as integral to the established methods of the organisation in question, is of much disputed origin. Commentators seem anxious, indeed over-anxious, to show that it is not a simple sexual vulgarism and, of course, if it were, it is hard to see how the phrase acquired its present meaning. Perhaps the 'cock' meaning 'catchpenny publication' recorded by Mayhew has some bearing or even 'cock and bull' story? However, according to those who profess to know, 'cock up' is an innocuous technical term meaning 'error' used by printers/ brewers/Civil Servants/poachers and many others. My own preference is for the poachers because, as a wily old countryman once explained to me, 'If you're creeping up on a pheasant and startle him, he'll squark "Cock up".' And it would be one too.

cold war   This phrase, which so vividly characterises the 'No war, no peace' situation which existed for so long after 1945 between the USSR and her former Western allies, is attributed to US commentator Walter Lippmann and dates from 1947. It has been adopted into Russian and no doubt other languages.

cop, *It's not much*   Meaning 'It's not much good' this is one of the best-known 'Cockney' expressions, though probably not originally confined to London. 'Cop' meaning 'to catch' goes back to the seventeenth century if not beyond and has had many developments. A 'copper' is one who catches you. 'Cop hold' means 'Get hold of this'. 'It's not much cop' has about it something of the sentiment 'Big deal!'

cracks, *papering over the*   Although the actual practice is no doubt much older, this first attained general currency after the Prusso-Austrian defeat of Denmark in 1864. There were deep differences between the two allies but in the Convention of Gastein, Bismarck, then dominant in Prussian politics, made no effort to resolve them, being content to 'paper over the cracks' until it suited him to launch his own attack on the crumbling Austrian Empire.

creek, *up the*   Used nowadays merely to indicate that someone is hopelessly wrong on some disputed issue, 'the creek' was once a much nastier location. Our phrase is a modified version of a military original which surfaced during World War II. Someone in a very awkward predicament was described as being 'Up Shit Creek with no paddles'. See also WAVES, DON'T MAKE for similar imagery.

'Days of wine and roses'   Sometimes used to imply a life of uninhibited pleasure, this line from Victorian poet Ernest Dowson's 'Vitae Summa Brevis' is in fact a lament. 'They are not long/ The days of wine and roses.' It was better used by Hollywood as the title for a classic study of the decline of an alcoholic. A line of Dowson's also provided the film title *Gone With The Wind*.

dinkies   One of the acronymic coinages of the contemporary 'City and wine bar' culture in which one's financial potential is seen as the key factor in social assessment. 'Dinkies' stands for 'Double income, no kids'.
   See also OIK.

dog   Man's best friend (as they say) is much put upon by the phrase maker. Look, for example, at this passage from John Taylor's *A Dogge of Warre* (1630).
   'I have heard a man say, I am hot as a Dogge, or, as colde as a Dogge; I sweat like a Dogge (when indeed a Dog never sweates), as drunk as a Dogge, hee swore like a Dogge.'
   The trend continues. Modern usage knows 'sick as a dog' (though 'as a cat' is a common variant), 'dog tired' and 'dirty dog'. Used in a favourable sense we have 'putting on dog' for attempting 'to cut a dash'. Quite apart from its associations, real or alleged, dog itself is a very curious word. The normal Old English word was 'hund' and 'dog' first appears as the name of a specific breed or type, probably the mastiff, and went into continental usage with the attribute 'English' – the French poet du Bellay, for example, praises *'le genereux dogue anglais'*.

292

drum up, *to drum up support* The phrase today usually refers to taking active measures to mobilise support for some cause or even for a social event. The meaning was once quite literal and relates to the days when military recruiting parties set out from their rendezvous to seek volunteers and advertised their arrival in street or market place with fife and drum. Their duty was described as 'drumming up recruits'.

drunkenness, *(terms for)* Our vocabulary today is undoubtedly impoverished as compared to that of the seventeenth century. Consider the wealth of expressions for being drunk found in *The Drunkard Opened* of 1635. 'He is foxed, he is flustered, cupshot, he hath swallowed a tavern token, he hath whipt the cat, he hath been at the scrivener's, he is bit by a barn weasel, he hath seen the French king.' This last must relate to the folktale of the missing drinker who claimed to have been miraculously transported to the French king's cellar and back again – all without any effort of his own! Our modern 'tired and emotional' has never really made it into general use but the Irish 'electrified' and 'legless' are notable contributions to a grand tradition.

ducks, *lame* Said to have originated on the Stock Exchange (where stags, bulls and bears are found) to describe a dealer or firm that has 'gone under'. Its common usage in recent years has been for an enterprise or even an industry that needs repeated public subsidy to keep in business. There is much debate on the evolutionary utility of this. The unlamed are much in favour of 'the survival of the fittest'. However, one cannot help thinking that these ducks might once have been dogs, for it is the lame dog that is forever being helped over stiles by the compassionate or sentimental.

Establishment, *the* A useful term for 'the powers that be' in all their institutional, social and cultural ramifications, it was popularised by Henry Fairlie in *The Spectator* from the mid-fifties. It is an extension of the narrower ecclesiastical aspect of a similar idea, the Established Church.

flying saucers   In 1947, while flying over America's Mount Rainier, Kenneth Arnold saw (or thought he saw) 'nine gleaming discs' in the sky. He said they looked like 'flying saucers' and a great phrase, even an industry, was born.

Fourth World   This is the name given to themselves as a movement by adherents of the philosophy that 'Small is beautiful', the title of Fritz Schumacher's best-selling book published in 1973. The 'Fourth World' Assembly and Forum met to develop these ideas in London in 1981. Fourth Worlders advocate small nations, small communities and economics on a human scale.

friends, *God protect me from my*   Now proverbial, this sentiment seems to have been first penned by William Blake in his 'Milton' (1804–8) in which Palamabron, driver of the Chariot of the Sun, says:

O God, protect me from my friends, that they have not power over me.
Thou hast given me power to protect myself from my bitterest enemies.

GIGO   'Computerese' acronym for 'Garbage in, garbage out', a principle that lies at the very root of wisdom and which seems to be ousting our beautiful old phrase about not being able to make silk purses from sows' ears. The GIGO principle is still not appreciated by the general public, who see computers as miracle machines rather than as what they really are, wonderfully fast workers but limited by the quality of their raw material.

gilt edged   A late nineteenth-century slang term for 'safe as houses' securities such as government stock and major colonial issues. The term derives literally from the gilt edges of the handsomely designed certificates, prestige documents for prestige holdings. Many old stocks and shares certificates are now traded in as collectors' items, of aesthetic interest in their own right.

Gipper, *win one for the* President Reagan's favourite nickname for himself, 'the Gipper' was, like so much of his Presidential style, rooted in Hollywood. It derived from his rôle as a doomed football star in the bio-pic *Knute Rockne: All American.* Rockne was the original Gipper and his dying plea to his team, 'Win one for the Gipper', was revived as a catchphrase at New Orleans in 1988 when President Reagan handed over his leadership of the Republican cause to George Bush.

glasnost A word much bandied about by commentators on the Russian scene in general and the Gorbachev revolution in particular, it is simply the Russian word for 'openness', a key aim of the new regime.

Gucci socialists The spectacle of the liberal rich patronising revolutionary factions in order to appear progressive has always been a bizarre one. It has called forth a number of vividly descriptive phrases, all in the vein of oxymoron – Gucci socialists, Lamborghini Marxists, etc. Sometimes cited in this connection are Brendan Bracken's 'Bollinger Bolshevik', 'ritzy Robespierre', 'lounge-lizard Lenin' – these shafts were directed at Aneurin Bevan who was Lord Beaverbrook's frequent house-guest. Bracken, if not accusing Bevan of downright hypocrisy, was at least pointing out his fascination for upper-class glamour.

hacking Now the established term for unauthorised utilisation of a computer system, 'hacking' began as American student slang for heroic dedication to one's studies. Perhaps computer students showed more of this than others. Perhaps the dream of successfully entering other people's systems

295

inspired aspirants to 'hack' the harder. The word found a wider British public when a hacker demonstrated his skill by breaking into the BBC's Telecom Gold account during a live TV transmission. His intruded message ran: 'This is more than just a game/ It's hacking, hacking, hacking.'

hammered This now obsolete business term had its origin in a custom of the old London Stock Exchange. An attendant, known as a waiter, called for silence by striking the rostrum three times with a hammer. An announcement was then made that a named member was unable to meet his obligations. To be 'hammered on the Stock Exchange' was on a par with being declared bankrupt. The word 'hammering' is now often used to mean any beating, whether literal or metaphorical.

hatter, *mad as a* There seems to be support for the view that the mad hatter simile did have some objective foundation in the use of nitrate of mercury by traditional beaver hat makers which led to an industrial disease, with disorientation and confusion as typical symptoms. The term was known in the early nineteenth century, before Lewis Carroll gave it worldwide circulation in *Alice*.

hors d'oeuvre Despite the published opinion of a well-known TV cook that hors d'oeuvre means 'outside work' and derives from the predilection of French chefs for subcontracting all that tedious chopping and slicing, the real origin of the term is in the fine arts where it described an adjunct or side piece which, though an acceptable 'garnish', was not part of the main composition. Since cooking is also an art, a transference of terms was natural and hors d'oeuvre gained its now normal meaning of a 'starter' to whet the appetite before the main course of the meal. The old theatrical 'curtain raiser' provides another analogy – a short, light piece before the main play.

hoodlum The main text's explanation of this word, as derived from a reversal of the name 'Muldoon', still commands much support but rival theories have been advanced. One such calls attention to the juvenile street gangs of the 1870s who raised the cry of 'Huddle 'em' when they crowded round and jostled pedestrians in order to rob them in the resultant confusion – the same technique as that of our contemporary 'steamers'. A scholar has also called attention to the Bavarian *hodalum* – a scamp. Origins can converge to strengthen a usage that at first had only a precarious place in the language.

hot line The original 'hot line' was that installed between the Kremlin and the White House after the Cuban Missile Crisis of 1962. Kennedy and Khrushchev, both having looked into the abyss, were equally anxious that World War III, so narrowly averted, should not start as the result of any accident or misunderstanding. Hence the direct telephone link at the very top.

knocked, *into a cocked hat* In early days, when a ship's position was being determined, three bearings were plotted on the chart. The ship should be at their point of intersection. If the observations were not quite accurate the lines would not meet at a point but would instead form a small triangle known as 'a cocked hat'. In its earliest usage, to be 'knocked into a cocked hat' meant to be not at all sure where you were.

Kwok's disease Perhaps from time to time we all blame an 'ethnic' meal for what is in fact no more than an unwise overindulgence. The US coinage 'Kwok's disease' signifies the near institutionalisation of this excuse. Kwok must owe something to 'wok', the now fashionable Chinese-style cooking pan.

loadsamoney Although this 'phrase in a word' is the original catchphrases of comedian Harry Enfield, it has more significance than most in this category. It neatly sums up much of the social ethos of Thatcherite Britain and has been extensively used in speeches by British Labour leader Neil Kinnock.

Logoranto   A 1988 coinage by Professor Adam Holdrime for the new 'language of signs' that has evolved mainly in connection with the motorway network but which is also found at transport termini and, indeed, other places of public resort. The new term is a variation of Esperanto, the name of a synthetic international language first published by Dr Zamenhof in 1887.

menstruation *(euphemisms for)*   Language, it has been said, is to enable us to conceal our thoughts, and euphemism is that branch of language that helps us give 'a fair name' to topics still not discussed openly in general company. Menstruation, that great fact of women's lives, is still something of a mystery to many males, not least because of the cloud of euphemy in which it dwells. Enquirers have noted many examples hinging on the fact that blood is red. 'The captain's at home' is an old one. The captain is a redcoat. 'The flag is up' can be shown as a reference to a red flag by the Americanism 'She's flying Baker', a clear allusion to the international code of signals (plain red flag represents B, read as 'Baker' or 'Bravo'). 'It's flag day' is a whimsical variant. The French '*Les Anglais sont arrivés*' brings us back to our beginning. 'The redcoats have landed!'

money, *(Give him the money, Barney)*   An elderly phrase now but one still used in the Press. At the height of the 1982 train drivers' dispute, a writer in *The Guardian* newspaper said, 'The message emerging from Whitehall is that the days of "Give them the money, Barney" are now at an end.' For older readers recognition was instant. Wartime radio news-reader Wilfred Pickles later developed his own quiz show *Have a Go* in which contestants, frequently pensioners, answered simple questions for cash prizes. They rarely failed to make the grade and associate Barney Colehan was always standing by ready to respond to the famous words.

naff off! A curt dismissal or, as Dr Johnson would have said, 'a formula of ablegation' and one said to have been favoured by Princess Anne. (One wonders, do other Chancellors of Universities talk like this?) This widely current, though objectively meaningless, phrase seems to be one of the languages few proven 'synthetics' – a created word, here given meaning by its mode of delivery, but at which no one can really take offence – sanitised obscenity as it were. Launched in Ronnie Barker's TV series *Porridge* in 1974, it goes back to Keith Waterhouse's novel *Billy Liar* and beyond that to Waterhouse's service with the RAF. That worthy organisation NAAFI has been blamed for giving rise to, first, a disparaging adjective and then, by development, the verbal form. Had all this not existed in authoritative sources, I would have guessed 'naff' to be a curtailment and then reversal of 'fanny'.

Nelson touch, *the* In his *Memoirs of Nelson* (1849) Thomas Pettigrew twice quotes letters from Nelson (25 September and 1 October 1805) in which the phrase occurs, apparently in reference to his plans for attacking the combined French and Spanish fleets. 'It was,' said Nelson (never inhibited by any false modesty) 'warranted never to fail.' Nor did it when the final clash came.

nouvelle cuisine The term 'nouvelle cuisine' first appeared in the *Gault Millau* gastronomic magazine in 1973 to describe the new 'lighter' style of chefs emulating the work of the late Fernand Point of La Pyramide, Vienne. Stress was laid on the freshness and high quality of the ingredients which were displayed on rather than concealed under the sauce. Think of NC (to which it is sometimes abbreviated) as a combination of healthier eating with the concept of 'plate art' – the careful arrangement of the food to appeal to eye as well as palate.

Obscuranto A name coined for the opaque, bureaucratic jargon seemingly preferred to plain speaking by the European Commission, especially when dealing with consumer affairs. In 'Obscuranto', nuts can be 'shell fruit' and flowers 'non edible vegetables'. The debate about 'Obscuranto' involves whether its usage is a deliberate effort to conceal unpopular aspects of proposed policies or whether it is no more than the result of filtering all material through the nine languages of the European Community. (See LOGORANTO for the origin of the form and, in the main text, BAFFLEGAB for an analogous coinage.)

ocker A useful Australian term for the ignorant pub know-it-all: hairy-chested, work-shy, racist and opinionated, and exemplified in other cultures by such creations as Andy Capp, Alf Garnett and Archie Bunker. The word was popularised if not invented by Australian comedian Paul Hogan in the mid 1970s.

oik This unlovely word, once used to denote an ignorant lout, has re-emerged as part of the post-Big Bang city-speak to describe the lowest level of money-making life 'One Income, Kids'.

OK *(— rules. OK?)* This ubiquitous graffiti phrase which has now even spawned parodies of itself ('Dyslexia lures, KO?') had its origins in Glasgow's gangland whence it spread to parallel subcultures in Liverpool and Belfast. I well remember seeing it appear in London's dock area, making its way up towards Aldgate in the 1950s. Its first form was 'Tartans rule, ya bas! OK?' – 'This is Tartans' territory, you bastards, and don't you forget it.'

parrot, *sick as a* This unlikely comparison was first used by Liverpool footballer Phil Thompson after his team's Cup

Final defeat in 1978. Since then it has become a standard part of the sports writers' vocabulary. Previously, indeed for centuries, the phrase had been 'sick as a dog' or 'sick as a cat'.

perestroika The other key note of the Gorbachev revolution (see GLASNOST), 'perestroika' is the restructuring of the Soviet state and economy, seen to be needed in order to implement the new ideals of a democratic communism.

pilot, *dropping the* A phrase used to indicate the only dubiously wise departure from the tested and tried policies of a respected elder statesman, it was the title of a Bernard Partridge cartoon in *Punch* when the young and inexperienced Kaiser William II dismissed that master statesman Prince Bismarck in 1890. The symbol that lies behind the cartoon is, of course, that of the ship of state.

pipe down In Britain's Royal Navy this was the last call of the day on the bosun's pipe, the signal for lights out and silence. In 'navalese' it became a forceful suggestion to the noisy or argumentative that they should 'shut up' and be quiet.

pits of the world This disparaging phrase, an esoteric metaphor for 'the worst' was at first linked with Woody Allen in the late 1970s, but was made famous by the 1981 Wimbledon men's singles tennis champion, John McEnroe. The Wimbledon that failed to accept his outbursts in the spirit in which he offered them was compared to that most unsavoury location 'the armpits of the world', a modern weakening surely of the classical *anus mundi*. However, there is still more to be said. 'Pits' can be fruit stones as in 'olive pits' or 'cherry pits', hence the Victorian line 'Life is just a bowl of cherries' sometimes evoked the follow-on 'How come I always get the pits?' It could well be that the grosser explanation overlies an equally valid earlier one.

301

plain sailing 'From there on it's all plain sailing' we are frequently told, meaning that there should be no problems and no tricky bits to deal with. The phrase has its roots in early navigation when 'plane' charts were used; that is, charts based on the assumption that the earth's surface was flat. Plane, or as it became in later usage 'plain', sailing did not involve the calculations of more sophisticated systems.

plugging a song This phrase for attempting to popularise a song and increase its sales by repeated mention and, if possible, performance on radio is said to derive from the activities of Leonard F. Plugge, a pioneer of commercial radio. Although Plugge certainly pushed new records in his Radio Normandie days in the 1930s, I feel that the natural meaning of 'plug' in the sense of filling a gap must have encouraged acceptance of the term.

preppy A vogue word of the early years of the Reagan Presidency and apparently coined by Erich Segal of *Love Story* fame, preppy indicates the qualities of those fortunate enough to have been, by virtue of their 'old' money and inherent good taste, to the right prep schools and so set on course for living happily ever after at their upper end of the social scale. (Compare IVY LEAGUE in main text.) Lisa Birnbaum's *Official Preppy Handbook* exists for those who cannot rely on their own inherently sound instincts to follow the style. The English 'county' has something of the same ring about it and that ubiquitous interior decorators' wooden duck (originally a decoy duck from the world of 'Huntin', shootin' and fishin'') seems to have been of preppy ancestry. Although President George Bush is heavily disguised as a Texan, he is, of course, the preppiest of preppies.

pseud, pseudish Usually claimed as a coinage by Richard Ingrams' *Private Eye* magazine and indicating the intellectually pretentious, it has also been traced back to his early days at Shrewsbury School. It was perhaps even then an anti-pseud cliquish adoption, for pseudo-intellectual was well known long before Mr Ingrams went into print.

radical chic US novelist Tom Wolfe's sarcastic term for the attitude of some of New York's 'conscience stricken rich' who in the 1970s held smart parties to raise funds for the revolutionary Black Panthers organisation. See also GUCCI SOCIALISTS. 'Parlour Pinks' was an earlier American term for a similar phenomenon.

Ramada socialism Labour MP Dennis Skinner's coinage for his view of leader Neil Kinnock's proposed 'new image' for their Party. The Labour leadership stayed at the up-market Ramada Renaissance Hotel for the 1987 conference. To Dennis Skinner this seemed ominous.

right as ninepence There is nothing specially 'right' about 'ninepence', but if we take the view that it might once have been 'nine pins' – upright and standing as they should be, ready for the next game – then it begins to make a bit of sense. The associations of 'ninepence' are quite otherwise. A proverbial saying goes 'He's ninepence short of a shilling' – far from being all there. Compare the American equivalent 'Fifty cards to the pack'.

roger An ancient word that has resurfaced in recent years as yet another semi-veiled term for copulation. It was well known in the eighteenth century and employed by Boswell ('Shall not a soldier roger for fourpence?') but goes back well before his time. 'Roger' was the name often given to a bull. Whether activity or typical name came first must be a moot point. The limerick's 'Roger the Lodger' must also have kept the old term at the back of many minds as well.

Roseland Estate agents' and media men's term for 'Rest of South-East England' as distinguished from the horrendously expensive London property market.

rover A romantic name this, and one much favoured in sentimental Victorian fiction; Ralph Rover, for example, or faithful Rover the dog. One 'roved the world' or 'the Seven Seas'. Perhaps, if homeless and rootless, one does well to make a virtue of it. The word derives from the Dutch *zeerover* – a 'sea robber' or pirate.

sacred cows Commonly used to indicate things that are generally agreed not to be touched by the rude hand of reform, the phrase comes from Hindu India where the cow, although living, breathing and above all eating, is more symbol than beast. For the orthodox Hindu the cow is symbolic of life itself and although milk is drunk and butter made, cows may not be slaughtered, even when seriously ill. To eat beef is the ultimate defilement. In village India a cow could pillage market stalls or lie across the railway track but could not be disturbed. Every society has its sacred cows though it is often difficult to recognise one's own for what they are. It is curious that Siam's equally venerated white elephant has given rise to a phrase of such a radically different character.

schmaltz 'Showbiz' term for the sickly sweet and sentimental stuff 'laid on with a trowel' that seems to go down so well with some sections of the public. It is from the Yiddish for (extra) chicken fat sometimes added to other dishes to make them more palatable to diners who like that sort of thing.

schooner A vessel with fore and aft sails on all her masts. The rig is said to have originated at Gloucester (Mass.) in 1713 and the name to derive from a cry of 'There she scoons' from a spectator at her first trials. The Scots verb *scoon* is 'to bounce over the water as a flat stone does'. (Does this suggest that scones – surely a related word – once had something in common with Mother Frisbee's pies?) The Scots-American usage is said to be the origin of the similar words for this type of ship in northern European languages. 'Schooner' as a measure of, for example, wine is of quite unknown origin but, one wonders, could there be some connection with the now obsolete 'bumpers' of ale?

Seymour   Contemporary 'Cityspeak' for a six figure salary, allegedly based on the name of an advertising agency employee (Saatchi and Saatchi is sometimes specified) who was the first to receive a salary in excess of £100,000.

sexual intercourse *(euphemistic phrases for)*   Mentioning the until recently unmentionable has often called forth unsuspected veins of imagination and even downright poetry, though 'having some dog and duck' is not in this last category. 'Giving the ferret a run' approaches a higher plane of symbolism as does 'dipping the adder' and 'dipping the wick', though the latter suggests rhyming slang and evokes memories of an old pub music hall parody. 'Putting in the ferret' is an established rural sport and 'rocking the boat' needs little comment. However the Welsh 'soaking Molly Meggins' quite baffles this lexicographer as does the question 'Did you see the king last night?' which was put to the youthful (and mystified) John Mortimer.

shanghai   Although essentially of American usage, this term for the kidnapping of real (or even only potential) seamen to make up the numbers of a ship's crew is of quite obscure origin and may well derive from the Australian *shangai* meaning 'a catapult'. Unofficial recruiting agents called 'crimps' got their hands on men by any means, fair or foul, took their commission and shot the victims off to sea before the unfortunate men, frequently too drunk to resist, knew what was happening to them.

slate, *a clean*   This means a new start, with all previous considerations wiped out, and is usually given, like so many

English phrases, a straight shipboard origin. During each watch the course steered and distance covered was recorded on a slate. When the watch changed, all this was entered into the logbook and the next watch began with a clean slate. An alternative view relates the expression to 'chalking up' pub debts on a slate which would then be wiped clean when the debt was settled.

Sloane Ranger   Descriptive term, coined in the mid 1970s by Peter York for an urban equivalent of the rural 'county' type – 'posh' young ladies, graduates of the public and finishing schools, 'filling in' with a not too demanding secretarial job in London and from time to time (even every weekend) returning to their 'place in the country'. Named from their preferred residential area (Sloane Square), they are the British equivalent of America's 'preppies'.

small is beautiful   This phrase was originally the title of a book published by Fritz Schumacher in 1973. In it Schumacher argued the case against 'giantism' and the case for decentralised 'human-scaled' institutions. (See FOURTH WORLD.)

soaps *(originally soap operas)*   Such popular TV programmes as *Coronation Street*, *EastEnders* and the glossy imports *Dallas* and *Dynasty* have as their remote ancestor a 1927 US radio serial called *Amos and Andy*. Sent out at prime times, with each episode ending in a 'cliff-hanger', it gave the sponsors (in this case the soap giants Proctor and Gamble) just what they wanted – a guaranteed audience for the commercials which were the whole point of the operation. A second soap opera *Today's Children* brought in the family theme that has since been employed so many times that it is almost a characteristic of the genre. Major British radio 'soaps' were *The Robinsons*, *Mrs Dale's Diary* and, greatest of them all, *The Archers*, which began as a vehicle for Ministry of Agriculture advice to farmers and survived to become a radio legend, more real for many than actual rural England.

stags   Now used to mean speculators who buy new shares hoping to resell them at a quick profit, the name comes from the fringe dealers in early railway issues who congregated in what was then called Stag Alley behind the old London Stock Exchange.

Stroke City   Sectarian sentiment in Ulster is quick to infer a leaning to 'the other side' even from one's use of placenames. To distance itself from this situation the Peace Movement of the 1970s began referring to Derry/Londonderry. The BBC's Radio Ulster disc jockey, Gerry Anderston, shortened this to Stroke City and the name has gained some currency.

summit   The use of this term to indicate dealings at Head of Government level goes back to the days of the Korean War and the debate on German rearmament when, in 1950, Winston Churchill called for 'a parley at the summit' as a possible way forward.

Sunny Jim   Often used ironically for someone whose temperament is far from sunny, the name derives from a jingle created by Ed Ellsworth to popularise the cereal 'Force' at the turn of the century. It ran as follows:
> Jim Dumps was an unfriendly man
> Who lived his life on the hermit plan
> Till 'Force' one day was served to him,
> Since then they've called him Sunny Jim.

Sunny Jim was depicted on the cereal packets as an athletic oldster sporting an eighteenth-century pigtail.

take it with you, *you can't*   This piece of homespun wisdom gained wide circulation as the title of a play by Moss Hart and George S. Kaufman, first presented at the Booth Theatre, New York City, in December 1936. Warner Brothers made a screen version which won the Academy Award for 'Best Picture of 1938'. The phrase has since entered the language.

Tom and Jerry   The names of the chief characters of the popular cat and mouse cartoon films were not just chosen at random. The original Tom and Jerry featured in *Life in London*, the famous guide to Regency nightlife produced by Irish sporting journalist Pierce Egan. Egan's gimmick was to involve his fictional 'Jerry Hawthorn and his elegant friend Corinthian Tom' with real figures from the London underworld. Egan died in 1849.

Ugandan affairs   A coinage of *Private Eye* magazine as a jocular euphemism for sexual activities. It derives from the (apocryphal?) story of a journalist who, when bored at a party, was told that upstairs he would find a black diplomat deeply versed in Ugandan affairs. He did find him up there, vigorously copulating with another guest. Hence the phrase.

United States of America   The first use in print of the name United States of America seems to have been by that ubiquitous figure Tom Paine in the second of his *Crisis* pamphlets published in January 1777.

vortices, *vile*   Said to be a network of dangerous 'anomalic' areas around the globe but in fact based on no more than the allegedly significant locations of the Bermuda Triangle and The Devil's Sea. Since the bases of the concept are themselves highly suspect, the system of 'vile vortices' must on present evidence be deemed fanciful. The expression was first used by Ivan T. Sanderson in 1968.

Wall Street   Now used in the wider sense as symbolising American big business and investment interests, Wall Street originally denoted the New York Stock Exchange at the junction of Wall and Broad Streets. (Compare the way in which British Harley Street and Whitehall have come to symbolise similarly powerful institutions.) The cynical 'folk-tale' is that the street took its name from a wall built by the first New Yorkers to keep out wolves!

wally, wimp These two are often used interchangably for, to dignify the subject, a stupid person lacking not only all the signs of manliness (wimp) but even simple common sense (wally). Their origins are quite different though their usage converges. 'Wimp' must ultimately derive from the character J. Wellington Wimpy in the original *Popeye* cartoons. Wimpy was a harmless, inoffensive fellow, best known for his addiction to the hamburger (which has led to his name being used by the well-known fast food chain). But wimp perhaps suggests 'whimper' and even 'limp'. Wimpy could never have become a tough, ruthless character. 'Wally' has a native British origin in the pickled gherkins sold to accompany the traditional fish and chips. They were gruesomely compared to pickled penises ('wallies' in London's vernacular) and the name struck. Compare the usage of 'dill' in the US.

warts and all Meaning 'with all the visible imperfections and nothing glossed over', these words are from an anecdotal version of Oliver Cromwell's instructions to the portrait painter Lely. The official record is rather more elaborate. 'Remark all these roughnesses, pimples and warts, and everything as you see me, otherwise I will never pay a farthing for it.' Admirable sentiments from one of the greatest of Englishmen.

water bewitched The cry of 'water bewitched' that I often heard as a child when someone wished to protest (at least half humorously) about the weakness of, for example, tea had puzzled me for many years until an unlikely chance brought enlightenment. Like so many quasi-proverbial expressions, it was quoted in part only, letting the hearer's own silent completion of the phrase be his own condemnation. Revelation came from an anecdote passed on by travel writer

Lawrence G. Green concerning an American captain's wife visiting St Helena who called for brandy and water, found it too weak for her liking and cried out (to the consternation of her hostess) 'Water bewitched and brandy begrudged!'

waves, *don't make*   Meaning 'Don't make a nasty situation any worse by thoughtless intervention', the reference is to a phrase attributed to the Vichy French collaborator Pierre Laval. Towards the end of his days of power he is reported as saying *'Je suis dans le merde jusqu' au cou. Ne faites pas des vagues'* – 'I'm in it up to the neck. Don't make waves!' Compare CREEK, UP THE for a similarly edited phrase.

whim-wham *(a whim-wham to wind up the sun)*   When a child persistently asks what something is, or what something's for, and a parent for whatever reason does not feel inclined to answer, resort is frequently made to a traditional 'put off', a reply so surrealistically bizarre that the child retreats baffled. Sound psychological parenting it may not be but it has certainly been going on for a long time. The interest of this example, one of the best known, is that a 'whim' was in fact a primitive winding engine. The variant 'A wig-wam for ducks to peck on' is, I suspect, a mere corruption of the more elegant original.